MUSLIM WOMEN AND ISLAMIC TRADITION
STUDIES IN MODERNISATION

MUSLIM WOMEN
AND
ISLAMIC TRADITION
Studies in Modernisation

Edited by
MARIAM ALLANA

KANISHKA PUBLISHERS, DISTRIBUTORS
NEW DELHI 110 002

KANISHKA PUBLISHERS, DISTRIBUTORS
4697/5-21 A, Ansari Road, Daryaganj,
New Delhi 110 002
Phones: 327 0497, 328 8285,
Fax: 011-328 8285

First Published 2000

ISBN 81-7391-344-7

PRINTED IN INDIA

Published by Madan Sachdeva for Kanishka Publishers, Distributors, 4697/5-21 A, Ansari Road, Daryaganj, New Delhi 110 002; Lasertypeset by Baba DTP Services, Delhi, and Printed at Nice Printing Press, Delhi.

Preface

The push and pull of tradition and modernity exercises decisive influence on orthodox communities, or groups with rigid social and hierarchical mores. The Muslim communities of India have contributed immensely to the development effort and socio-economic progress of the country. It has produced some of the finest academicians, educationists, artists, social reformers, men of law, parliamentarians, social activists and a host of other able, creative people. On the other hand, the communities have also seen persistent backwardness, traditional resistance to change, and a secluded and sheltered existence for the majority of their women. A case in point was the widely discussed entry of women into mosques in a city in Uttar Pradesh. In the end analysis, the forces of emancipation and constructive change have had the edge over the rigid, unbending and extremely fundamental proponents.

The significant social context of the 'major minority' community in India needs no elaboration. That Muslims are more traditional than other communities has to be viewed in a historico-religious perspective and the role and status of women of Muslim faith in various countries of the world is the subject of numerous very scholarly and erudite works. The present publication attempts in a modest way to throw light on the several aspects of traditional Islamic views on matters pertaining to such vital aspects of women's life as divorce, custody of children, support and maintenance after divorce, and the laws on property and inheritance. The book also highlights some relevant aspects of the role and status of women in the rural communities and marginalised groups in Bangladesh and Pakistan. The work would be of particular interest to students and researchers in the sociology of minority communities, as well as academicians, theologians and religious personages wishing to revisit and review the salient features of Islamic tradition and women.

MARIAM ALLANA

Contents

1

Aspects of Islamic Law: Third Country Interpretations of Marriage Conventions

MAINTENANCE AND OBEDIENCE

The complex of rights and duties assigned to the wife by virtue of the marriage reflects a balance adapted to the patrilineal and patriarchal structure of the family. The wife is obliged to move to the husband's dwelling, to stay at his house (*mulāzamat baytihi*) and not leave it without his permission; to obey him (*tāa*); to fulfil her marital duties (*istimtā*); to bring up the children, and attend to the household. On the other hand, she has property rights *vis-a-vis* the husband. She is entitled to maintenance; to kind treatment (*husn al-mu'āshara*); to the legally specified number of visits to and from her relatives, and such like.[1]

Legal Background

Maintenance (*nafaqa*) includes food (*ta ām*), clothing (*kiswa*) and a legal dwelling (*maskan shar'i*). As between the spouses, the right to maintenance is vested in the wife alone. She is not required to bear the cost of her and her children's subsistence and of the household, even if the husband is unable to do so and she has means of her own. According to Islamic law, the property of the spouses is separate and the wife may manage her property independently.[2]

The amount of maintenance is fixed by agreement between the spouses or, in the absence of agreement, by the *sharī'a* court. The *qāḍi* appoints experts (*mukhbirūn*)—representatives of the parties and of the court—to assess the amount. They are religious functionaries and public figures of accepted authority, such as *imāms, mukhtārs,* heads of local councils, advocates and secretaries of *sharī'a* courts.[3] The amount is fixed in accordance with the economic position of the spouses, the cost of living and the needs of the wife and the family. The concept of maintenance has greatly widened in present-day Muslim society: it now comprises also the cost of the education of the children, medical treatment, including sick-fund dues, expenditure in connection with childbirth, travelling expenses, etc.[4] Maintenance was usually paid in money, but occasionally in kind, in the shape of staple foods (such as oil) and essential household articles (such as soap). Sometimes it consisted in property bearing a yield (such as olive trees). Payment might also be made in promissory notes.[5]

The wife can enforce a judgment for maintenance by execution, but few instances are attested of her doing so.[6] On the other hand, numerous cases are on record of husbands failing to comply with the judgment. Such failure is apparent from recurrent actions for maintenance and from judgments for divorce by agreement, by which the wife waived maintenance accumulated in her favour since the judgment awarding it.[7] If the husband is unable to support the wife or is absent, having left her without maintenance, the wife may, with the approval of the court, borrow money (*istidāna*) in his name which he will have to repay. Cases are recorded where a relative of the wife, who, but for her marriage, would have owed her maintenance, granted her a loan at her request[8] or where she collected maintenance out of her absent husband's property.[9]

If the woman left her husband for any reason, she commonly went to the house of her father or some other agnatic relative, who supported her until she returned to her husband's house.[10] A frequent way of collecting maintenance was by transferring the insurance pension of the children or the old-age pension from the husband to the wife.[11] In urban areas, sometimes it was found that wives were the supporters of the family, including, in some cases, the husband.[12] There were instances of wives being compelled to work because the maintenance paid by their husbands was insufficient for their upkeep.[13]

Causes of Claims for Maintenance and of Disobedience

The wife's duty of moving into the husband's dwelling is conditional on receipt of the prompt dower. If the dower is not without paid, she may leave his house his permission without being regarded as a rebellious wife (*nāshiza*), in which case she would lose her right to maintenance.[14] In many cases, the wife left the husband's house on the ground that all or part of the prompt dower or some stipulations connected therewith, such as household effects and various appurtenances, had not been forthcoming[15]; she claimed maintenance, refusing to return until she had received her due. In some instances, it was expressly stated that the wife had not moved in with the husband (*zifāf*) at all and that the marriage had not been consummated.[16] But usually the wife left the husband after *zifāf* had taken place and sometimes even after children had been born.[17] Other property items which frequently gave rise to a claim for maintenance and to disobedience were the *jihāz* (equipment, clothing and household effects which the wife brought with her from her father's house on her marriage),[18] the *maṣāgh* (jewelry) and the *ḥaly* (ornaments). A wife would claim ownership thereof, accuse the husband of taking them from her against her will, sometimes by force, and demand their return.[19] The aforesaid grounds obtained in towns and villages, where women were alive to their property rights, but not in Beduin society.

Non-receipt of maintenance was, of course, the principal motive for a claim. A wife might sometimes allege that her husband was delaying (*yumāṭil*) her maintenance,[20] that the amount of maintenance was insufficient and that an addition (*ziyāda* or *raf*) was required,[21] or that her husband had left the house and gone to live elsewhere without arranging for her maintenance.[22]

Disputes concerning the dwelling were another cause for claims. The husband is obligated to provide the wife with a legal dwelling (*maskan shar'i*), containing all the equipment she requires, at a place chosen by him. A legal dwelling is a separate house (*dār 'alā ḥidatihā: i.e.,* separate from the house of the husband's family) if the couple are well off, and a separate apartment within the husband's family's house (*bayt min dār 'alā ḥidatihi*) if they are not. The dwelling must have all the legally required facilities, as well as neighbours of a social level which accords with the couple's standing. The husband must not accommodate his relatives—except an undiscriminating (*ghayr mumayyiz*) minor—in the dwelling without the wife's consent, nor may the wife accommodate therein her children (even minor) by another husband or her relatives without the husband's consent. If the husband installs his wife in a separate dwelling in his family's house, she is not entitled to demand a different dwelling unless his relatives "harass her by word or deed."[23] In fact, the characteristics of the legal dwelling correspond to the principle of patrilocality (dwelling within the husband's family's residence).[24]

Hundreds of maintenance and obedience judgments indeed reflect a complex set of relationships between the spouses within the framework of the extended family, with all its typical manifestations and tensions. The wife might assert that the dwelling was not legal, *i.e.,* that it was not a separate entity within the husband's family's dwelling[25]; that the catering and meals were shared—in other words, that she was completely dependent on her mother-in-law[26]; or that some household utensils, clothing and other appurtenances were lacking.[27] But her main complaints in this connection were that her husband's relatives (her mother-in-law, father-in-law, brothers-in-law, sisters-in-law, etc.) "harass her by word and deed," *i.e.,* insulted and beat her (sometimes so seriously as to force her to flee the house);

locked her up in the house; turned her out of the house; prevented her from entering the house or her room: charged her with immoral conduct, and so forth. The wife frequently demanded that the husband prevent his relatives from entering her dwelling and interfering in her life.[28]

Tensions between the wife and the husband's relatives were important factors in the disintegration of the extended family.[29] There is evidence of this and especially of attempts by the wife to achieve a structural solution by which she would escape the control of her in-laws: she might leave the husband's house and refuse to return to him and obey him until he provided her with a dwelling away from his family, in a house owned by him; there were cases in which such attempts were successful.[30] Sometimes a woman made her consent to the marriage conditional on the husband providing her with a separate dwelling; this mostly meant a dwelling in the house (*dār*) of the husband's family, but occasionally express stipulation was made for a "completely separate house."[31] The wife at times agreed to live in her husband's father's house, but stipulated that "if anger erupts" between her and the husband's family or "if she is compelled to leave the house for any reason" the husband should provide her with a dwelling "away from the family" or pay her a sum of money with which to build a new house.[32]

The practice of making the marriage conditional on the provision of a separate dwelling was particularly widespread in urban types of settlement and in the Little Triangle villages. Cohen in his study of Bint al-Ḥudūd in the Little Triangle found that the wife demanded a separate dwelling when there was no blood-relationship between her and her husband,[33] that is to say, that the grip of the extended family was stronger in the case of endogamous marriages. This finding is not confirmed by the sources of the present work. On the contrary, in more than half the cases in which the wife stipulated for a separate dwelling the spouses belonged to the same clan (*ḥamūla*) or were even first cousins.[34] The endogamous marriage was thus no serious obstacle to the wife's striving for a separate dwelling, *i.e.*, to the breakup of the extended family. The stipulation in the marriage contract was particularly widespread in relation to the contents of the dwelling, *viz.*, the various household effects (*'afsh al-bayt, athāth*): furniture, bedding, a sewing-machine, "a complete drawing-room suite," bedroom and kitchen equipment, and all this "after the latest fashion."[35] The value of the household equipment usually ranged between IL 1,500 and IL 2,000.

The wife sometimes refused to move into a dwelling because in her opinion it did not suit her social status or might lower her prestige. Thus, in one case, a woman contended: "[Girls] who are my equals (*mathilāti*) obtained separate conjugal dwellings," and in another case the woman said that the *maskan* was not legal "considering their status and the kind of people they are"; she asked that a house of concrete be built for her. In yet another case, the wife refused to live in the *maskan* because it was situated in the village main street, "lest her good name be impaired."[36] In several cases, the wife alleged that her husband would leave her in the house by herself so that she felt lonely (*tastawḥish*). This, too, is a legal ground for maintenance in certain circumstances, and the husband must either provide a female companion (*mu'niṣa*) to keep her company and cheer her up or transfer her to a place where she will not feel lonely.[37] In one case, a woman from Ramla said that her husband went to his other wife in Gaza every Saturday morning and returned only on Monday, leaving her to herself in the meantime; "and there are no neighbours nearby so that I am afraid." In a further case, a woman from Galilee reported that her husband went to work near Jerusalem, leaving her to herself, and that she "felt lonesome." The husband provided a *mu'niṣa* to relieve her boredom on the nights when he was away from home, but the wife refused to accept her because she belonged to the husband's *ḥamūla* and harassed her.[38]

The wife is bound to follow the husband to whatever locality he chooses.[39] She generally raised no objection as to the type of settlement, the neighbourhood or the like. But in several dozen cases wives did raise objections although their dwellings were legal and their husbands had not withheld any of their conjugal rights or ill-treated them, but on the contrary, had been kind to them. However, these women were not willing to live with their spouses in certain localities or geographical areas even if they were treated "in the best possible way" and provided with "the best of dwellings."[40] The chief cause of this phenomenon was the unwillingness of the wives to change the way of life, habits, standards, type of housing, etc., to which they had been accustomed before their marriages. Two-thirds of the cases involved townswomen who were not prepared to live in the country,[41] in a Beduin encampment[42] or even in a town regarded as inferior in social, economic or other respects.[43] Sometimes a townswoman was unwilling to move to another quarter of the same town.[44] A countrywoman might not be prepared to live in a village less developed or farther from urban centres than her home village or might wish to live in another quarter of the same village.[45] In one case, a Beduin woman who had married a Beduin of another tribe refused to live in his encampment.[46] A countrywoman might refuse to live in town, despite better housing conditions, and a higher standard of living, because of her attachment to her original environment and her family and because of her fear of change, and of confrontation with a modern way of life.[47]

A townswoman married to a Beduin or villager could stipulate in the marriage contract that the conjugal dwelling should be in her home locality.[48] She sometimes added that if the husband infringed this stipulation he should have to pay her a sum of money for the purchase of a dwelling there.[49] In isolated cases, countrywomen stipulated that their townsmen husbands reside in their villages.[50] In one case, the couple lived for a time near the residence of the wife's family at Lod. Because of disputes between the husband, a Negev Beduin, and the wife's family, and because he worked near Beersheba, he suggested that they go to live with his tribe, but she would have none of it "even if he gives me a palace."[51] This case is instructive because it involved a phenomenon approximating matrilocality. It was a consequence of intensified commuting of rural and Beduin manpower to urban and economic centres, especially since the late 1950s, when restrictions on movement imposed by the Military Government were gradually relaxed and eventually abolished. In the encounter between rural and Beduin commuters and urban women, the latter had the upper hand, and as a result, the couples took up residence in town. Significant in this connection, though rare, was the husband's resort to a stipulation in the marriage contract in order to ensure that the conjugal dwelling be in his home locality,[52] although the *shari'a* already required it to be there.

Sometimes a wife reached a goodwill agreement—without binding force—with the husband establishing the conjugal dwelling in her home locality. Thus, in one case, the couple lived for a time in the husband's village but then, following a quarrel, they made an agreement under which the permanent dwelling was to be in the wife's township and she was to supply his meals when he was staying with her in return for a fixed maintenance payment. In another case, the spouses agreed to move from the countryside to the city where the husband worked. He sold his property, but at the last moment he changed his mind, whereupon the wife left his house and went to live in the city. In a further case, the husband moved to the wife's dwelling in a Beduin settlement after she had repeatedly left his house, situated in a village. Later he was compelled to return to his village, but his wife refused to follow him.[53]

In several cases, the husband lived in the wife's dwelling (not in her family's); in almost all such cases she was a townswoman and he from some other type of settlement.[54] Sometimes the wife stipulated in the marriage contract that the dwelling should be her property or the common (*mushtarak*) property of the spouses or that half of the house should be her property as part of, or in addition to, the dower.[55] In all these cases, the wife came from one of the mixed towns (Jaffa, Ramla, Lod) or from a Little Triangle village. In one case, the spouses were first cousins who had inherited the plot and house where they lived from their parents. In another case, the wife required the husband to register the dwelling in her name and to give her "whatever she might demand in the future, without any restriction."[56]

Cruelty toward the wife or "lack of good treatment" by the husband was frequently a cause of disobedience. A wife might complain that her husband ill-used her in various ways: cursed her, humiliated her, treated her rudely and harshly, burdened her with work beyond her strength, beat her violently, sometimes to the point of grievous injury necessitating medical attendance and hospitalization, or even threatened or attempted to kill her.[57] Sometimes women called the police or filed actions in the civil courts.[58] Under such circumstances, the wife mostly left the husband's house and refused to obey him on the ground that she was not "safe in the dwelling with him."[59] The husband frequently ejected the wife from the house, alone or with her children.[60] Occasionally he himself left the house and disappeared without leaving a trace[61] or stayed away for a long time, especially for purposes of work. In one case, the wife said that the husband spent five hours every day travelling to work and back to his village and that damage was caused her thereby[62]; such disruption of family life was typical of the increased commuting of manpower from towns and villages to centres of employment.[63] Imprisonment of the husband or his confinement, by police order, to a place outside the locality in which the couple lived could also be a ground for a claim for maintenance.[64] Sometimes the wife complained that her husband was insulting her by charging that she "loved someone else" or was unfaithful to him.[65] In one case, the wife took offense at the fact that her husband had not himself come to take her to his house "in accordance with custom and tradition"; had he done so, she said, she would have willingly obeyed him. In another case, the wife had waited three years in vain at her brother's house for the husband to ask her personally to return to him; then she had sued him for maintenance.[66]

It has happened that a husband forced his wife to work and hand over her earnings to him and beat her soundly when she started out late for work.[67] A wife might assert that she was ill and unable to work.[68] In the Little Triangle villages, the wife frequently stipulated in the marriage contract that she would go "veiled or keep indoors" (*mukhad-dara*) and "not have to work away from home."[69] Changes in the occupational structure, especially the large-scale commuting of rural manpower, had caused a serious shortage of agricultural labour. As a result, there was an increased need for the employment of women and children, and since agricultural work was hard, many women preferred to marry landless men. The liberation of women from agricultural work has in recent years become a matter of prestige. A woman who did not work away from home, or who in consequence of her marriage had stopped doing so, covered her face with a veil.[70] The author did not encounter conditions of this kind in other parts of the country, except for one case involving a woman from Acre.[71] The fact that this custom was peculiar to the Little Triangle was probably due to the advanced social position of women in this area compared with other agricultural regions. In most cases, the women in question had an elementary or secondary education.[72]

Polygamous marriages were another cause of claims of maintenance and disobedience. Islamic law requires the husband to practice justice and equality (*'adl*) toward his wives as regards maintenance and the apportionment (*qasm*) of his time between them. He must also install each of them in a separate dwelling. This applies even in so far as a wife does not claim that a rival in the same house (*dār*) harms her by word or deed.[73] Wives often complained of discrimination as to maintenance or marital relations.[74] Another frequent complaint by a wife was that the husband had installed her and her rival in the same dwelling or adjoining dwellings and that this caused her so much suffering or injury that she sometimes fled from the house; her flight might also has means of exerting pressure on the husband to grant her a separate dwelling[75]. There have been cases in which a husband, after taking a second wife, turned the first wife out of the house[76] or left the house and went to live elsewhere with the other.[77] It has also happened that a wife left her husband's house because of his taking another wife, with the declared intention of not returning to him and without claiming maintenance.[78]

One of the commonest causes of the wife's leaving the husband's house and refusing to return to him—sometimes despite numerous approaches by the husband through mediators (*wusaṭā'*) and "people of good will" *(ahl al-khayr)*[79]—were disputes between the two families and interference by them in the life of the couple. The dispute could be quite unconnected with the spouses themselves; it might be over some criminal matter or some land.[80] Then, again, it might be between the husband and the wife's family.[81] Shaykh Ḥasan Amīn al-Ḥabash said that most of the disputes were due to incitement (*taḥriḍ*) by the wife's family.[82] Shaykh Amīn Qāsim Mudlij, on the other hand, tended to stress the role of the husband's relatives. The latter seemed to think that since the wife was bought with their money, she ought to be their slave (*'abda*) and servant (*khādima*) rather than serve and obey her husband. They regarded themselves as "a political and legislative authority and the son [the husband] as an executive authority" whose task was to implement the decisions of his family regarding his wife. The wife's relatives, on the other hand, were distressed about her being severed from her family and felt that she was entitled to a married life in freedom, without outside interference. These opposing views might even find expression on the very first day of the marriage, especially among unintelligent people. The immediate cause of disputes of this kind was the proximity of the conjugal dwelling to the residence of the husband's family.[83]

In such circumstances, the wife usually displayed loyal, sometimes even fanatical, attachment to her family. Thus, in one case, a wife who had left her husband's house contended: "My children's honour is not greater than that of my brothers."[84] Sometimes the wife was not prepared to return to the husband's house until the families had made peace (*taṣāluḥ*) or her father had given his consent.[85] But it also happened that she might openly admit that her father or brother forced her to leave her husband's house, that she did not deny that the dwelling was legal and that her husband had given her everything due to her, and that she wanted to return to him but was afraid that her relatives would harm her.[86] In one case, the wife said that her father "will slaughter her if she crosses him" and asked that the court issue an order for obedience and that she be handed over to her husband by the police "so as to escape punishment by her father."[87]

In the case of exchange marriages (*shighār, tabādul al-zawjāt*) it is difficult in everyday life to maintain strict equality between the exchanged women as to food, housing, clothing, and so on. Shaykh Ḥasan Amīn al-Ḥabash said that it was sufficient for one of them to think that she was less favourably off than her *badīla* (the one for whom she had been exchanged) to make jealousy and envy spring up immediately, which would in turn lead to a distorted outlook and spoil relations between the spouses.[88] Exchange marriage created a mutual dependence between the two families: the falling out, for any reason whatsoever, of one couple, as a result of which the wife left the husband's house and he applied for a judgment for obedience or she claimed maintenance, would almost automatically entail similar steps on the part of the other couple. A wife frequently admitted that she had no complaints against her husband regarding the dwelling, dower, or any other matter, and that she only left his house because her *badīla* had quarrelled with *her* husband and because "according to custom," when one *badīla* left her husband, the other was expected to do likewise.[89] A woman sometimes stipulated that she would only return to her husband on the condition that her *badīla* return to hers.[90] And indeed, if and when the first couple made up its quarrel, the other wife would also return to her husband.[91]

Other manifestations of the mutual dependence created by exchange marriages were the payment of maintenance at like rates to the two wives[92] and actions for maintenance and obedience between the respective partners, ending in the divorce of both wives at the same time and on the same terms.[93] The women were pawns in the game between the families: their moves were usually determined against their will.[94] In only one case did a woman seek release from the rules of mutual dependence, but the matter ended in divorce contrary to her wishes.[95] The only way to break the dependence between the two marriages was to pay dower, and in several cases a *badīla* in fact announced her willingness to return to her husband if dower was paid.[96] Exchange marriages were particularly frequent in rural and Beduin society, but did occur in urban society as well.[97]

Chief among the causes of non-payment of maintenance, and of claims for obedience, were conditions in which the wife had left the house without the husband's permission and gone to see her father, brother, mother, children or other relatives or her neighbors,[98] refused to return to the husband and to obey him,[99] was "rebellious," did not fulfil her duties toward the husband, the children and the household,[100] gave her own family and her children preference over the husband,[101] had her children by another man live in her husband's house,[102] or had misbehaved herself[103]; sometimes the husband was unable to pay maintenance or to provide a separate dwelling to the wife owing to poverty, unemployment, or insufficient income.[104] The wife might work away from home against the husband's will[105] or demand to live in her original locality.[106] Some of these causes attest to innovations in the status of women, such as their working away from home and supporting their families.[107]

The Rebellious Woman

A wife who leaves her husband's house without his permission and without a legal reason is considered rebellious (*nāshiza*) and loses the right to maintenance for the duration of her rebelliousness (*nushūz*).[108] The declaration of a wife as rebellious is the customary legal sanction against her refusal to obey. The concept of the *bayt al-ṭā'a* (house of obedience) does not exist in Israel, where a judgment for obedience is not legally enforceable.[109] Moreover, the prohibition of polygamy and of divorce against the wife's will had deprived the husband of two severe sanctions that once would have deterred the wife from disobedience. Shaykh Ḥusnī al-Zu'bī and other *qāḍīs* were of the opinion that women now took unfair advantage of the reforms in their legal status and that the rules of obedience were no longer effective.[110]

The *sijills* do not contain many declarations of rebelliousness, but many women were actually in a state of rebellion in the sense that they did not obey their husbands and did not receive maintenance. In many cases, though women told the courts that they would not obey their husbands, they were nevertheless not declared rebellious; and many judgments for obedience were not enforced for many years, if at all.[111] For both traditional and modern reasons, the economic sanction did not seem to deter women from disobedience. As stated, a woman who left her husband usually went to her agnatic relatives, who provided for her and for her children (if she had taken them with her) until she became reconciled with her husband and returned to him. If the dispute ended in divorce, the burden of maintenance devolved on her family until she was remarried. Sometimes a wife made her return to her husband conditional on his reimbursing the maintenance paid by her father during her stay with him.[112] Moreover, the urban woman enjoyed a sense of economic security. She was not dependent on her father; she worked for her living and was able to support her children and might even live alone.[113] She might waive maintenance for herself and her children and undertake to provide for her children "at her own expense."[114]

Furthermore, in some cases the wife, on her own initiative, demanded to be considered rebellious and denied the right to maintenance.[115] In about half the cases in which the wife was declared rebellious, the spouses, or at least the wife, came from an urban type of settlement. Reasons for the wife's being declared rebellious included unwillingness of a townswoman to live in the husband's home locality (if rural or a Beduin encampment)[116]; disputes between the spouses over property, such as jewelry, livestock and immovables[117]; the wife's working away from home; her living in a separate dwelling with her children by another man[118]; and her reaction to being ill-treated by the husband in various ways.[119] In one case, the husband alleged that the wife's father incited her against him "for reasons of village party politics."[120] In the vast majority of cases, there was no blood relationship between the spouses, and it seems reasonable to assume that in an exogamous marriage the wife enjoys greater freedom in her relations with the husband than in an endogamous one.

The traditional equilibrium between the rights and duties of husband and wife had thus been greatly upset in Israeli Muslim society. This was due to the disintegration of the extended family, to the changes in the position of women and to the intervention of the Knesset. It seems that more than in the past the husband in recent times has resorted to legal action to get his wife to obey him. It is characteristic that in one case the husband sought a judgment for obedience because he feared that the wife was about to slip across the border into some Arab country; he asked for her to be tied to him by a IL 3,000 guarantee and with the help of the police.[121] However, since judgments for obedience were not enforceable, the husband had no choice but to apply the traditional methods of establishing domestic peace by means of arbitrators and mediators.

Sometimes disputes between spouses were indeed terminated by reconciliation. An important part was played in this connection by arbitrators, mediators, "people of good will," the children of the spouses, and *qāḍīs*.[122] In the case of reconciliation, the wife withdrew her claim for maintenance or asked that the judgment for maintenance given in her favour be rescinded,[123] and the husband withdrew his action for obedience.[124] Reconciliations were sometimes accompanied by detailed agreements between the spouses, specifying the duties and rights of each toward the other. The husband might undertake not to be late in paying maintenance to his wife and children; to assure their subsistence and well-being; to allot a specific daily amount to the wife for household expenses (to be supplemented by him if insufficient, while any surplus was to be kept by her in a special fund); to treat the wife well; not to beat or curse her; to prevent his relatives attacking her or interfering in her life; to divide his time equitably between his wives, to provide a separate dwelling for his wife, to build her a new house with a kitchen and modern facilities, to set up a partition between her dwelling and that of his family, to provide a separate entrance to her dwelling; to permit the wife to visit her relatives from time to time. On the other hand, the husband was entitled to bring up his children and ensure that they obeyed him, and to determine the location of the dwelling. The wife would undertake to be "extremely courteous" toward the husband, not to annoy him "and to remember that he is the head of the family"; not to interfere in matters pertaining to his personal freedom, such as the times of his going out and coming home; to obey him, not to go out without his permission; to fulfil her marital duties; to manage the household, cook his meals and look after the children; to see that her relatives did not call without his invitation or consent, and so on.[125] Sometimes it was provided that one of the wife's relatives should offer surety for the fulfilment of her obligations under the agreement or that if the husband infringed a condition of the agreement he should pay maintenance or—which was very rare—the wife might be delegated by the husband to divorce herself.[126] On the basis of such agreements, the *qāḍī* would give a judgment for obedience by mutual consent of the parties.[127]

Maintenance of Women within the Wider Family Circle

Maintenance out of the estate is unknown in Islamic law. The widow is not entitled to maintenance out of her husband's estate; according to the *sharī'a,* she takes a share of it.[128] Her maintenance is the responsibility of her children. However, unlike the wife's right to maintenance, which exists even where she is rich and the husband poor, the mother's maintenance is fixed in accordance with her economic position: only a destitute mother is entitled to maintenance, and on the other hand, children are only liable to pay it if they have the necessary means.[129] The Knesset interfered in the matter of maintenance as far as the wider family circle is concerned, which includes the parents and grandparents of the spouses, the grown-up children and their spouses, the grandchildren, and the brothers and sisters of the spouses. There was no interference as to maintenance within the immediate family (*i.e.*, the spouses and their minor children), to which religious law continues to apply. The Family Law Amendment (Maintenance) Law, 5719-1959, provides, *inter alia*, that the extent, measure and modes of provision of maintenance within the wider family circle shall, in the absence of agreement between the parties, be prescribed by the court "according to the need of the person entitled and the ability of the person liable." This principle is consonant with the Islamic legal concept. Another section provides that the law "shall add to, and not derogate from, maintenance rights accruing under any law administered by a religious court, or under the personal law applying to the parties."[130]

More than 200 claims for maintenance within the wider family circle were filed in *sharī'a* courts in the period under review. About one-third were filed by the widowed mother, the remainder by the father (sometimes maintenance was sought by both parents) and other relatives. All the applications by widows were directed against sons, not one against daughters. The mother based her application on the plea that she was old, ill and poor, that she had no property or source of income, that the National Insurance pension was insufficient, that she was incapable of earning a living, that she had no supporter and that no one but her son (or sons) owed her maintenance.[131] She sometimes alleged that her son had seized control of the family property and thereby deprived her of her means of subsistence.[132]

Some of the actions ended with maintenance being awarded to the mother by mutual agreement of the parties. The sons might undertake to provide their mother, in addition to maintenance, with a suitable dwelling in which to spend the rest of her days.[133] Failing mutual agreement, the rate of maintenance was fixed by *mukhbirūn* (experts). Sons who refused to pay maintenance to their mothers contended that their commitments toward their own families did not allow them to assume additional burdens and that their mothers had property—shares in the estates of their family heads—sufficient for their subsistence.[134] There was a definite correlation between the extent of the sons' readiness to pay maintenance to their mothers and the state of property relations after the death of a family head: where the mother held the family property or her share in the estate, the sons were less ready to grant her economic assistance. A similar attitude governed relations between sons and their aged father. In some cases, a father claimed maintenance from his sons on the ground that he had registered all his property in their names.[135] In one case, the sons made it an express condition for their paying maintenance to their father that he should transfer part of his property to them, and in another case they rejected their father's claim for maintenance on the ground that he had registered all his property in the name of his wife, their mother.[136] All the maintenance claims of widowed mothers arose in rural or urban, but not Beduin, types of settlement.

A small number of maintenance claims were filed by women of other degrees of relationship: by sisters against brothers, by nieces against paternal uncles, by granddaughters against grandfathers and so forth. The maintenance claim of a minor in the custody of her mother was usually filed by the latter,[137] but sometimes by the claimant herself.[138] In claims by sisters, it was occasionally contended that the brother had usurped their share in the father's estate.[139] In some cases men were ordered to pay maintenance to their daughters-in-law or granddaughters because their husbands were unable to support them, the maintenance was then regarded as a debt of the husbands.[140]

The *Qāḍīs* and Maintenance and Obedience

The salient feature in the *qāḍīs'* dealing with maintenance and obedience claims was their effort to reconcile the spouses and restore domestic peace. This sprang from their deep-rooted belief in the importance of the marital union and family life. Shaykh Tawfīq Maḥmūd Asaliyya stressed the heavy responsibility of the courts in this connection: "The family is the nucleus of society, and the greater its integrity and inner equilibrium, the co-operation between its members, and its purity, the greater is the *umma's* [Muslim community's] progress on the road of civilization."[141] Shaykh Ḥusnī al-Zu'bī said that "the marital bond is a solid bond between the spouses, and the *sharī'a* wants it to subsist and the comradeship and love between the spouses to endure."[142] Shaykh Amīn Qāsim Mudlij, Shaykh Mūsā al-Ṭabarī and observers close to *sharī'a* court affairs likened the *qāḍī* to the family doctor.[143] Almost all maintenance and obedience judgments note that the court made efforts to bring about reconciliation and compromise settlement between the spouses. Frequently the hearing was adjourned in the hope that the spouses would meanwhile reach agreement.[144] The *qāḍī* might invoke the blood-relationship of the spouses to smooth out their differences.[145] Indeed, his efforts were sometimes successful without his having to render judgment for maintenance or obedience.[146] The striving for compromise was probably connected with an established tradition of avoiding application of the *sharī'a* for fear of distorting it.[147] This tendency turned the *sharī'a* court into a kind of arbitral agency, as customary in traditional society; in fact, the *qāḍīs* occasionally called in outside arbitrators to settle disputes between spouses.[148] They refrained as far as possible from handing down decisions and applying legal sanctions. The judgment was very often intended to validate an agreement or compromise reached by the parties.[149]

If the court's efforts to reconcile the parties failed and there was no escape from passing judgment, the *qāḍī* did so reluctantly.[150] He might add that the judgment for obedience was conditional on the husband's treating the wife well and fulfilling all his conjugal duties, or he might warn the husband not to ill-use his wife in any way, to respect her rights, not to touch her property, to grant her "full freedom so long as no infringement of Islamic law is involved," to enable her to visit her relatives, not to force her to wait on him or his relatives and to avoid petty jealousy, malicious gossip and the like.[151] He would sometimes threaten that if the husband did not comply with his directions he would award maintenance to the wife or permit her to act against the husband's will, for instance, in the matter of visits to relatives.[152] Sometimes the *qāḍī* exhorted both spouses to fulfil their mutual duties, to prevent their respective families from meddling in their affairs.[153] Shaykh Mūsā al-Ṭabarī and Shaykh Tawfīq 'Asaliyya occasionally made a judgment for obedience conditional on the husband's providing sureties for good behaviour toward the wife.[154]

The *qāḍīs'* approach in judgments was extremely formal; they decided in scrupulous adherence to the provisions of the *sharī'a* and sometimes invoked Qurānic verses and commentaries to support their judgments.[155] With regard to maintenance, this approach was usually favourable to the wife. The *qāḍīs* took no account of changes in the social and economic status of women and continued to regard the husband as the head and supporter of the family. Thus, in one case, Shaykh Ṭāhir Ḥamād awarded maintenance to the wife although she had admitted that she was well-off and lived without assistance from her husband, "because maintenance is one of her legal rights and the husband is not exempt from providing it." In another case, he ordered the husband to pay maintenance "because according to the *sharī'a* a wife cannot be forced to put up the husband in her house . . . if she does not do so of her own free will."[156] Shaykh Ḥasan Amīn al-Ḥabash decided that maintenance of the wife was the responsibility of the husband alone even if he was poor.[157] Shaykh Tawfīq Maḥmūd 'Asaliyya held that unemployment of the husband did not relieve him of the duty to provide maintenance to the wife.[158] These decisions conformed to the spirit of Islamic law. The foregoing also applied whenever the husband failed to fulfil one of his other obligations toward the wife, such as the payment of prompt dower, or to conform to any stipulations connected therewith, the provision of a legal dwelling, good treatment of the wife, and so on; in all these cases, the *qāḍīs* were careful to award maintenance to the wife.[159]

On the other hand, the formal approach was sometimes to the wife's disadvantage. Thus, the claim of a woman in the last month of pregnancy for maintenance from the day, six months earlier, when she had been driven from her husband's house was dismissed by Shaykh Amīn Qāsim Mudlij on the ground that according to the *sharī'a* maintenance is not awarded for the time preceding the filing of the application.[160] Shaykh Ṭawfīq Maḥmūd 'Asaliyya distinguished between wife-beating "contrary to the principles of the *sharī'a*" and wife-beating "after the manner of husbands." He accordingly awarded maintenance to a wife who left her husband's house only in the case of the former type of wife-beating.[161]

Nevertheless, in some cases the *qāḍīs* deviated from the rigid formal approach in view of the husband's economic position. Thus, for instance, Shaykh Mūsā al-Ṭabarī directed a wife to file a claim for maintenance for herself and her children against her grown-up sons and dismissed her application for maintenance from her husband because the latter was poor and unemployed, had no property and was supported by his sons. In another case, he ordered the husband's father to pay maintenance to his daughter-in-law and her children because the husband worked for his father as a shepherd and was not able to support his family.[162] The *qāḍīs* at times had recourse to the welfare services of the State rather than to the institutionalized organs entrusted with the provision of maintenance to the wife and family in traditional society. In some cases, they took into account pensions from the National Insurance Institute or the Ministry of Social Welfare or even asked that such pensions be increased to make things easier for husbands who found it difficult to meet their obligations.[163]

The *qāḍīs* usually heeded the wife's troubles concerning the dwelling as far as was consistent with the *sharī'a,* and when they departed from this practice it was not necessarily to her advantage. They decided that the dwelling was not legal when it was not separate *within* the house (*dār*) of the husband's family, as when sanitary facilities were shared, where there was no separate entrance to the wife's dwelling, when there were no decent neighbours, or when furniture and other essential accessories were lacking. They also decided so when physical or mental injury was caused to the wife or when her safety was threatened.[164] The husband was sometimes ordered to provide a dwelling *outside* his family's residence when his relatives harassed his wife in any way, as he was indeed required to do according to the *sharī'a.*[165] Nonetheless, in several such cases, the *qāḍīs* sought solutions within the joint dwelling of the extended family, having regard to the husband's circumstances and the housing shortage.[166] On some occasions, they were in favour of a separate dwelling even though no legal grounds for it existed. Shaykh Amīn Qāsim Mudlij was alert to the fact that interference in the couple's life by the husband's parents caused great suffering to the wife and that it was difficult for her to find witnesses to her harassment since the husband's relatives were not usually eager to testify against him. He therefore suggested that if the *qāḍī,* by examining the spouses (and not by evidence required under the *sharī'a*), gained the impression that the proximity of the dwelling to the residence of the husband's parents was the direct cause of the disputes between the spouses he should have to decide that the dwelling was not legal.[167] This suggestion was not reflected in judgments, and its very making seems to indicate that the *qāḍīs* did not follow it.[168] The same *qāḍī* suggested that the wife stipulate in the marriage contract that a dwelling near the residence of the husband's parents shall not be legal.[169] Such stipulations, though invalid according to the Ḥanafī school,[170] have met with the full support of the courts, and so have stipulations to the effect that the conjugal dwelling shall be situated in the wife's home locality.[171]

The question of the separate dwelling was particularly serious in the case of a polygamous marriage. The *qāḍīs* usually insisted on a separate dwelling (*dār*) for each wife,[172] although there were deviations from the *sharī'a* in this matter: for instance, Shaykh Ṭāhir Ḥamād decided that the dwellings of the rival wives need not be fully separate unless the spouses were people of means,[173] and Shaykh Ḥasan Amīn al-Ḥabash rejected an application by a wife for a separate dwelling although her rival was living in an adjoining room.[174]

The *qāḍīs'* approach to the question of obedience was likewise formal. They were careful to order obedience (*tā 'a*) when the wife had *prima facie* obtained all her matrimonial rights, such as dower and a legal dwelling, and there was no legal ground for her leaving the husband's house.[175] Wife-beating "for the purpose of chastisement" (*biqaṣd al-ta'dīb*) was considered legitimate from the *sharī'a* point of view and not a sufficient reason for leaving the conjugal dwelling.[176] The *qāḍīs* were not prepared to recognize the departure of one *badīla* in an exchange marriage from her husband's house as a legal ground for the other to do the same; in each case they ordered obedience[177] unless it was proved that the wife had not received dower.[178] Shaykh Ḥasan Amīn al-Ḥabash sharply attacked this type of marriage, calling it "a malignant disease" since, in his opinion, it was a cause of trouble, of disputes between the families and of divorce: as the couples could not, by the nature of things, be alike in character, temper and economic circumstances, there would always be jealousy and resentment between the two women. He recommended a form of marriage not linking the two couples to each other.[179] The exchange marriage is a striking example of a clash between social custom and religious norm. The *qāḍīs* sided with the *sharī'a,* which in this case represents a more progressive concept than custom. A more frequent example is the conflict between the wife's loyalty to her father's house, which did not cease after her marriage, and her loyalty to her husband, enjoined on her by the *sharī'a*. Here, too, the religious norm did not stand the test of reality owing to the strength of the blood-tie, and here, too, the *qāḍīs* sided with the religious norm. When a wife refused to return to her husband's house on the ground that her brothers were no less important to her than her children, Shaykh Tawfīq Maḥmūd 'Asaliyya said that "such a view point is recognized neither by the *sharī'a* nor by the [secular] law."[180]

The *qāḍīs* were chary of judging a woman rebellious (*nushūz*) even when required to do so according to the *sharī'a*. In such circumstances, they contented themselves with a judgment for obedience; in fact, even when it was apparent that the wife did not comply with the judgment, they were in no hurry to subject her to the full rigour of the law. It seems that they did not wish to exacerbate relations and give a kind of legitimation to their severance. Moreover, they were aware that the denial of maintenance to a rebellious wife was no longer a deterrent. Shaykh Ḥusnī al-Zu'bī said so expressly,[181] and this awareness was probably the reason why he had not given a single *nushūz* judgment. In some cases, the *qāḍīs* contented themselves with a threat that if the wife did not obey the husband she would be declared rebellious, but when she persisted they did not carry out their threat.[182] In other cases, they rejected the wife's claim for maintenance "because of her rebelliousness" or because she had failed to comply with an order for obedience, but still did not positively declare her rebellious.[183] Only in about a score of cases was the wife actually declared rebellious, and this mostly at her own request[184] or because she had failed to comply with an order for obedience.[185] Most of the *nushūz* judgments were rendered by Shaykh Mūsā al-Ṭabarī,[186] who sometimes gave as the reason his inability to compel the wife's obedience.[187]

The *qāḍīs* were alive to the fact that judgments for obedience were practically meaningless because they could not be enforced. Shaykh Mūsā al-Ṭabarī would explain to the husband that he had no power over the wife after passing a judgment for obedience or *nushūz* and was not allowed to interfere in her affairs.[188] Shaykh Ḥusnī al-Zu'bī considered that the Knesset should intervene with regard to obedience since its criminal legislation in matters of marriage and divorce had deprived the husband of the two sanctions traditionally available to him against the rebellious wife in addition to denial of maintenance. Shaykh Ḥusnī suggested inserting a provision in the Penal Law Amendment (Bigamy) Law, 5719-1959, to the effect that if the wife did not comply with a judgment for obedience this should be a good defence for the husband to a charge of polygamy. He believed that such a sanction would deter the wife and cure her waywardness.[189] Shaykh Amīn Qāsim Mudlij suggested enacting a provision whereby rebelliousness of the wife should also be a good defence to the charge of divorcing her against her will if the divorce were to take place under a special permit from the *sharī'a* court.[190] Shaykh Ḥasan Amīn al-Ḥabash also noted the helplessness of the husband where the wife refused to comply with a judgment for obedience, rebelled and transgressed "the bounds of the *sharī'a,* good sense, reason, and benevolence." "There are women," he said, "whose extortion must be guarded against," who "are instigated to rebellion by human beings and demons," and for whom detailed and precise laws must be devised in accordance with each kind of rebelliousness.[191]

With regard to maintenance within the wider family circle, there is no clear distinction between positive, legally-binding norms and ethical norms, the latter being more in the nature of charity.[192] This encouraged *qāḍīs* to forego the exercise of judicial power and to try and settle claims by way of compromise and agreement between the parties. They often acted as real arbitrators[193] and, when an agreement had been reached, gave it the force of a judgment.[194] It was only when the parties did not reach agreement or when the defendant did not appear in court that the *qāḍī* was compelled to exercise his power and have maintenance fixed by *mukhbirūn*.[195] Almost all the maintenance suits filed by widowed mothers or other women in the wider family circle were allowed. The *qāḍī* might also decide, for instance, that a grown-up son should provide a suitable dwelling for a widowed mother or separate his dwelling from hers.[196] Only in a few cases did the *qāḍī* dismiss a woman's maintenance claim after it had been found that she had property, a share in an inheritance or an income sufficient for her livelihood.[197]

Notes and References

1. See *FRL*, arts. 69-74. For more detail see Qadrī, arts. 17, 150-9, 206-16.
2. See Qadrī, art. 150; Linant de Bellefonds, pp. 258 *seq.*; Schacht, p. 167; Abu Zahra, p. 145; Fyzee, p. 203.
3. See, *e.g.*, *Ṭbll*, p. 157: no. 21-f.23/59, p. 160: no. 1-f.3/60, p. 167: no. 8-f.15/60, p. 170: no. 11-f.22/60; *AcD8*, p. 97: no. 14/70-f.125/69; *JfQ4*, p. 103: no. 115-f.83/68.
4. See, *e.g.*, *AcI3*, p. 28: no. 17-f.47/56, p. 29: no. 19-f.55/56, p. 85: no. 19-f.78/58; *AcQ5*, p. 45: f.109/64; *AcD8*, p. 39; no. 39-f.77/68; *NzI4*, p. 195: no.1/5-f.13/59; *JfQ2*, p. 590: no. 623-f.29/63. Cf. the Syrian Law of Personal Status, No. 59 of September 17, 1953, art. 71(1).
5. See, *e.g.*, *AcI2*, p. 5: f.3/51; *AcD6*, p. 51: f.121/64; *NzI4*, p. 141: no. 6/2-f.15/53 (the husband undertook to give the wife a promissory note for the balance of maintenance due to her for one year and she "is free to use it as she pleases . . .").
6. See, *e.g.*, *AcD6*, p. 41: f.94/65; *JfQ3*, p. 131: no. 206-f.82/64; *JfQ5*, p. 4: no. 7-f.12/69.
7. See the chapter "Divorce," p. 159.
8. *FRL*, arts. 96, 98. See Abu Zahra, p. 145; Goitein and Ben-Shemesh, p. 225. See. *e.g.*, *AcD7*, p. 62: f.21/67.
9. See, *e.g.*, *NzI4*, p. 62: no. 1/1-f.2/50, p. 67: no. 1/13-f.25/50.
10. See, *e.g.*, *TbI1*, p. 156: no. 20-f.3/59, p. 281: no. 2-f.4/65.
11. See, *e.g.*, *JfQ4*, p. 2: no. 2-f.80/65, p. 134: no. 160-f.125/68, p. 145: no. 174-f.134/68; *NzI4*, p. 289: no. 4/14-f.64/66.

12. See, *e.g.*, *JfQ1*, p. 216: no. 338-f.48/55 (the husband had a pension insufficient even for coffee and tobacco; he was unfit for heavy physical work and the wife was a seamstress); *JfQ2*, p. 432: no. 418-f.12/60; *JfQ4*, p. 55: no. 51-f.97/67 (the wife went out to work and was the sole supporter of the family; the husband had another wife in Gaza), p. 130: no. 153-f.132/68 (the wife said that she did not want the husband and that "he provides support [for himself] and I provide support [for myself]"), p. 134: no. 160-f.125/68.
13. See, *e.g.*, *NzI4*, p. 227: no. 1/19-f.60/63.
14. *FRL*, art. 71; Qadrī, art. 214.
15. See, *e.g.*, *JfQ2*, p. 335: no. 527-f.5/85, p. 406: no. 570-f.35/59.
16. See, *e.g.*, *JfQ4*, p. 108: no. 122-f.77/68; *AcD6*, p. 12: no. 12/65-f.174/64; *AcD7*, p. 23: f.132/65; *TbIL*, p. 10: no. 1/11-f.25/50.
17. See, *e.g.*, *JfQ1*, p. 6: no. 12-f.10/51; *AcI2*, p. 45: f.42/53. Cf. Granqvist, vol. 2, p. 226.
18. See, *e.g.*, *NzI4*, p. 53: no. 1/16-f.27/49, p. 98: no. 3/8-f.17/51, p. 113: no. 5/5-f.14/52 (the wife was willing to obey if the husband gave her *nuqūṭ* (bridal gifts) to replace those he burnt); *AcD8*, p. 17: no. 17/68-f.143/67.
19. See, *e.g.*, *JfQ2*, p. 529: no. 583-f.39/62; *AcD6*, p. 28: f.24/65 (the husband complained that the wife had fraudulently taken jewelry from him that belonged to him), p. 71: f.71/64; *NzI4*, p. 139: no. 2/4-f.8/53; *Ṭ̣bI1*, p. 156: no. 20-f.31/51 (unless the husband returned to her her gold, of which he had possession, the wife would not obey him in any house "even though his house were of gold"), p. 224: no. 16-f.15/63 (the wife refused to hand over her jewelry to the husband and he beat her and locked her up in his house until she was rescued by the police; he was arrested and she brought a criminal action against him).
20. See, *e.g.*, *JfQ4*, p. 2: no. 2-f.80/65 (the husband delayed maintenance so long that the grocer, contrary to his habit, refused to give the wife credit: the husband neither gave her money nor bought the commodities himself); *AcD7*, p. 62: f.21/67.
21. See, *e.g.*, *AcI1*, p. 82: f.54/50 (the wife contended that she "also smokes"): *AcD6*, p. 65: f.153/65.
22. See, *e.g.*, *JfQ3*, p. 310: no. 449-f.130/66; *NzI4*, p. 345: no. 10/47-f.138/67.
23. *FRL*, arts, 70-2; Qadrī, arts, 184-8; See Fyzee, pp. 119-22.
24. See Baer, p. 64.
25. See, *e.g.*, *JfQ4*, p. 46: no. 46-f.123/67 (the husband's mother slept in the passage, which also served as kitchen, to the couple's room); *Ṭ̣bI1*, p. 232: no. 21-f.36/63 (the doorway between the wife's room and the residence of the husband's relatives was not properly stopped

up: she asked for it to be stopped up with stones and clay and that none of the husband's relatives should come near it); *NzI4*, p. 85: no. 1/42-f.110/50 (the wife had been installed near the room in which the husband's parents and relatives lived, p. 119: no. 2/15-f.59/52 (shared sanitary facilities), p. 272: no. 2/26-f.89/65 (no partition or roof separating the wife's dwelling from the residence of the husband's relatives), p. 290: no. 5/15-f.50/66 (no separate entrance to the wife's dwelling), p. 307: no. 2/37-f.154/66 (the husband had established a barber shop in the dwelling); *AcD7*, p. 13: f.48/66 ("a place dark in the daytime," not fit for permanent residence), p. 55: no. 14-f.?/67 (no running water in the kitchen; the landlord, a bachelor, lived on the premises and there were no separate sanitary facilities).

26. See, *e.g.*, *JfQ4*, p. 94: no. 97-f.38/68 (the wife alleged that the husband supported her through the intermediary of her mother-in-law, who "gave her food when she wanted to and none when she did not"), *NzI4*, p. 127: no. 25-f.98/52); *ṬbI1*, p. 261: no. 14-f.28/64 (the wife wanted no "partnership (*shirka*) with the husband's relatives in kitchen and household because it gives her headaches").

27. See, *e.g.*, *JfQ3*, p. 266: no. 406-f.24/66; *JfQ4*, p. 94: no. 97-f.36/68; JfQ5, p. 132: no. 217-f.263/69; *ṬbI1*, p. 139: no. 2-f.43/58.

28. See, *e.g.*, *NzI4*, p. 128: no. 26-f.104/52 (the father-in-law had cursed the wife and sworn a *ḥarām* oath that she would not enter his house), p. 136; no. 4/36-f.121/52 (the mother-in-law accused the wife of adultery with the father-in-law and of being pregnant by him), p. 139: no. 1/3-f.12/53 (the son of her rival insulted and beat the wife), p. 188: no. 1/7-f.25/58 (the dwelling was near the residence of the husband's relatives and not near that of Muslim neighbours who might save her when she cried for help or was attacked), p. 358: no. 7/21-f.39/68 (the wife's brother-in-law frequently chased her out of the house; her husband did not protect her because he was under his brother's thumb); *AcI1*, p. 76: f.47/50 (the husband and mother-in-law beat the wife); *JfQ1*, p. 34: no. 58-12/52 (the wife was "harmed by the proximity" of the residence of the husband's relatives and asked for them to be warned and ordered to use the back door); *ṬbI1*, p. 69: no. 7-f.8/55 (the mother-in-law and sister-in-law forbade the wife to enter her room "and to make use of my freedom . . . their behaviour is such that even an animal could not endure it"), p. 102: no. 10-f.29/57 (the wife and her sister were married to cousins of theirs (brothers), and the two couples lived in the same house, together with the father of the husbands, who was mentally ill and had committed a heinous crime on her sister; the wife feared for her life).

29. See Rosenfeld, *Peasants*, pp. 32-3, 87-9; Cohen, p. 54.
30. See, *e.g.*, *NzI4*, p. 360: no. 9/23-f.49/68 (the husband left his family's home and rented a separate house to bring his wife back to him and "ensure a quiet married life"); *ṬbI1*, p. 122: no. 10-f.4/58, p. 208: no. 4-f.39/62; *AcD*8, p. 17: no. 17/68-f.143/67.
31. *JfMC68*, no. 9513 (special dwelling—*maskan khāṣṣ*), no. 12617; *ṬbMC68*, no. 8276 (a room and sanitary facilities), no. 8278 (a stipulation that the husband should have the upper storey of his father's house); *AcM*C68, no. 2437 (separate legal dwelling—*maskan shar'i mustaqill*); *NzM*C68, no. 6110 (separate house standing by itself—*dār mustaqilla waḥdahā*). Cf. Cohen, p. 54; Rosenfeld, *Peasants*, p. 36; Yūsuf Dasūqī, *AI*, vol. 8(1962), Nos. 1-2, p. 3.
32. See, *e.g.*, *JfQ3*, p. 363: no. 504-f.60/67; *AcM*C68, no. 2612 (the husband undertook to pay the wife IL 10,000 for the construction of a house in the village if she should be compelled to leave his house for any reason).
33. Cohen, p. 54.
34. See, *e.g.*, *ṬbI1*, p. 122: no. 10-f.4/58, p. 202: no. 24-f.36/62, p. 208: no. 4-f.39/62.
35. See *JfMC68*, no. 10316. See also *AcM*C68, nos. 2636, 2644, 2830.
36. *ṬbI1*, p. 249: no. 5-f.8/64, p. 164: no. 5-f.9/60; and *NzI4*, p. 297: no. 8/24-f.82/66, respectively. See also *NzI4*, p. 139: no. 2/4-f.8/53.
37. See Qadri, art. 187.
38. *JfQ4*, p. 185: no. 239-f.57/69; *NzI4*, p. 135: no. 3/35-f.3/52. In another case, the *qāḍī* ordered the husband to spend every night at home "to allay the wife's fear of attacks." See *AcQ5*, p. 65: f.71/63.
39. *FRL*, arts. 70-1.
40. *AcQ5*, p. 74: f. 192/63. See also *NzI4*, p. 101: no. 1/14-f.99/51, p. 182: no. 1/12-f.43/57.
41. See, *e.g.*, *JfQ2*, p. 475: no. 499-[f.39/60] (a woman Jaffa refused to live at Bāqa al-Gharbiyya. She contended that life was penurious there, that she went hungry and, in addition, the dwelling was shared with her husband's parents); *AcI3*, p. 68: no. 40-f.85/57; *AcQ5*, p. 74: f.192/63; *AcD*8, p. 50: f.50/68 (a woman from Acre refused to live in Qalansuwa village "because of the discrepancy between her habits and the traditions of the village people"); *NzI4*, p. 117: no. 1/12-f.53/52, p. 300: no. 1/27-f.106/66.
42. *JfQ2*, p. 545: no. 543-f.68/62 (wife from Jaffa, husband from the al-Huzayyil tribe; the husband was willing to provide her with a dwelling at her choice in Ramla, Jaffa or any of several other places).
43. See, *e.g.*, *JfQ4*, p. 34: no. 32-f.102/67, p. 126: no. 145-f.104/68 (the husband had moved from Jaffa to Lod for reasons of work); *NzI4*, p. 101: no. 1/14-f.49/51 (wife from Nazareth not willing to live at Shafā Amr).

44. See, *e.g.*, *NzI4*, p. 182: no. 1/12-f.43/57 (Nazareth).
45. *ṬbI1*, p. 7: no. 4/8-f.16/50, p. 89: no. 9-f.31/56; *AcD*8, p. 5: f.5/68; *NzI4*, p. 122: no. 1/18-f.74/52.
46. *NzI4*, p. 358: no. 7/2f-f.39/68.
47. See, *e.g.*, *AcD*8, p. 29: f.29/68; *NzI4*, p. 107: no. 2/18-f.72/51, p. 297: no. 9/25-f.74/66, p. 328: no. 4/24-f.88/67 (the wife refused to move from the eastern Muslim quarter of Nazareth to a relatively luxurious quarter mostly inhabited by Christians).
48. See, *JfQ4*, p. 88: no. 87-f.3/68, p. 117: no. 132-f.84/68, p. 141: no. 168-f.135/68 *AcD*6, p. 71: no. 71-f.138/64; *AcD*7, p. 13: f.48/66, p. 52: f.11/67; *AcMC*68, nos. 2846, 2945; *NzMC*68, no. 6539; *JfMC68*, nos. 10132, 10294.
49. See, *e.g.*, *JfMC68*, no. 10132 (wife from Jaffa, husband from the al-Huzayyil tribe; the amount to be paid to the wife in the event of an infringement of the stipulation was IL 10,000).
50. *JfMC68*, no. 10099; *AcMC*68, no. 2987 (it was stipulated that so long as the husband was tied to Nazareth by his work they would live in town, but that when he had to leave town because of his work they would both make their permanent home in her village).
51. *JfQ3*, p. 370: no. 511-f.511/67.
52. *AcMC*68, no. 2937 (husband from Nazareth, wife from Haifa), no. 1850: *NzMC*68, no. 6380.
53. *AcI3*, p. 50: no. 12-f.2/57; *NzI4*, p. 287: no. 1/10-f.48/66, and p. 382: no. 5/52-f.173/68, respectively.
54. *JfQ1*, p. 88: no. 138-f.8/53; *JfQ2*, p. 434: no. 421-f.27/59; *JfQ3*, p. 137: no. 214-f.?/64 (the wife lived on the ground floor of the house and the husband on the upper floor; the wife paid rent out of her own money); *JfQ4*, p. 117: no. 132-f.84/68.
55. *JfMC68*, nos. 10027, 10291, 10322; *ṬbMC68*, nos. 8030, 8047, 8049; *AcMC*68, no. 2848.
56. *AcQ4*, p. 8: f.2/61 (each of the spouses had rights in the property in accordance with his or her share in the inheritance); and *AcD*6, p. 15: f.29/65, respectively. See also *ṬbI1*, p. 273: no. 21-f.39/64 (the wife refused to obey the husband because the house was not registered in her name).
57. See, *e.g.*, *JfQ1*, p. 57: no. 91-f.30/51 (the wife demanded a separate bedroom during her menstrual period), p. 107: no. 172-f.48/53 (the husband beat the wife till she bled because she was negligent in her housework and reviled him); *JfQ2*, p. 405: no. 568-f.50/59 (the husband beat and reviled the wife; she would not be content with a "certificate of guarantee for her life" from the police); *JfQ3*, p. 239: no. 377-f.49/66 (the husband beat the wife "after the manner of husbands"); *JfQ4*, p. 46: no. 46-f.123/67 (the husband beat the

wife while the court proceedings were in progress); *Ṭbl1*, p. 24: no. 8-f.21/51 (the husband threatened to kill the wife), p. 167: no. 8-f.15/60 (the husband beat the wife severely and burdened her beyond her capacity with work "contrary to humanity, religion and law"), p. 173: no. 14-f.34/60 (the wife fled the husband's house after he had tried to set her alight and strangle her), p. 259: no. 12-f.25/64 (the spouses accused each other of attempting to set the other alight), p. 260: no. 13-f.31/64 (the husband spent his time gambling in coffee-houses); *NzI4*, p. 62: no. 2/2-f.4/50 (the wife said that her husband beat and harassed her "when I have done wrong and when I have not"), p. 127: no. 25-f.98/52 (the husband beat the wife until she had a miscarriage); *AcI2*, p. 10: no. 8-f.10/51 (the husband got drunk and beat the wife).

58. See, *e.g.*, *JfQ4*, p. 46: no. 46-f.123/67; *Ṭbl1*, p. 173: no. 14-f.34/60, p. 259: no. 12-f.25/64; *NzI4*, p. 127: no. 25-f.98/52, p. 256: no. 1/9-f.39/66.
59. See, *e.g.*, *Ṭbl1*, p. 173: no. 14-f.34/60; *NzI4*, p. 88: no. 6/47-f.118/50, p. 107; no. 2/18-f.72/51, p. 127; no. 25-f.98/52; *AcD6*, p. 50: f.120/65.
60. See, *e.g.*, *JfQ3*, p. 287: no. 427-f.80/66; *JfQ4*, p. 46: no. 46-f.123/67; *NzI4*, p. 53: no. 1/16-f.27/49, p. 218: no. 1/11-f.8/62; *Ṭbl1*, p. 18: no. 4-f.10/51, p. 225: no. 17-f.7/63.
61. *JfQ3*, p. 310: no. 449-f.130/66; *JfQ4*, p. 78: no. 74-f.141/68; *NzI4*, p. 371: no. 7/37-f.81/68, p. 383: no. 2/55-f.125/68.
62. *NzI4*, p. 88: no. 47/6-f.118/50.
63. See, *e.g.*, *JfQ4*, p. 7: no. 7-f.94/67; JfQ5, p. 33: no. 56-f.141/69 (the couple lived in Abū Ghūsh; the husband worked in Jerusalem and Bethlehem and spent one night a week at home; his brother provided the wife's maintenance and received a monthly payment from him); *NzI4*, p. 287: no. 1/11-f.53/66 (the husband worked in Tel Aviv and came home to his Galilee village once a week, as he used to do before his marriage), p. 345: no. 10/47-f.138/67.
64. See, *e.g.*, *JfQ1*, p. 68: no. 6-f.2/55; *AcI3*, p. 59: no. 26-f.82/57; *Ṭbl1*, p. 271: no. 20-f.5/64.
65. *NzI4*, p. 60: no. 4/28-f.49/49 (in consequence of his accusation, she was "not respected by the people"), p. 329: no. 5/5-f.96/67; *Ṭbl1*, p. 18: no. 4-f.10/51 (the husband denied having accused the wife of prostitution and said that she was "modest and pure").
66. *NzI4*, p. 181: no. 3/11-f.38/57; and *JfQ4*, p. 85: no. 84-f.22/68, respectively. See also *AcD*8, p. 1: no. 1/68-f.146/67. For the ill-tempered woman (*ḥardāna* or *za'lāna*) see Granqvist, vol. 2, pp. 218 *seq.*; Rosenfeld, *Peasants*, pp. 43-5, 145-6; Cohen, p. 124; *JfQ1*, p. 273: no. 422-f.19/57, p. 282: no. 436-f.30/57.

67. *JfQ2*, p. 300: no. 464-f.5/58; *AcI3*, p. 13: no. 16/55-f.49/55.
68. *AcI2*, p. 13: no. 10-f.15/51; *Ṭbl1*, p. 33: no. 17-f.41/51.
69. See, *e.g.*, *ṬbMC68*, nos. 8101, 8119, 8227, 9318.
70. See Cohen, pp. 34-6, 50.
71. *AcMC68*, no. 2631 (the veiling of the face and the confinement of the wife to the house are not referred to).
72. See, *e.g.*, *ṬbMC68*, nos. 8114, 8115, 8119, 9323.
73. *FRL*, art. 74; Qadrī, arts. 152-5, 186.
74. See, *e.g.*, *JfQ1*, p. 61: no. 97-f.50/51, p. 273: no. 422-f.19/57 ("the rival wife is bitter"—*al-ḍarra murra*); *JfQ4*, p. 55: no. 51-f.97/67, p. 84: no. 83-f.16/68, p. 94: no. 97-f.97/68, p. 185: no. 239-f.57/69; *AcI2*, p. 5: f.3/51 (the wife at first demanded that the husband exercise justice and equality as to marital relations, housing conditions and subsistence, but later declared that she accepted the existing rate of maintenance provided he exercised justice as to marital relations).
75. *JfQ1*, p. 273: no. 422-f.19/57; *JfQ3*, p. 311: no. 450-f.135/66; *JfQ4*, p. 92: no. 95-f.121/67, p. 113: no. 126-f.82/68 (the wife had been installed in her rival's house and "ate out of her hand"); *Ṭbl1*, p. 127: no. 15-f.3/58, p. 131: no. 19-f.20/58 (when one of the wives was talking in her room, the other heard her, which was a source of incessant quarrels between them), p. 188: no. 9-f.15/61, p. 201: no. 13-f.34/62 (a partition two metres high should be erected between the wives' rooms); *NzI4*, p. 32: no. 47-f.86/47, p. 121: no. 4/17-f.58/52 (the wife asserted that at the time of the inspection (*kashf*) the husband had deceived the court emissaries as to the legality of the dwelling, for all the furnishings had been borrowed from her rival's quarters, to be returned after the inspection); *AcD7*, p. 11: no. 11/66-f.165/65. Cf. Granqvist, vol. 2, pp. 191-2.
76. See, *e.g.*, *JfQ4*, p. 92: no. 95-f.121/67; *Ṭbl1*, p. 12: no. 4/14-f.28/50, p. 42: no. 1-f.6/53; *NzI4*, p. 373: no. 3/40-f.98/68 (the wife had found shelter with one of her children).
77. *Ṭbl1*, p. 160: f.31/60; *AcI2*, p. 18: no. 15-f.19/51; *AcD8*, p. 76: f.97/69.
78. *JfQ3*, p. 32: no. 54-f.111/63, p. 340: no. 470-f.12/67; *JfQ4*, p. 94: no. 97-f.38/68; *JfQ5*, p. 103: no. 172-f.244/69.
79. See, *e.g.*, *Ṭbl1*, p. 180: no. 1-f.40/60.
80. See, *e.g.*, *AcQ5*, p. 30: no. 20-f.121/62, p. 70: f.182/63; *Ṭbl1*, p. 91: no. 12-f.37/56; *NzI4*, p. 314: no. 3/4-f.8/67 (the wife was beaten and expelled from the husband's house "because of a family quarrel unconnected with her"), p. 372: no. 1/38-f.110/68.
81. See, *e.g.*, *Ṭbl1*, p. 151: no. 9-f.16/57.
82. See, *e.g.*, *NzI4*, p. 321: no. 6/13-f.49/67, p. 327: no. 3/23-f.85/67,

p.343: no. 7/44-f.147/67, p. 360: no. 9/23-f.49/68; *JfQ5*, p. 70: no. 121-f.140/69.

83. *AI*, vol. 11 (1968), Nos. 1-2, pp. 3, 8-10.
84. *JfQ5*, p. 65: no. 110-f.198/69.
85. See, *e.g.*, *NzI4*, p. 161: no. 1/9, p. 245: no. 6/16-f.75/64.
86. See, *e.g.*, *JfQ3*, p. 32: no. 54-f.111/63, p. 113: no. 177-f.66/64 (the wife was turned out of her house "screaming" by her brother).
87. *JfQ2*, p. 523: no. 501-f.65/62.
88. *AI*, vol. 11 (1968), Nos. 1-2, p. 3.
89. *NzI4*, p. 125: no. 3/23-f.96/52, p. 127: no. 25-f.98/52, p. 288: no. 2/12-f.49/66 (the wife left the husband's house "in return" for her *badīla* having done so); *ṬbI1*, p. 88: no. 8-f.30/56 and p. 89: no. 9-f.31/56; *AcQ5*, p. 41: f.120/61. Cf. al-Ārif, p. 132.
90. *NzI4*, p. 360: no. 9/23-f.49/68; *JfQ4*, p. 174: no. 219-f.90/68; *JfQ5*, p. 119: no. 201-f.177/69; *ṬbI1*, p. 31: no. 16-f.38/51; *AcD7*, p. 31: f.31/66 [71/66], p. 49: f.8/67.
91. See, *e.g.*, *JfQ4*, p. 115: no. 130-f.71/68 and p. 116: no. 131-f.74/68; *ṬbI1*, p. 31: no. 16-f.38/51 (after the man had taken back his wife, who was his daughter's *badīla* and whom he had repudiated by revocable divorce, his daughter also returned to her husband).
92. See, *e.g.*, *ṬbI1*, p. 213: no. 8-f.32/62 and p. 214: no. 9-f.48/62; *NzI4*, p. 131: no. 1/30-f.129/52 and p. 132: no. 2/31-f.130/52.
93. See the chapter "Divorce," pp. 129-30.
94. See, *e.g.*, *JfQ3*, p. 172: no. 282-f.159/64.
95. *JfQ4*, p. 174: no. 219-f.90/68 (after the wife had learnt that her father, who was her *badīla's* husband, wished to divorce his wife, she declared that she objected to a divorce and that, as far as she was concerned, there was nothing to prevent her from returning to her husband; the *qāḍī* ordered obedience, but the matter ended with the divorce of both women). See *JfQ4*, p. 184: no. 238-f.88/69 and p. 184: no. 237-f.87/69.
96. *NzI4*, p. 87: no. 4/45-f.114/50; *JfQ3*, p. 97: no. 154-f.21/64. Cf. al-Ārif, p. 132.
97. Cf. Rosenfeld, *Peasants*, pp. 108, 122-5, 136, 138; Cohen, pp. 113-14; Marx, *Bedouin*, pp. 102, 121, 150, 160.
98. See, *e.g.*, *JfQ1*, p. 59: no. 93-f.39/51 and p. 270: no. 418-f.25/57; *ṬbI1*, p. 30: no. 15-f.35/51, p. 126: no. 14-f.17/58, p. 256: no. 10-f.13/64, p. 258: no. 11-f.20/64; *NzI4*, p. 268: no. 3/19-f.65/65, p. 271: no. 2/24-f.61/65.
99. See, *e.g.*, *NzI4*, p. 299: no. 2/26-f.13/66; *JfQ4*, p. 103: no. 115-f.53/68.
100. See, *e.g.*, *JfQ4*, p. 32: no. 31-f.128/67 (the wife did not live maritally with him and did not prepare his meals).

101. See, *e.g.*, *NzI4*, p. 94: no. 2/3-f.10/59 (the wife distributed the food the husband gave her to *her* family, neglecting *his* family).
102. See, *e.g.*, *NzI4*, p. 193: no. 1/1-f.2/59.
103. See, *e.g.*, *Ṭbl1*, p. 4: no. 1/5-f.15/50 (the wife "ill-treats me by word and deed, by curses and spitting in my face, and this is contrary to the *sharī'a*"); *NzI4*, p. 306: no. 2/35-f.137/66; *JfQ3*, p. 128: no. 201-f.83/64 ("because of her long tongue"), p. 310: no. 499-f.130/66 (she used "ugly expressions"); *JfQ4*, p. 1: no. 1-f.81/67 (she beat her husband), p. 64: no. 109-f.195/69.
104. See *e.g.*, *NzI4*, p. 93: no. 1/2-f.4/51, p. 355: no. 1/15-f.33/68; *JfQ2*, p. 437: no. 424-f.2/60; *JfQ3*, p. 202: no. 333-f.1/66, p. 250: no. 389-f.42/66, p. 333: no. 473-f.29/67; *JfQ4*, p. 2: no. 2-f.80/65.
105. *Ṭbl1*, p. 4: no. 1/5-f.15/50 (the wife worked in the fields "like the other village women"), p. 173: no. 14-f.34/60, p. 207: no. 3-f.44/62 (wife working as a school teacher); *JfQ1*, p. 246: no. 382-f.36/56 (the husband was willing to increase the wife's maintenance on condition "that she stops working as a hired employee and stays at home"); *JfQ4*, p. 55: no. 51-f.97/67 (wife worked as a poultry plucker). See Rosenfeld, *Peasants*, p. 37.
106. In one case, the husband gave as the reason for his inability to provide his wife with a dwelling separate from that of his family that as the eldest son he could not leave his parents and brothers. See *NzI4*, p. 310: no. 5/40-f.159/66. Cf. Rosenfeld, *Peasants*, p. 85.
107. See, *e.g.*, *Ṭbl1*, p. 271: no. 20-f.5/64; *JfQ4*, p. 122: no. 144-f.103/68 (the husband said that the wife wasted all his earnings by issuing cheques).
108. *FRL*, art. 101; Qadrī, arts. 166-71. Cf. Schacht, p. 168.
109. *JfQ4*, p. 146: no. 5/17-f.111/68. See Yūsuf Dasūqī, *AI*, vol. 7(1959), Nos. 2-3, p. 14; *AI*, vol. 10(1966), Nos. 3-4, p. 3; Baer, p. 35.
110. *AI*, vol. 8(1963), Nos. 3-4, pp. 1-2; *AI*, vol. 9(1954), Nos. 1-2, p. 8: *AI*, vol. 11(1968), p. 6.
111. See, *e.g.*, *ṬBl1*, p. 30: no. 15-f.35/51, p. 69: no. 8-f.11/55 (the wife was not prepared to return to the husband's house "for the time being"; she wished to "chastise him properly" but considered the possibility of returning to his house in a year "if he treats me better"), p. 70: no. 9-f.12/55 (the husband undertook to treat the wife well "and to honour her as his life companion," but she refused to return to him on the ground that she had heard such promises before), p. 153: no. 17-f.28/59, p. 180: no. 1-f.40/60 ("my blood any body do not match and do not mix with his"; she "will never" return to him); *JfQ4*, p. 173: no. 217-f.65/69; *AcQ5*, p. 5: no. 5/63-

f.26/62; *AcD6*, p. 6: f.8/65. See Shaykh Ḥusnī al-Zu'bī, *AI*, vol. 11(1968), Nos. 1-2, pp. 6-7.

112. See, *e.g.*, *NzI4*, p. 157: no. 2/4-f.1/54.
113. *AcI2*, p. 32: f.76/51 (the wife worked and deposited her money in a bank); *AcI3*, p. 10: no. 13/55-f.33/55 (the wife worked "independently of him" and lived alone with her daughter); *JfQ1*, p. 62: no. 98-f.56/51.
114. See, *e.g.*, *JfQ1*, p. 228: no. 353-f.15/56; *JfQ2*, p. 545: no. 543-f.68/62; *JfQ3*, p. 327: no. 468-f.16/67; *NzI4*, p. 163: no. 1/12-f.47/54.
115. See, *e.g.*, *NzI4*, p. 140: no. 1/5-f.13/53, p. 52: no. 2/19-f.58/53, p. 156: no. 2/2-f.4/54, p. 161: no. 3/8-f.17/54, p. 169: no. 1/2-f.4/56, p. 186: no. 2/4-f.16/58, p. 188: no. 1/7-f.25/58; *JfQ1*, p. 186: no. 307-f.36/55.
116. *NzI4*, p. 140: no. 1/5-f.13/53, p. 169: no. 1/2-f.4/56; *AcI2*, p. 38: f.125/51.
117. See, *e.g.*, *AcI2*, p. 37: f.116/52, p. 39: f.133/52, p. 71: f.34/54; *AcI3*, p. 4: no. 4/55-f.9/55 (a village woman was unwilling to accept that the property should belong to her townsman husband; she claimed five cows); *AcD6*, p. 15: f.29/65.
118. *AcI2*, p. 32: f.76/51; and *ṬbI1*, p. 54: no. 5-f.8/54, respectively.
119. *ṬbI1*, p. 39: no. 8-f.19/52 (her husband beat her and she refused to return to his house "even if it were a palace in Paradise"), p. 234: no. 23-f.42/63; *AcI2*, p. 33: f.84/51; *AcI3*, p. 1: no. 1/55-f.3/55.
120. *ṬbI1*, p. 152: no. 16-f.27/59.
121. *JfQ2*, p. 552: no. 552-f.73/62. In another case, a husband whose wife had fled to Shaykh Salmān al-Huzayyil sought to get her back by an order for obedience for fear that she was "to be divorced from him and married to another man." See *JfQ2*; p. 528: no. 510-f.93/61.
122. See, *e.g.*, *JfQ3*, p. 145: no. 230-f.108/64 (arbitrator— *ḥakam*); *ṬbI1*, p. 180: no. 1-f.40/60 (mediators—*wusaṭā*), p. 186: no. 7-f.14/61; *NzI4*, p. 194: no. 3/4-f.12/59 (men of good will — *ahl al-khayr*), p. 220: no. 2/7-f.21/63 (the arbitrators' agreement included IL 50 "reconciliation fee"—*badal muṣālaḥa*); *AcD6*, p. 1: no. 1/66-f.172/65. On the *qāḍīs* see below, p. 106.
123. *JfQ4*, p. 133: no. 158-f.130/68. See also *JfQ4*, p. 72: no. 68-f.20/68, p. 92: no. 95-f.121/67; *NzI4*, p. 46: no. 1/3-f.7/49; *AcQ5*, p. 19: f.61/61.
124. See, *e.g.*, *JfQ4*, p. 133: no. 158-f.130/68.
125. See, *e.g.*, *JfQ3*, p. 145: no. 230-f.108/64; *ṬbI1*, p. 239: no. 27-f.75/63; *NzI4*, p. 220: no. 2/4-f.32/63, p. 231: no. 5/25-f.75/63,

p. 253: no. 2/31-f.141/64, p. 253: no. 3/23-f.137/64, p. 262: no. 1/8-f.1/65; *AcQ5*, p. 15: f.59/62; *AcD6*, p. 76: f.188/64.

126. See, *e.g.*, *JfQ3*, p. 145: no. 230-f.108/64; *NzI4*, p. 220: no. 2/4-f.32/63; *AcQ5*, p. 15: f.59/62. For delegated repudiation see the chapter "Divorce," pp. 153 *seq*.
127. See, *e.g.*, *NzI4*, p. 236: no. 1/1-f.1/64, p. 243: no. 3/13-f.65/64; *AcQ4*, p. 29: f.12/59, p. 51: f.188/59.
128. *FRL*, art. 152. See Fyzee, p. 204.
129. For more details see Qadrī, arts. 408 *seq*.
130. Family Law Amendment (Maintenance) Law, 5719-1959, *SCH*, No. 276 of March 12, 1959, secs. 1-6, 19(b). See also Explanatory Note to Family Law Amendment (Maintenance) Bill, 5716-1956 (*Bills*, No. 267 of June 4, 1956, p. 126), and Explanatory Note to secs. 122-36, 198 of *IFB*.
131. See, *e.g.*, *JfQ3*, p. 251: no. 390-f.61/66; *JfQ4*, p. 28: no. 27-f.104/67; *TbI1*, p. 49: no. 10-f.24/53; *NzI4*, p. 248: no. 4/22, p. 308: no. 3/38-f.160/66; *AcI1*, opposite p. 25: f.12/49, p. 47: no. 40-f.28/49.
132. See, *e.g.*, *ṬbI1*, p. 194: no. 15-f.25/61 (the widow had three daughters).
133. See, *e.g.*, *ṬbI1*, p. 85: no. 4-f.7/56.
134. *JfQ1*, p. 78: no. 121-f.91/52; *JfQ3*, p. 199: no. 327-f.84/65; *ṬbI1*, p. 49: no. 10-f.24/53, p. 196: no. 18-f.25/61; *AcI2*, p. 64: f.26/54 (the sons contended that the mother could sell her share in the estate of the family head).
135. *JfQ4*, p. 173: no. 216-f.117/69, *ṬbI1*, p. 53: no. 3-f.4/54, p. 256: no. 9-f.12/64.
136. *JfQ2*, p. 316: no. 493-f.40/58; and *JfQ3*, p. 199: no. 327-f.84/65, respectively.
137. See, *e.g.*, *JfQ2*, p. 336: no. 528-f.7/59; *ṬbI1*, p. 194: no. 15-f.25/61, p. 253: no. 7-f.3/64; *NzI4*, p. 149: no. 1/15-f.43/53, p. 172: no. 1/6-f.31/56, p. 288: no. 3/13-f.56/66; *AcI2*, p. 35: f.4/52; *AcI3*, p. 17: no. 21/55-f.88/55, p. 21: no. 30-f.105/55.
138. See, *e.g.*, *JfQ1*, p. 218: no. 341-f.80/55 (the brothers s*AI*d they were prepared to pay their sister a higher rate of m*AI*ntenance than she demanded if she would live with them ag*AI*n in the same house; she and her small daughter were living at a strange woman's house).
139. See, *e.g.*, *AcQ5*, p. 9: f.16/63.
140. See, *e.g.*, *AcI3*, p. 60: no. 28-f.62/57; *NzI4*, p. 1: no. 9-f.12/47, p. 20: no. 34-f.60/47.
141. *AI*, vol. 11(1968), Nos. 1-2, p. 10.
142. *NzI4*, p. 223: no. 1/10-f.2/63. See also *NzI4*, p. 220: no. 1/2-f.5/63; *AI*, vol. 8(1963), Nos. 3-4, p. 1.

143. *AI*, vol. 11(1968), Nos. 1-2, pp. 9-10; *AI*, vol. 6(1957), Nos. 1-2, p. 15; *AI*, vol. 7(1959), Nos. 2-3, p. 16; *AI*, vol. 1(1950), No. 2, p. 4. For a more extensive discussion see the chapter "Divorce," pp. 180-1.
144. See, *e.g.*, *JfQ1*, p. 284: no. 442-f.33/57; *JfQ2*, p. 477: no. 503-f.48/60; *NzI4*, p. 254: no. 5/34-f.146/64.
145. See, *e.g.*, *JfQ3*, p. 266: no. 406-f.24/66; *JfQ4*, p. 122: no. 141-f.103/68.
146. See, *e.g.*, *JfQ4*, p. 32: no. 31-f.128/67; *JfQ5*, p. 7: no. 11-f.100/69; *JfQ1*, p. 477: no. 503-f.48/60; *NzI4*, p. 200: no. 1/3-f.13/60; *JfQ3*, p. 273: no. 412-f.94/66.
147. See, Goitein and Ben Shemesh, pp. 39-40.
148. See, *e.g.*, *NzI4*, p. 220: no. 2/7-f.21/63; *AcQ4*, p. 51: f.188/59; *AcD6*, p. 1: no. 1/66-f.172/65; *JfQ3*, p. 145: no. 230-f.108/64 (in the event of an infringement of the terms of the agreement brought about between the spouses by the *qāḍī* and a Beduin Shaykh, the latter was to serve as an arbitrator between them and his decision was to be final); *JfQ4*, p. 116: no. 131-f.74/68.
149. See, *e.g.*, *AcI2*, p. 50: f.88/53, p. 71: f.81/74; *AcI3*, p. 16: no. 20/55-f.56/55, p. 26: no. 12/56-f.31/56; *AcQ4*, p. 64: f.231/59; *AcQ5*, p. 15: f.59/62; *AcD6*, p. 76: f.188/64; *NzI4*, p. 220: no. 2/4-f.32/63, p. 231: no. 5/25-f.75/63; *JfQ3*, p. 145: no. 230-f.108/64; *ṬbI1*, p. 239: no. 27-f.50/63.
150. See, *e.g.*, *JfQ3*, p. 128: no. 201-f.83/64, p. 145: no. 230-f.108/64; *JfQ4*, p. 1: no. 1-f.81/67; *AcD6*, p. 71: no. 71-f.159/65 (Shaykh Amīn Qāsim Mudlij ordered obedience only after the wife had rejected reconciliation—*muṣālaḥa*—with the husband "even on terms which she might propose"); *AcD7*, p. 8: f.37/66; *AcD8*, p. 59: no. 120/68 (obedience was ordered because the wife refused to appoint a family council for the purpose of reconciliation—*ṣulḥ*).
151. As did especially Shaykh Ḥusnī al-Zu'bī. See, *e.g.*, *NzI4*, p. 264: no. 1/13-f.33/65, p. 270: no. 2/21-f.75/65, p. 271: no. 1/31-f.80/65, p. 304: no. 4/32-f.31/66.
152. See, *e.g.*, *NzI4*, p. 307: no. 1/36-f.158/66; *AcI2*, p.46: f.48/53; *AcI3*, p. 27: no. 14-f.37/56, p. 40: no. 39-f.127/56, p. 51: no. 13-f.33/57, p. 82: no. 15-f.72/58; *ṬbI1*, p. 195: no. 16-f.28/61.
153. See, *e.g.*, *NzI4*, p. 220: no. 1/2-f.5/63; *ṬbI1*, p. 4: no. 1/5-f.15/50; *AcI2*, p. 35: f.93/51.
154. *AcI3*, p. 55: no. 19-f.67/57; *NzI4*, p. 206: no. 1/4-f.10/61; *JfQ3*, p. 116: no. 131-f.74/68 (the surety also served as arbitrator—*ḥakam*—between the spouses).
155. See, *e.g.*, *JfQ1*, p. 57: no. 91-f.30/51, p. 279: no. 432-f.36/57; *AcQ5*, p. 72: f.176/63.

156. *JfQ3*, p. 30: no. 49-f.7/52; and p. 88: no. 139-f.10/53, respectively.
157. *Ṭbl1*, p. 205: no. 2-f.30/62.
158. *JfQ3*, p. 333: no. 473-f.29/67; *JfQ4*, p. 7: no. 7-f.94/67, p. 20: no. 18-f.114/67, p. 118: no. 134-f.91/68.
159. See, *e.g.*, *JfQ1*, p. 37: no. 64-f.21/52, p. 128: no. 217-f.17/54; *JfQ2*, p. 559: no. 466-f.62/62; *NzI4*, p. 73: no. 3/22-f.57/50, p. 119: no. 2/15-f.59/52; *Ṭbl1*, p. 5: no. 2/6-f.16/50, *AcI2*, p. 38: f.117/52.
160. *FRL*, art. 95; *AcD8*, p. 1: no. 1/68-f.132/67.
161. *JfQ3*, p. 239: no. 377-f.49/66; *JfQ4*, p. 103: no. 115-f.53/68.
162. *AcI4*, p. 16: f.74/59; and *AcI3*, p. 51: no. 14-f.35/57, respectively.
163. See, *e.g.*, *JfQ4*, p. 2: no. 2-f.80/65; *AcI4*, p. 92: f.94/60; *AcD8*, p. 37: f.37/68.
164. See, *e.g.*, *NzI4*, p. 99: no. 1/10-f.27/51, p. 119: no. 2/15-f.59/52, p. 127: no. 25-f.98/52, p. 219: no. 1/1-f.1/63; *JfQ1*, p. 57: no. 91-f.30/51 (the wife lacked cosmetic equipment); *JfQ2*, p. 472: no. 493-f.30/61, p. 498: no. 458-f.75/61 (a dwelling not owned by the husband was not legal); *JfQ3*, p. 287: no. 427-f.80/66, p. 291: no. 431-f.120/66; *JfQ4*, p. 34: no. 32-f.102/67, p. 88: no. 87-f.3/68; *Ṭbl1*, p. 126: no. 14-f.17/58, p. 149: no. 12-f.20/59; *AcI3*, p. 18: no. 23-f.73/55, p. 49: no. 11-f.31/57; *AcQ5*, p. 72: f.176/63 and p. 82: f.201/63; *AcD7*, p. 13: f.48/66.
165. See, *e.g.*, *JfQ2*, p. 414: no. 582-f.74/59, p. 431: no. 417-f.81/59; *Ṭbl1*, p. 102: no. 10-f.29/57, p. 122: no. 10-f.4/58.
166. *AcQ4*, p. 95: f.127/60 (Shaykh Mūsā al-Ṭabarī dismissed the wife's claim for a separate dwelling "because dwellings are scarce these days and involve high key-money . . . and there is nothing wrong with a *maskan shar'ī* housing two or three families, with shared sanitary facilities"). See also *JfQ1*, p. 100: no. 161-f.37/53 (Shaykh Ṭāhir Ḥamād); *Ṭbl1*, p. 162: no. 3-f.8/60 (Shaykh Ḥasan Amīn al-Ḥabash directed the husband to provide provisional dwelling arrangements until he was better off).
167. *AI*, vol. 11(1968), Nos. 1-2, pp. 8-10.
168. See, *e.g.*, *AcD6*, p. 71: f.138/64 (Shaykh Amīn Qāsim Mudlij himself dismissed a wife's claim for another dwelling because she had not succeeded in proving (by witnesses) that the husband's relatives harassed her).
169. *AI*, vol. 11(1968), Nos. 1-2, pp. 8-10.
170. See the chapter "Stipulations Inserted in Contracts of Marriage," p. 30.
171. For references to *sijill* entries concerning stipulations as to the dwelling see above, pp. 95 *seq*.

172. See, *e.g.*, *ṬbI1*, p. 12: no. 4/14-f.28/50, p. 42: no. 1-f.6/53, p. 127: no. 15-f.3/58; *AcD7*, p. 11: no. 11/66-f.165/65.
173. The judgment was set aside by the Court of Appeal. *JfQ1*, p. 273: no. 422: f.19/57; Ap1, p. 25: no. 31.
174. *ṬbI1*, p. 131: no. 19-f.20/58.
175. See, *e.g.*, *ṬbI1*, p. 25: no. 9-f.24/51; *AcQ5*, p.65: f.71/63; *AcD8*, p. 17, no. 17/68-f.143/67.
176. See, *e.g.*, *JfQ1*, p. 107: no. 172-f.48/53 (the wife alleged that the husband had beaten her until she bled, but Shaykh Ṭāhir Ḥamād, accepting the husband's plea that he had struck her with his hand "in order to chastise her" and not for revenge, ordered obedience).
177. *ṬbI1*, p. 31: no. 16-f.38/51, p. 88: no. 8-f.30/56 and p. 89: no. 9-f.31/56; *AcQ5*, p. 41: f.120/61; *AcD7*, p. 31: no. 31/66-[f.71/66]; *JfQ4*, p. 174: no. 219-f.96/68; *JfQ5*, p. 119: no. 201-f.177/69; *NzI4*, p. 125: no. 3/23, p. 288: no. 2/12-f.49/66, p. 360: no. 9/23-f.49/68.
178. See, *e.g.*, *NzI4*, p. 87: no. 4/45-f.114/50; *JfQ3*, p. 97: no. 154-f.21/64 (the wife alleged that she had not received the dower, but Shaykh Ṭāhir Ḥamād ordered obedience because the marriage contracts indicated that the two *wakīls* of the *badīlas* had received the dower).
179. *AI*, vol. 11(1968), Nos. 1-2, pp. 3-5.
180. *JfQ5*, p. 65: no. 110-f.198/69.
181. *AI*, vol. 8(1963), Nos. 3-4, pp. 1-2.
182. See, *e.g.*, *JfQ1*, p. 34: no. 58-f.12/52, p. 186: no. 307-f.36/55; *JfQ3*, p. 131: no. 206-f.82/64; *AcI3*, p. 95: f.127/60; *AcQ5*, p. 7: f.5/61, p. 17: f.50/61; *NzI4*, p. 205: no. 1/18-f.90/60.
183. See, *e.g.*, *ṬbI1*, p. 39: no. 8-f.19/52, p. 54: no. 5-f.8/54, p. 132: no. 21-f.27/58, p. 176: no. 17-f.43/60; *NzI4*, p. 169: no. 1/2-f.4/56, p. 250: no. 4/28-f.80/64.
184. See, *e.g.*, *NzI4*, p. 152: no. 2/19-f.58/53, p. 188: no. 1/7-f.25/58.
185. See, *e.g.*, *AcQ5*, p. 2: f.2/63; *AcI2*, p. 29: f.61/51.
186. See, *e.g.*, *AcI2*, p. 32: f.76/51, p. 72: f.85/54; *AcI3*, p. 1: no. 1/55-f.3/55; *AcD6*, p. 15: f.29/65 (Shaykh Amīn Qāsim Mudlij); *ṬbI1*, p. 207: no. 3-f.44/62, p. 234: no. 23-f.42/63, p. 273: no. 21-f.39/64 (Shaykh Ḥasan Amīn al-Ḥabash).
187. See, *e.g.*, *AcI3*, p. 4: no. 3/55-f.7/55.
188. See, *e.g.*, *AcI3*, p. 4: no. 4/55-f.9/55.
189. *AI*, vol. 8(1963), Nos. 3-4, pp. 1-2; *AI*, vol. 9(1964), Nos. 1-2, p. 8; *AI*, vol. 11(1968), Nos. 1-2, p. 6. Such an amendment in the law was also urged by Advocate Maḥmūd al-Māḍī, the then director of *sharī'a* courts: see *AI*, vol. 9(1964), Nos. 1-2, p. 9.
190. *AI*, vol. 9(1964), Nos. 1-2, pp. 2-3. Cf. Yūsuf Dasūqī, *AI*, vol. 7(1959), Nos. 2-3, pp. 13-18.

191. *AI*, vol. 9(1964), Nos. 1-2, pp. 5-10.
192. See Fyzee, p. 202.
193. See, *e.g.*, *JfQ2*, p. 336: no. 528-f.7/59 (in a woman's action for maintenance against her sons, both sides asked Shaykh Ṭāhir Ḥamād to act as arbitrator).
194. See, *e.g.*, *JfQ1*, p. 277: no. 427-f.43/57; *ṬbI1*, p. 48: no. 8-f.22/53; *NzI4*, p. 374: no. 4/41-f.117/68; *AcI1*, p. 92: f.67/50.
195. See, *e.g.*, *JfQ3*, p. 251: no. 390-f.61/66; *JfQ4*, p. 119: no. 136-f.101/68; *ṬbI1*, p. 253: no. 7-f.3/64, p. 59: no. 11-f.21/54; *NzI4*, p. 190: no. 2/10-f.31/58.
196. *JfQ1*, p. 218: no. 341-f.80/55; *AcQ4*, p. 61: no. 29-f.130/57.
197. *ṬbI1*, p. 196: no. 18-f.25/61; *AcQ4*, p. 59: no. 25-f.46/57.

2

Muslim Women in the Indian Subcontinent

I

Marginal Communities: Poor Muslim Women in Rural Bangladesl

The thematic shift in social sciences to understand women's subjugation and oppression is encouraging. The shift, however small, towards woman's studies is a move from a fractional to an integrated understanding of society. The woman is usually considered as the second sex and there are a number of myths (Janeway, 1971) and stereotypes which support the woman's inferior status. The position of the woman is one of second order citizen in the human society. But even while it is so, there are variations in her status across societies or cultures. There are cultural variations in the modes of subordination and oppression as well as differences in the cosmologies that support them.

In addition, the position of women within a given society may also be contrasted between women of different classes, castes, religions, etc. Goode (1963:2) and others argue that women of the lower classes exercise more rights than their counterparts in the educated upper classes—who least exercise them. Further that women of the lower strata are employed and have *de facto* more power, although their men have more conservative ideas on the role of women.

There is an old saying: It's a man's world and woman's place is in the home. This divides the world by sexes. If women have only a place, the rest of the world must belong to someone else, and therefore, to men. But the women employed outside the household, especially those belonging to the lower classes, do not seem to substantiate this dictum. Such women virtually belong to two different worlds—the family on the supposedly natural world of women, and the man's world which exists outside the family. The latter is usually the sphere of women's employment. The familial domain has been transmitted to women as their domain through the ages. But the extra-familial domain or the sphere of productive work outside the household is a recent development and is certainly not as old as the traditional patriarchal family. The separation of the family from a consumption-production unit and its relegation to a mere consumption unit have produced the values that place women indoors. Both the domains expect conflicting performances from the same woman.

Standardised Roles

Every society has a set of standardised prescriptions for proper behaviour of its members belonging to different sexes. It assigns different duties and ways of living to men end women with an assumption that they have differing psychological attributes and capabilities, moral, social, intellectual as well as physical. Scriptures and rituals support such a division of society. The ideal patterns of behaviour are transmitted through customs and traditions. The normative behavioural prescriptions constructed around physical facts of sex differences are central to the lives of individuals and vital to society. There exists a whole set of traits, attitudes, prescriptions and proscriptions which women have accepted as proper to them. These are deeply internalised to become stable parts of their identity. The mode of oppression supported by a related cosmology interpellate women to their given situation. Thereby they come to acquire a world view which governs and nurtures their ways of feeling and seeing the world. There is a system of interlinked thought and behaviour. Women's behaviour can be partially understood in terms of this world view which consists of a set of beliefs and sentiments that define their role.

The purpose here is to understand the thought and behaviour of the poor, landless women in their social setting. To analyse how they struggle to fulfil the social, cultural and reproductive roles expected of them by tradition and society. And to understand the cosmology derived from the scriptures, mythology, religion, rituals, institutions, etc. what are the problems and dilemma encountered by the woman in her effort to behave normatively. Belonging to the bottom rung of society how does she resolve the conflicting demands of an ideal wife–mother on the one hand, and the bread-earner in the face of severe economic compulsion on the other. The life-taking pressure of poverty threatens the traditional values, and thus impede the process of her becoming an ideal woman. How does she manage to combine the two contradictory roles into complementary ones? How are the compromises made? How does she face the outer world in the face of strong sex-role stereotypes while stepping into the man's domain by taking up economically productive ventures? Does she conclude her fate to be preordained, given by God and simply resolve by accepting what comes her way (or what her husband and others inflict on her) or does she struggle, or experience anger and resentment at how things shaped up for her, and that they could have been handled otherwise. What future does she cherish or contemplate for her daughters as future women of the same society?

The paper tries to analyse these issues from the opinions, attitudes, plights, and actual behaviour of the poor, rural, and landless women of Tangil district in Bangladesh. The women belong to that stratum of society where life is full of sorrow, suffering, pain, agony, scarcity, hunger and starvation. A house usually means a hut which may have a roof. In the case of a few fortunate ones, the house has all the four walls. Women dream of a future when their children would get some food to eat and their faces would look radiant. It is a great achievement if the family can get rice three times a day. Some wildly growing vegetables can be plucked from others' fields, and firewood for cooking may be foraged. Occasionally a small fish may be brought in by children. The *fitra* given to the poor during *Id* brings hopes for some good food and also clothing to cover their nakedness.

The analysis is based on the case studies of 16 women compiled in the form of an edited book entitled, "Jorimon of Beltoil village and others; in search of a Future". Although the case studies have been collected in the wake of an experimental Grameen Bank Project to give loans to the poor and landless, the anthropological case history method provides rich ethnographic material and biographical accounts of the women. What makes the volume valuable is the care taken by the editor and the translators to keep the bare appeal of the biographical sketches and experiences as were narrated by the informants. Each case study unfolds a detailed life story, exactly as seen, felt and judged by the women to have happened to them. In addition, there is first hand information from the narrator's point of view of her life's past, present and the future Plans and hopes. The researcher, in each case study, provides an almost live picture of the house, dress, food and a few things placed in the sheds or huts. (The page numbers indicated here refer to the above book.)

II

A woman rarely has an independent identity of her own. Her status is dependent upon her andro-centric context. She is seen as a daughter, wife or mother of a male member of the society. All these positions revolve around the familial domain. Each of these positions is governed by a set of norms which prescribe an ideal behaviour. Each role is woven into an intricate web of ideas regarding rights and delegations which subordinate the women to it. The birth of a daughter is not always desired and more so if there happens to be a daughter already in the family. Very early in childhood, the daughters are made to share their mother's tasks such as jobs in the kitchen and the household. They take a substantial responsibility along with the cult of domesticity at a rather early age.

As a child Sakhina has spent most of her time in the fields tending cows and goats and gathering firewood. The only brother who was also the youngest did not do any work. After the death of her father things changed. Besides her own household work. Sakhina's mother started husking paddy in other peoples house...Sakhina started to accompany her mother to work (p. 62). Shumari learnt to help her mother in the household chores from early childhood. She used to sweep the floor, wash the dishes and bring water in a pitcher from the well. In addition, she used to help with the cooking. She also tended the kitchen garden, helping to clear the weeds and keeping an alert eye for the cows, goats, ducks, chickens that spoilt the plants. Furthermore, she used to look after the cowshed and make fuel cakes from cowdung and dry them (pp. 161-62). Collecting cowdung, twigs, firewood and wildly growing vegetable substitutes like spinach and *Kochu* is usually done by small girls, although it means a great deal of strain for them. Daughters are not only trained in the domestic chores, they are also taught to become responsible towards the whole family early in their lives. At the age when rich children go to school, Koituri had to earn her own bread by doing odd jobs at neighbours' houses (p. 240). As Bachaton's husband was disabled, her two daughters, Amena and Maleka, not only helped her in her work, the two carried loads of paddy and chilli from the market to the house and also carried these loads to retail in market (p. 51). They were like two strong men to their parents. Tara *bewa's* daughter Royeka felt bad for her mother and helped her to husk, spread and dry paddy. Her whole body would be wet from perspiration and smeared with sand while she made *muri*. Her mother felt proud of Royeka's capabilities and help and commented that she had been working like this from early morning. It was past mid-day and she was still working alone without taking any breads (p. 269). The young daughters are well equipped to perform their duties and take up the tasks expected of a woman in the household.

The parents are keen to marry them off at a very tender age. Although the age at which these women were married ranges between 7 to 16 years, most of them were married around 11 years of age. The groom's position always had an edge over the bride's irrespective of parents' economic position, capabilities of the prospective spouses and even physical appearance. The three eldest girls were married off before Shumari was born. The only sister's wedding that Shumari saw was that of her immediate elder sister, Noori. Shumari was then 10 years old. As soon as Noori was married off, Rajjab Khan the father started making plans for getting a good groom for her (pp. 162-63). The only desire of the desperate parents is to marry off their daughter to any one. Halima's complexion was dark. Which meant that proposals were not really forthcoming. Her widow mother was prepared to pay substantial dowry but a groom was hard to find. This caused endless worries to her widow mother and brother. Finally, owing largely to her mother's efforts, Halima was married at the age of 13 to Alauddin who was slightly deranged and people called him Mad Ala (p. 149). Same was the problem with Mafia's parents who took great care to keep their son-in-law happy (p. 180). Poverty, sorrow, pain and suffering had made Alekha's mother extremely weak. When Alekha reached 15 her parents' worry was her marriage. Dowry had to be given even though it was a terrible hardship for the poor family. The few proposals that come always demanded one thing or the other. One such proposal came up. Without probing anything, Alekha's father hurriedly arranged to give a dowry of Taka 1100 by selling 4 decimals of cultivable land for Taka 500 and added to it his own savings plus some money he borrowed from a relative (pp. 133-36). Despite doing all the household work Asia could not satisfy her husband's family because her father had not spent much on her marriage (p. 273).

Some brides were taken with an understanding that the erratic and irresponsible behaviour of the son would be set right. The son rarely gets set and instead the bride's future is ruined. Khalil Mian being the only son became rather spoilt under his father's fond indulgence. He squandered both his father's and his own hard earned money. When Hatim Mian realised this he arranged a marriage for his son, who did not change (p. 96). Thus, the bride a child herself is expected to be a social worker or a counsellor. The girls understand their marriage to any boy or man as a matter of course. The socialization and training is such that nothing else seems normal. In Parson's (1951) view children learn about the world and the culture in which they live by growing up in the sub-system. The daughters too learn what a woman ought to be in her different roles. Her role is imputed to her and she must prove upto the mark. The prospect of a married life is so charming to the girls that they dream about their married world and expect it to be better than their present. This is an important sentiment in a society that constantly threatens a woman's position as a wife at the mercy of her husband and his family members.

Jorimon, the ten-year-old little girl, comes to her new home with heart beating in fear and eyes filled with rosy dreams. But within a few days, all her dreams faded into thin air, "I never had any wish fulfilled at my father's home. Neither did I have any better luck at my husband's," says Jorimon (p. 18). Some of the girls are more realistic and do not dream high of their married future. Asia Begum's is a story of pain, suffering, humiliation and broken dreams. She never had any ambition, the only thing she wanted was a happy family life. This was not a great expectation but Asia had to go through three marriages in search of this receding mirage. She ended up in a morass of dejection and self-pity (p. 271). The patterns of behaviour expected of a girl in her conjugal family were all clear to the girls. Their training at their matal homes instill, in them the feeling that only by keeping their busbands and his kinsmen happy can they establish themselves in their conjugal homes. As a newly married bride, Bachaton tried to please every one as best as she could. She used to sweep the courtyard, cook, and serve food, and do practically every thing else (p. 34). Hazera and Mafia were no different as brides. Daughters are brought up to be subordinate. They come to believe the values of society that conditions them into the habit of timidity. They are persuaded to be submissive and frivolous and are made to believe that this will get them more out of life.

The myths create the belief of female weakness. Under their influence women put up willingly with exploitation and accept a role which subjects them to the will of others. They tend to live frivolously and continue to ignore their personal satisfactions. They submit to outrage and victimization. They are flogged and accept this lying low. They are trained to inculcate the ability to grant a pardon, and absolve the man who inflicts the outrage. Women idealise this. They receive recognition and praise for being feminine. This maintains the *status quo* as it is. These myths, values and ideals uphold an orthodoxy.

If anything went wrong or happened against expectation, the blame is put on the newly-wed bride. Bachator was labelled as 'jinxed' when the horses died due to an epidemic (p. 35). Asia's father would turn wild if his meal was not waiting for him after he had taken his bath, irrespective of the fact whether there were any provisions for a meal in the house. He would let out his fury by slapping, beating up and kicking the offender. Asia's mother bore the brunt of his torture. She gave birth to seven children without ever being spared of his beating (p. 272).

Home making and house keeping are central to the numerous roles expected of an ideal married woman. Her credit lies in her ability to keep things moving forward *i.e.* to be able to run the house efficiently. The task is extremely challenging for the poorest of the women who rarely have house made of four walls and a roof, let alone other items required for a mere survival.

In Kashen munshi's hard-up family life, quarrels were regular occurrences. Asia's parents used to fight with each other over trifling matters. Her father sometimes beat up her mother. Her faults were small—a slight delay in cooking, failure to sweep the yard clean enough...Asia's mother had the burden of preparing food for so many hungry mouths. When rice was in short supply she used to borrow or beg from the neighbours. Naturally she could not always prepare the meals in time. But the mushi would go crazy if his meal was not waiting for him after he had taken his bath (p. 272). As trained to bear all household responsibility, women manage to make ends meet even in the face of irresponsible husbands.

Mamtaz and her husband were the only members of their small family. She had always wished to build a nice happy family. All her life Mamtaz had been free from the duties and responsibilities at her parents' home. But now she herself took up the burden of building her own home and family. Sheikh Ali was not much concerned about his family he had no thoughts about the future. Mamtaz used to argue with him every day and tried to make him face the reality (p. 215).

Rabeya lived with her in-laws for three years after the marriage. Kuddus did not do any work and used to loaf around. His father had tried to reform the boy but Kuddus did not care for his father. Finally, Kuddus was separated from the family. But this did not change his habits. He still preferred not to work. He did not stay at home much. So Rabeya had to starve. She stayed on, although it meant enduring hunger and pain. Sometimes she confronted her husband when he came home: "Where do you go every day? Who would give me food if you leave me like this? Kuddus would reply, 'If you don't like it, you are free to go' (p. 225). Later he sold off his wife into prostitution. Tofazzal Mian had the habit of beating her up for every little thing. Tofazzal's father tried to pacify him and requested Fuljan to go back with him. Fuljan thought, I am pregnant now. In a few days I'll have a baby and that will only complicate matters. Let me go back and try to live in my husband's home in whatever way (p. 101). It was her rightful peace despite inhuman treatment. Women are treated as commodities that can be dispensed or done away with or allowed to stay at home as their men please. As it is, the hoary traditions expect them to do all that pleases the male members in the family and the society. Most of the women live pathetic lives under the constant threat of being thrown out of the house. Divorce is the worst form of insult inflicted on a woman. It robs her of her prestige and belittles her into a lesser human being. Most of the younger women have been harassed for dowry. It is not so for the older ones as it was not so institutionalised a few decades ago. These women have become victims of the dowry system. Asia could not satisfy her husbands' family despite all her efforts. The main reason was that the wedding ceremony was not colourful as they expected and Asia's father did not give dowry to Hamid, Asia's husband. His step-mother was after her right from the day she stepped into their house. All her complaints were listed to Hamid. She gave him plenty of examples of others who gained by marriage. Hamid started disliking his in-laws. He was displeased with them. He divorced Asia a year after marriage. Hamid kept all her ornaments. Asia came back to her father's house with nothing but the sari she was wearing. She was burden in the year of drought and crop failure (pp. 273-74).

The reproductive role of women is a major obligation. It is absolutely normal to expect the wife to produce children for her husband. There is a fear of being turned cut or having to put up with the husband's second wife if she cannot bear children within a few years of marriage. For 8 years after her marriage, Sakhina did not have any children. People called her barren and infertile. Afaz Ali himself thought so and did not spare any opportunity to make remarks about this. But after 8 years she silenced all her critics by giving birth to a child, a baby daughter. In the midst of so much sorrow there was not enough food for Sakhina and Afaz: Sakhina's face lit up with joy and satisfaction (p. 65). Abdul Ali married seven times. Rabeya's mother was his last wife, the only one to have produced children. She gave birth to three daughters and a son before becoming a widow (p. 223).

The value of a son is more than that of a daughter. The woman certainly improves her status by bearing a son for her husband. She is insecure about her future in the conjugal home if she has no son. After Asia was divorced by Hamid, her father arranged her marriage with Buzrat Ali who had married thrice earlier. His first wife died after giving birth to a son. The second wife was very lazy and was also not good looking. She did nothing but eat, sleep and socialise in the neighbourhood. Buzrat Ali divorced her on these grounds. He also divorced his third wife because she was a shrew and quarrelsome woman. She was also accused of hating Mansur Ali, Buzrat's son by his first wife. Asia was his fourth wife. After about a year of her marriage, Asia gave birth to a daughter. The birth of a female child did not much please him. Later Asia gave birth to a second daughter, who soon died. The birth of two daughters did not go well with Buzrat Ali. His love and affection for Asia began to cool. Asia once again gave birth to a daughter. It was the turning point in her life. Buzrat Ali did not hide his disgust and anger. He became alternately angry and indifferent. He often beat up Asia.... A mean villager counselled Buzrat to divorce Asia. "She will never give you a son, you must realise that if you hang on to Asia, your own son Mansur will not much care for you in old age. Who will then give you food or look after you if you are ill? Buzrat tortured Asia and divorced her one day (pp. 274-76).

Rabeya's eyes glistened with tears revealing her fear of being deserted by her husband. With deep regret Rabeya remarked that if she had a son she could lead the rest of the life with him. There was no meaning in life without a son and a fear of her husband leaving her to her own self. This is the plight of a woman who sacrificed every thing possible and worked for the well-being of her husband to experience constant fear that he would leave her (pp. 237-38).

Women have also been divorced because their husbands did not find them appealing or took fancy for some other woman. Divorce and desertion generate the most dreadful fear in women's minds. Removing of the 'married', label and putting the label of 'divorce' is a doom in more than one way. In addition to the economic problems, the divorced woman is thrown into the world without any social status. Her remarriage is more difficult as compared to that of an unmarried girl. She is a burden on her parents who are already hard pressed. Divorce is prestige withdrawn. It is a doom for woman. She is thrown out to face the insecurities of the larger society.

The cruelty of world is no less for a widow. She has to face the challenges and burdens of life all by herself and worse if she has very small children. Women thus believe that it is better to accept the tortures of one man, the husband, than to suffer the wrath of the whole society. Jorimon's husband was a terribly ill-tempered man. In her words, "He is a Khan in name as well as in deed." He used to beat her up on the slightest pretext and threatened to divorce her all the time. At times Rustom's beating left Jorimon's entire body bruised and bleeding. Yet she suffered every thing in silence for the sake of children. Fuljan had serious problems of housing after she was divorced even though she had no problems in earning for herself and her son from her tailoring skill. She shifted from house to house and to other villages before she could find a quiet place to earn a living (p. 103). The mother of Rabeya was evicted from their homestead and had to beg on streets after she became a widow (p. 224).

Alekha's parents tried very hard to get her married again. But it was extremely difficult to find a husband for a girl who has been divorced. Although one or two proposals did come. A lot of problems of dowry arose and everything fizzled out (p. 138). Asia was prepared to put up with a life of humiliation only if it meant a secure home. But Kudrat Ali moved decisively to put Asia away for good. He divorced her and sent her home to her brother. Hazera was at that time and Moktar only two (p. 278).

A frivolous woman is virtuous. She accepts as proper to her whatever her husband has to offer her: love, beating, kicking, abuse and threat. She should not cause any displeasure to him or else bear the brunt. Afaz Ali seized the wooden lampstand and cursing loudly fell upon her beating her ruthlessly. There was not an inch of her body that did not bear the brunt of his wrath. Finally her outraged husband put his weight on her chest and began strangling her. Sakhina lost consciousness and lay in a bloody mess all that night. Her head was wounded and she was seriously hurt. The next three days she lay helplessly in bed. But Afaz Ali did not even once inquire about her or bring her any medication. Sakhina's brother later took her home and her mother learnt everything that had happened. Sakhina cried and beggerd "Mother, please send me back to that house, I don't want to go there." Her mother, however, tried to make her understand the situation that a woman gets married only once, and has to face upto pain and sorrow. Sakhina understood that her mother's door was no longer open for her. She understood that there was no way but to accept what fate had in store for her (p. 64). She realised that her security was only in being someone's wife, whatever way she was treated was not so important.

Shumari's husband Ramjan had married a second wife and did not bother about Shumari. Her father accepted her misfortune and believed that she was not fated to have any happiness. He pleaded with Ramjan to give a place to Shumari in his house after he was dead along with a part of his land. But Shumari was forced to continue to stay with her brother. It was only when Shumari's husband and his wife were suffering from sorrow and hardship while Shumari was doing well by raising cows, that Ramjan wanted to bring Shumari to live with him. Despite all her suffering, humiliation and insult inflicted by Ramjan she agreed to join him and his second wife with a hope to help them out of their suffering (p.168).

In the process of a constant frivolous behaviour and the spirit of paroning most women tend to accept male tutelage as their fate. Now fulfilment of any wish for Fuljan and constant threats to Bachaton who was branded as jinxed; sorrow as the constant companion of Sakhina who commented that God had created and sent her to this world only to suffer, why should he then allow her to have a glimpse of happiness? (pp. 18-36). The non-appealing Alekha and Fuljan gradually came to accept their plight as their misfortune. Alekha hardly ever complained to her own parents about the beatings she was receiving for she knew she had to stay in her husband's home no matter what happened (pp. 101-37).

An important feature about the women's belief in fate is that it is through a process that they come to believe in fate rather than view it as an end produce dropped into their laps. Halima did not assign every problem to fate instantly.

It was after her struggle with child birth, loss of children, rearing them up, and the long drawn struggle to maintain her life that she invoked fate (pp. 147-58). Divorce of Koituri and abandoning of both her sons on roadside to be picked away drove Koituri crazy. She wept uncontrollably for deprived motherhood and commented that others could not feel her pain, a mother's pain at loss of her children. It was much later that she came to accept all that as misfortune and God given (pp. 239-52). Mafia's first child, a boy, died soon after birth. Her mother-in-law blamed Mafia for this and stepped up her ill-treatment. She was starved and thus could not carry a child. The child was either dead or died soon after birth. Mafia received deep scare from her husband's beatings, but did not want to leave him. She tried her best to pull along for a few years before she finally left him. It was at this point that she invoked fate (pp. 179-92).

Almost all the women have earnestly endeavoured to improve their circumstances and conditions. It is only after continuous failure to overcome suffering at the hands of in-laws, beatings, threats and divorce by husbands that these women assigned every thing to their fate. They did resist and tolerate cruelty with the hope of a better future. But fate came as a scapegoats only when all efforts of altering their marital and family life proved ineffective.

Belief in fate seems to have rescued them and offered some consolation. Thus they never thought of disbelief in the institutions of marriage, family, dowry and divorce existing as bastions of patriarchy in the larger society. As soon as a daughter reached 9 or 10 years of age, the mother's biggest worry was marrying her off. She hoped to find a decent husband for her and contemplated and wished for her happy married life. She dreamt of a life without sorrow, beating and suffering for her daughter, although deep inside there was a strong fear for this to happen.

As mentioned earlier, Asia's only dream was a happy married life for which she was married and divorced thrice. She blamed her fate in the end but had expected a better fate for her daughter, Hazera. Hazera was over-worked at her in-laws' place. They did not care for her when she fell ill. Asia brought her medication on learning about Hazera's suffering. Her husband spent his days in illness and her mother-in-law disliked and troubled her. Hazera was soon divorced and live with her mother. Asia's greatest worry is now her daughter. She could not imagine that her daughter's fate would be identical to hers (p. 282). This is the story repeated in most women's life experiences.

III

The potential to withstand suffering and struggle for a better deal as long as strength and will power permit is the source of hope in their lives. It is hope that keeps them alive amidst an open Pandora's box. Although they ultimately come to surrender to pressures of patriarchy and accept as fate all male tutelage in the familial domain. They are more strong in the extra familial domain. As already mentioned, even in the familial domain they rarely accept defeat in the beginning, despite being knit into a culture of female subordination. Their resistance is much greater in the extra familial domain, which has been an all male domain for ages. Woman's place is therefore in the home. There are sex role stereotypes that support such a territorial division (Sharma, 1980: 39-47). Even religion and scriptures are used to strengthen the separation of domains on sex lines.

The economic pressures of being landless, uneducated, unemployed, wage earning hands are easy to understand. More so, given the frequency of droughts and floods that ruin the crops and possibilities of work opportunities. Even when work is available, the wages are so low that it is not possible for a man to support his family. There is hardly any family who did not experience hunger and starvation for days at a stretch. Some of them have never had a hearty meal all their lives and mothers cherish a family of well-fed children. The suffering caused by poverty and hunger was not easy to put up with. It reached beyond the capacity of mothers to bear all this.

Women found themselves at cross roads in the face of such a mind-boggling situation. It was a mental turmoil for them. They could improve the situation, save their children from hunger if they could earn some thing in cash or kind. But the scarcity of work apart, they were faced with a strange dilemma. The values and norms confining the woman to the household prevailed strongly on the one hand and the emaciated faces of starving and naked children constantly chilled the mother's spine on the other.

At her husband's death, Sakhina's enormous pain and helplessness, however, did not confine her to the house for too long. The more she thought she would not leave the house, the more her empty stomach and the cries of her starving children compelled her to venture out. Only five days after her husband's death Sakhina had forgot her prestige and was at her neighbour's door soliciting help (pp. 68-69). In her words, when Shahinoor her son "...starts to bring up blood, all my strength and outrage disappear. I wish I had died earlier... There is no one on this earth who will look after this fatherless child. If he does not live, how can I keep myself alive?" (p. 65). The only path to survival for Sakhina was to work in neighbours' homes. During the harvesting season there was much to do in the farmers' households. Sakhina found work in cleaning, parboiling and husking paddy. Whatever she got in return somehow kept them alive. She never had the good fortune to eat a hearty meal. Besides the rice harvesting season, there was not much work available in the village, and at such times, Sakhina's family faced abject poverty and starvation. In utter helplessness she had to throw aside shame and delicacy and go about begging (p. 69). Many others also had to beg or borrow in worst times. The decision to step outside the house to support the family or add to the man's earnings meant doing away with decency.

The value that a decent woman remains indoors is incorporated as a desire and functions as a means to maintain the social structure, although women come to accept it as an end. Attitudes and beliefs reflect an ideal world, they show what women dream of having, doing and being. Thus they are subordinate to the beliefs and attitudes. Famuna had never asked for anything to any one, had never gone to work at others' homes. She had a strong sense of self-respect (p. 198). The women who worked in others' houses were clear in their minds that they had no self-respect or dignity as they stepped out to work.

To uphold the social values and live a life of dignity, the women thought of working outside only in utter desperation. They struggled their best to save their faces until they were virtually overpowered by starvation and bushed outside the house. Family property was also sold out to avoid women's work outside. When hard days came, Jammuna sold her ornaments. Her husband was the only earning member. If he earned anything, they ate, otherwise they went hungry. On top of this other adversities like natural calamities, floods, storms and the war of independence struck them one after the other. Their miserable life became more and more unbearable (p. 198). Like many others, Bachaton's family sold land to save themselves from starvation. Her days were spent in semi or complete starvation. The food she and her family ate would not be called food at all. When things become unbearable, she stretched out her hands to her brothers but even that had a limit.... So, she pitifully requested her neighbours to lend her money. However, she never had to pay any interest on the loans. She used to sell whatever chickens or goats she reared to repay the money (p. 43). Moyfal did the same when Abas Mia became the same and sick (p. 124).

When all avenues of survival were blocked, there was no other alternative but to venture out defying the social values of patriarchy. Women moved out under severe pressures. When Sagir Ali was ill and confined to bed all responsibilities fell on Bachaton. Her children were too small to earn a living. But so many mouths would not listen to reason alone. When starvation and suffering reached such a stage that they could not bear it any longer, Bachaton decided that she had to stand on her own feet. She could not be tied down to the prohibitions of society any more. And at night under the cover of darkness, she started cultivating their land. During this time the village elders became very busy in reminding her of the norms of society and the duties of a respectable woman, but she turned a deaf ear to them. At night she worked on her own land and during the day she husked paddy and worked in other people's houses in return for whatever little she got for the family (pp. 40-41).

Within a month of her marriage, Sakhina was compelled to look for work in neighbouring houses. She was not afraid of working outside. It was worse to suffer and worry inside the house (p. 63). Wazed Ali's protracted illness drove Tara helpless and the relatives became reluctant to offer further help. So Tara went to work at neighbours' houses without anyone knowing. Later, no one opposed her working out to earn a living (p. 258). Tara launched her career of working in others' houses under pressure and with a sense of hopeless dejection.

As this was a step away from the traditional roles of women, they did not have smooth sailing. This was objected to by their kinsmen and also by the elders in the society. The displeasure was directly revealed to those women who did not behave normatively. An important difference in the response of male members to women's ventures outside the household is the reflection of varying degrees of tolerance and displeasure of the larger society. It is pertinent to note that the pressure on women to stop coming out of their houses was not the same for all jobs that women did outside the household. The objection was covert and mild when women took up jobs as helping hands in others' houses and farms. The cases of Bachaton, Jorimon, Moyfal, Sakhina, Koituri and others reveal that they did not face major obstacles from their families or society's elders when they looked for the odd chores in neighbouring households.

The communication of disapproval was quite strong whenever women took up major roles outside the household. There was displeasure when women took up jobs which were customarily the exclusive tasks of men such as cultivating and ploughing land by Bachaton or petty trading done by Sakhina and Halima who peddled wares and other goods, or Moyfal's and Jorimon's paddy husking business, etc. People created all sorts of fears in the minds of the villagers. They called it a death trap and an instrument of killing poor people. They did not object when Bachaton was carrying head loads of firewood to sell. But when she began her independent husking trade they protested vehemently. The rich cultivators, the village elders, the headmen, the *mollahs*, all opposed the bank loan scheme. They spread malicious and absurd rumours and created a feeling of fear among women. The *mollahs* passed all kinds of religious verdicts aimed at restraining the women (p. 54). Some people frightened Moyfal. They warned her that if she could not repay the money properly, her house and land would be confiscated, and she would be tied up and thrown into prison, and so on (p. 126). When Alekha told her father about the bank loan, Kabil Mondal stubbornly opposed the idea. He told her sternly that it was impossible for her to use the money profitably and pay back the weekly instalments regularly especially since Alekha was a woman. It is not possible for a woman to run a business (p. 144). Shumari was deterred on the same ground (p. 173).

Mamtaz was barraged with the sentiments of neighbours and kinsmen against bank loans taken by women. "The women who visit the bank and hold meetings have no self-respect." The money lenders were furious and didn't care what they said about the bank and these women (p. 219). A few village elders did not like Rabeya's visits to the bank. They took her to task. "Shameless woman, you are not satisfied with your own shamelessness. You have to turn the head of a few other decent girls, too. If you dare to set foot to the bank once more, we will drive you off from the village." Rabeya was starving that day. She could not take the insult lying low. She had nothing to lose and did not fear any more the guardians of society. She told them, "When I starve with my family do you care to give me a morsel to eat? I have not taken anything for the whole day but do you seem to care? When I go to the bank you think I have done a crime against you..." (p. 223).

Both direct and indirect forms of disapproval of women's economic independence are revealed as women gather courage and cross the cordons of traditional values and boundaries. Men seem to be most ruthless and critical when women take over in the outer spheres. This seems to threaten male domination and patriarchal values exercised on women. Males seem to become dispensable when women tend to show signs of self-sufficiency or independence. It is in this context that one may understand the objections of society's elders to women's economic liberation. It would be worthwhile to further probc whether the practice of unequal wages for men and women for equal work is also an indirect form of disapproval and suppression.

Women's belief in fate, as mentioned earlier, does not drop from the blue. They do not easily surrender to the traditional institutions of exploitation whether it is in the household domain or outside it. In addition, the process of fighting back and struggling for an improvement in their situations reveals numerous emotions, turmoils, sorrow, suffering, joy and hope. In the whole process of ups and downs during their struggle against both the male and the economic oppression, women experience remorse, anger and resentment. The pangs of fighting out fortresses of tradition are not an easy task.

Most women suffered in silence at their husband's or in-law, cruelty. But suffering in silence is not always equal to absolute submission. The feelings and ideas that come to their minds during their non-protest or meek silence are significant indications of a deep pain and displeasure against the oppressor. Jorimon recalls her past when she went from village to village with a heavy load of firewood on her head. People used to ignore us all the time. No one ever looked at us with grace or favour. But today with an independent paddy husking trade Jorimon does not have to put up with any affronts or insults (p. 28). Bachaton's condition worsened after her husband was struck down with paralysis. She begged for *marh,* which is usually thrown away, from her neighbours for the children. She could not bear to see the famished look of their starving faces. She felt as if her heart would break. Their cries for food drove her mad. Utterly desperate, her frustration and resentment at her own helplessness caused her to beat them severely at times. And then, when she was alone she cried out to the heavens, beat her breast and wept bitterly (p. 40).

Sakhina had an argument with her husband who had misinformed that he owned property while he owned none. Words led to more angry words. Sakhina called him a cheat and wicked. She was struck immediately in the head and ruthlessly beaten. Helpless to move she suffered silently in bed (p. 64). Later at his death Sakhina did not carry hatred for him. Her tears had a deeper emotion of anger and remorse, a tussle in the process of questioning patriarchy. Rabeya at times confronted her husband, who was also her cousin, for being irresponsible (p. 225).

Fuljan was unhappy about her husband's interest in Bela. One night, they fought over this issue angrily. He beat her up. Fuljan was dejected and did not speak to him for days (p. 101). Shumari was not pleased with Ramjan marrying Shano. She continued to live in her father's house as a disapproval in the midst of pain, anguish and suffering. When the badly off Ramjan came to take her back she showed her anger, "I can't go to your house just because you wish me to. When I was starving, when I was wearing torn rags, when Sobur was dying from disease and neglect no one came forward to help me. But now you are here" (p. 175). Similar reactions are observed when women are stopped from moving out of their houses, especially when they take bank loans for economic independence. Rabeya's retaliation to village elders has already been mentioned (p. 233). Bachaton recalled how angry she was when she was absolutely helpless and wanted to earn a living. She commented that the children went practically naked '... I myself had no clothes. I had only a torn rag of a sari which I wore month after month. I was so ashamed I avoided going out in front of people' (p. 44).

Abuse at others, hands made Sakhina angry and she felt that she was not a human being any more. In her words, "Even cows and goats have some value to people but I did not have even that. I felt that if I had been born a cow instead of a person, perhaps I would have had some value" (p. 74).

Fuljan was very sad and dejected with her marital life, and her undesirability at her brother's house and later at her aunt's house. She was unhappy with the hurdles her aunt's family created for her despite her self-sufficiency as she earned her livelihood from stitching garments (p. 105).

The cruelty of social institutions of divorce and remarriage are at their apex when Alekha takes her life to avoid transfer of her father's property to Rahim, her prospective husband, to make up for her lower status of being divorced and also for having fallen in love with Rahim (pp. 142-43).

IV

Anger and resentment be it overt or covert is a response to the oppression of women when it becomes unbearable to them. They suffer in silence and resent as long as they can tolerate. They speak out when the seems of their toleration give way. Some totally withdraw from the scene as Alekha did. The tug of war continues.

In the higher and middle strata where property is inherited women are said to be more submissive and tolerant. Status of women in the section of the society which has no property is assumed to be better and those women less tolerant. One may analyse the variations in the experiences of torture and tolerance of women across classes in society. It would be interesting to explore this comparison, especially in the context of pitiful plights and turdly tolerances towards suffering and starvation of the lower class women as these. Another argument which Goode (p. 963) also supports is the ideal of conjugal family which is supposed to emancipate the individual from the domination of elders and the group. Also, the nuclear family's so-called egalitarian norms are considered to act as the strongest instrument for the emancipation of women from male tutelage. Does this hold good for the lower class families, where most families are conjugal as against joint? Are these women more emancipated owing to the wide prevalance of conjugal families?

The present paper has analysed the three structural principles governing women's oppression—gender, class, and community. The woman in the present study is poor but poorer than her husband because she is considered and treated as second sex (and a lesser human being therefore). That she is not indispensable and can be subjected to frequent divorces and remarriages is supported by the third principle of subordination, *i.e.,* the fact of her belonging to the Muslim community. The third principle, however, merely provides a large cosmology for male domination and female suppression. It is difficult to say that the latter is because of the former. It would be relevant to point out that one of the 16 women studied here is a Hindu and her plight is not very different when compared with other Muslim women.

Status of Women in Pakistan

The women in Pakistan seem to have no respite from medieval age patriarchy disguised under the garb of Islamisation. Hudood (propriety), blasphemy and witness laws can best explain the plight of the vast majority of women in Pakistan. Under these laws a rape victim must produce two pairs of eyes—of Muslim males—to prove the crime. If the witnesses happen to be non-Muslims or women, the required number increases to four. The result is that the victims themselves end up in jail for seven years after being convicted of adultery. If a Muslim husband wants to get rid of his lawful wife, he simply has to lodge a complaint under the blasphemy laws that his wife has challenged Islam. This finds her behind bars and she can even be hanged. According to a survey, 70 per cent of the women languishing in Pakistan's jails are victims of such laws.

As if these repressive measures were not enough, Pakistan has been witnessing a spate of 'honour killings' of women in the recent past. Their own families murder women if they are suspected of "immoral activities". These include among other things, marrying without the consent of the family, being seen with a person the family disapproves of, going out alone, disobeying the husband or the in-laws, adultery or just unfortunately being the subject of gossip. Honour is recovered only when the woman dies. The latest chilling case of 'honour killing' is the murder of Samia Sarwar, a woman seeking divorce, which was opposed by her family. She was shot dead on April 6, 1997 in Lahore by a gunman hired by her parents.

Samia, 29, mother of two children, aged four and eight, had been living with her parents for the past four years after leaving her husband due to his "violent nature". He beat her up regularly and had thrown her down the stairs when she was expecting her second child in February 1995. Pregnant Samia shifted to her parents' house—her mother is a gynaecologist while her father an industrialist. But they were opposed to a formal divorce and had threatened to kill her if she persisted. She tried for four years, and ultimately was left with no option but to leave her paternal home in Peshawar. She was given shelter at Dastak (the knock)—a house for women run by a sisters duo Hina Jillani and Asma Jahangir, well-known lawyers and human rights activists.

Incidentally, the BBC aired a documentary, *A matter of honour,* on 'honour killings' in Pakistan. According to this documentary, in the north-west of Pakistan in one year 350 women were killed in the name of honour. Many of the killers who were interviewed were unrepentant. They said there was no greater honour than killing a girl who dared to elope. The rulers of Pakistan decried the film as anti-Islam.

Surprisingly, 'honour killing' which considered a legacy of tribal culture, is not confined to some illiterate families residing in the remote and backward tribal areas of Pakistan. These are taking place in major cities, among the educated and affluent sections of Muslims. The Chairperson of the Human Rights Commission of Pakistan, Asma Jahangir, says that apart from the police and a dominant section in the Press, there are judges in the superior courts expressing this kind of sentiment towards women in Pakistan. Dr. Riffat Hassan, a well-known authority on Islam, who is often described as the first woman liberation theologist of Islam, believes that such killings have got impetus and legitimacy due to a wave of so-called Islamisation in Pakistan. This has resulted in the imposition of male-chauvinistic laws on Muslim women, which are detrimental for the healthy and democratic development of any society. Muslim women need to be educated about their rights under Islam so that they can fight these brutalities and oppression.

It has been argued by the reformists that gender-equality and gender-justice were so central to the world view of normative Islam that it had guaranteed women not only the right to live and other fundamental rights given to all human beings, but also special rights which—taking account of their vulnerability in pre-Islamic Arabian society (more than 14 centuries ago)—were intended to safeguard them from any kind of injustice. However, the condition of women in Pakistan and many other "Islamic" nations has no relation with Islam. It is the absolute violation of the sanctity of human life—the most fundamental of human rights—which cannot be condoned in the name of culture or religion.

It is true that a number of 'honour killings' have been reported in India, the latest incidents taking place in Haryana and Rajasthan. However, the situation in India is different in the sense that at least at the level of legislation, women are treated as equal. In Pakistan the theocratic state is itself prejudiced.

Documenting a Training Programme for Women

Documentation of a programme is a process by which the documentationist directly observes and personally couches the proceedings of a forum a discussion or a dialogue in a sequential and scientific manner. An assignment for documentation also carries with it an opportunity to participate in the programme, interact with the participants, learn from the resource persons, benefit by the discussions and to have close association with the organisers. Documentation essentially has two sides one is contributing by way of recording the transaction and in this process, the order pertains to the gaining of knowledge.

Documentation could be done by a simple method of recording the proceedings in a hand book or by taping the entire proceedings. Depending upon its significance and resource availability, it could also be video filmed in parts or full. Compared to the third method, the second method is considered to be more effective, economical and long lasting. Under the first method, we may miss certain portions of the speech and proceedings or fail to capture the feelings of the audience or speakers. The third method is costlier, cumbersome and bristles with scores of complications.

Documentationist's Role

Documenting can be by one or more persons, and by an outsider or insider. However, it must be done by a person who is familiar with the ideology of the sponsors and their organisation and knowledgeable the theme of the programme. He should fit in with the overall system of the programme and his work should be considered as an integral component of the total process. His presence should be felt neither too distinctly nor too inadequately. He should neither lag behind nor swim against the regular current but should be part of the running flow.

The author had an opportunity to document a 10 day seminar-cum-workshop intended to train the rural women on income generating projects, sponsored by the International Labour Organisation (ILO) and the Danish International Development Authority (DANIDA) and offered by the International Federation of Plantation, Agriculture and Allied Workers (IFPAAW). The participants comprised the active women members of trade unions, encompassing the plantation and agricultural sectors from India (Tamil Nadu, Andhra Pradesh, Kerala, West Bengal and Gujarat) and Sri Lanka.

Women's Training Programme

Organised in Tamil Nadu during September 1990, three methods were followed in this programme lecture method, group discussion and individual project preparation exercises. The author followed the second method of documentation namely 'tape-recording' the proceedings from the start to the end. Nearly two-dozen cassettes were used up in recording the proceedings, which were later replayed and transcribed.

On completion of the exercise, the author considered it useful to share his experiences with a wider audience, gained during the course of the 10-day programme, arranged to train women in developing proposals for income generating projects and initiating necessary follow-up activities when they get back to their respective unions. This paper, accordingly, focus on the general and technical difficulties inherent in using the tape-recording method of documentation and the precautions that the prospective documentationists should take prior to their documentation process.

We may collect the background materials regarding the training and objectives of the sponsoring as well as training organisation, along with the programme schedule. We might also know about the number of participants, their language, sponsoring organisation and other available details. In addition, information on the number and nature of resource persons, topics to be discussed and the possible methods to be deployed will also be helpful to us.

The fundamental aspect in the process of documentation is that we should know from the training organisers about the form and manner in which the proceedings should be documented. While some prefer a synthesised and synoptic account of the proceedings in an indirect speech, others expect a step-by-step verbatim account of the transactions in a direct speech form. Under such circumstances, the tape recording method readily comes to our rescue, for we can replay it any and report accordingly.

We should never slither down to other roles and assist or associate in any other tasks except observation and recording. Our total concentration is of utmost necessity and diversion for even a short while may be dearer to the documentation process. Circumstances may compel us to translate and clarify certain concepts, or plunge into dialogue with the training organisers; such forms of distractions need to be thoroughly avoided.

Handbook Maintenance

A programme in which there are mostly lectures with prepared scripts, we may simply record the discussion portions. However, in those programmes which consist largely of discussions and less of lectures, the documentationist's role becomes critical and exerting. He needs to be careful and alert in the latter situation and take suitable precautions.

In order to surmount such possible problems or even otherwise, we should keep track of the proceedings in a handbook, specifying the date, time of commencement, topic discussed, resource person with correct spelling, initial and his designation with full address, time of completing the lecture, duration of discussion and the name and organisation of the participants involved in the discussion. Barring the content of questions, answers and other clarifications raised, which might be getting recorded, we have to note down everything else in our notebook.

Sometimes the trainers go around the trainees, far away from the dais, and hence their speech goes unrecorded. Similarly, when they work out certain estimates, do calculations or draw pictures on the black board, the tape fails to capture them. Therefore, it is our duty to diarise them in our handbook.

In addition to the above, we should also adhere to the following instructions:

Collect every piece of paper, used by the lectures and participants in doing exercises, drawing pictures, or any other relevant scribblings made in the training hall.

At times, there are mistakes in their calculations or work sheets or proposals, which require rectification, or rehashing. We may do all these, without prejudice to their original intent.

When changes are made in the original programme schedule, such details should be entered in the same.

Tapes and Cassettes

Every cassette as well as its cover should have the details on the date and time, title of the programme (*e.g.* inaugural, valedictory, business session etc.) and the trainer's name as well as the topic discussed.

Entry of the above details in the cassette is far more important than its entry on the cover, although it is equally important. For, a cassette devoid of any details, when packed into a wrong cover, might cause greater confusion and waste our energy and time.

Tape recorder with numbers will be of greater convenience because, we can enter this number on the cassette as to where the previous ends and the next one begins. This would save out time at the time of replay.

Changing the sequence of the programme in the series of casettes causes greater confusion. For instance, when a casette recorded on the first day of the programme has some unrecorded portions on the 'B' side, we are tempted to use it for a small slot on some other day. Although they may be allowed in economic terms, technically such practices are not advocated, for this leads to embrarrassment at times.

Replay of Cassettes

In as much as the tape-recording system has advantages, replay of the recorded cassettes also has its disadvantages. Even the perfectly recorded proceedings might evade certain portions from our memory and thereby cause ambiguity in identifying the person, the content or its context. In order to avoid this problem, we should replay the cassettes as early as possible, without losing much time from the date of closing the programme.

Even recorded cassette takes more time for replay than what it originally took for recording. While well prepared speeches or standard lectures may take less time, discussions and clarifications take a long time for deciphering.

Those programmes in which the business sessions last for a few or fixed hours, for instance, from 10.00 A.M. to 1.00 P.M., and 1.00 P.M. to 5.00 P.M., it will be convenient for us to complete the task early. On the contrary, if it has a non-stop and marathon sitting every day, then our task is made tougher.

Residential programmes facilitate the organisers to have extended sessions and thus exhaust the energy of not only the participants but also the documentationists. In order to combat this problem and even otherwise, while recording the proceedings, we should be vigilant enough to avoid translations, repetitions and needless explanations. This would help us to be economical in time, energy and resources.

Noise Distortion

Noise free environment is a boon for recording exercises. Programmes held near public transport points, industrial workshops etc., cause heavy noise disturbance and thus distorts the message. The fan-generated air too contributes its share. The downpour of rain, movement of things and conversation between persons adjacent to the training spot or recording place cause noisy sounds during replay.

Conversation between persons on the dais and simultaneous translation of the lectures by those near the podium are audible loudly in the casette than the original lectures or proceedings. Consequently, it becomes very critical for us to comprehend the feeble voices heard at a distance, amidst the rough voices recorded in a close range.

Despite a complete recording of the proceedings, we might fumble in finding out who is the owner of the voice. Even in smaller gatherings, it is a testing time for us to locate the identical voice of two different participants. At such critical junctures, our handbook comes to us handy.

Occasions arise when just a single word, spelt out sufficiently unclear, especially by foreigners, causes hell of a problem to us. Failure to find out, even after repeated replays, will halt our progress in completing the process.

Technical Snags

Besides the problems expatiated above, certain technical problems confront us in the process of documentation. These are listed below:

1. Failure to release the 'pause' button, results in missing the recording of proceedings.

2. Delay in putting on the tape, leaves out some proceedings, from being recorded.

3. While changing the cassette, we miss a portion of the proceedings.

4. While recording, the volume in the tape should be completely put off.

5. When the battery becomes weak and exhausted it hampers the output.

6. Message recorded in the power-operated tape-recorder is noisy during replay.

7. At times, the cassette runs very fast during replay.

When the tape recorder becomes defective, it dislocates the process.

Associate Gains

Besides documenting the programme, this experience also helps us in the following ways:

1. We feel as one of the participants and absorb whatever they learn.

2. We are able to assess the strengths and weaknesses of every resource person and hence we can avoid such mistakes during our subsequent opportunities.

3. We can read the expectations of participants from various resource persons and we can charge ourselves suitably in future training.

4. While we are invited for a training programme, we know what kind of details we should gather from them before giving our consent.

5. We learn about the drawbacks of this programme and hence can arrange training programmes in future with less mistakes.

Documentation experience is thus not merely an assignment but also an opportunity, not just an exerting and exhausting task but an educative and enjoyable one too.

Notes and References

Janeway, E. *Man's World, Woman's Place,* New York: Penguin Books Ltd.

Parsons, T. *The Social System,* New York: The Free Press, 1951.

Sharma, U. *Women, Work and Property in North-West India,* London: Tavistock Publications Ltd., 1980.

Yunus, M. (ed.) *Jorimon of Beltoil Village and Others: In Search of a Future.*

Dhaka: Grameen Bank, 1984.

3

Equality and Enabling Legislation

Women's emancipation is based on concerted efforts to further the principle of equality and removing all legal discrimination *inter alia* between sexes. Our leaders have shown their acceptance of the view that to achieve liberty there must be complete liberty for women and "all legislative traces of the inequality of women without exception must be removed."

Stress on the removal of discrimination and special protective legislation for women was necessary, because the British policy in the field of family law had a crippling effect on women. Whatever the motivation, the British adopted a policy of letting Hindus be governed by Hindu Law and Muslims by Muslim Law in matters of family relations. This policy of relying on age-old personal laws has been described as "another act of enlightend policy," but the result of it was to encourage the feeling of separateness and prevent the unity of the two communities. The policy achieved such success that modernisation of most of these laws has proved difficult even today. Coupled with this policy was another one of non-interference or rather non-intervention (in family law) on the plea that 'as the British legislature cannot make Mohammedan or Hindu religion, so neither can it make Mohammedan or Hindu Law'. This resulted in stagnation with the result that the two systems could neither absorb nor adjust to socio-economic changes. Sociai tensions invitably arise in situations when 'law does not in fact answer the needs arising from major social change."

In the early part of the 19th century, due to the efforts of our social reformers some marginal adjustments were made in response to humanitarian considerations and social demands. Although female infanticide had been banned earlier, the most significant was the legislation which penalised the practice of Sati. The groundwork for this had been laid for a very long time and this was an example where legislative legitimacy was given to an accepted social norm. The then Governor-General, Lord Bentink, in referring to the proposed legislation, said that the government would be following and not going ahead of public opinion.

The prevalence, in 18th and early 19th centuries, of child marriage leading often to early widowhood was one of the major concerns of the social reformers. Their tireless efforts to curb this social evil finally resulted in 1856 in 'The Hindu Widows' Remarriage Act. But even such social legislation stopped after 1857. The social reformers realised that in the face of the government's refusal to legislate on social matters the only way open was to try and spread education more widely among the people, particularly women, in the hope that this would help to eliminate some of the inhuman practices and also act as an incentive to women to organise and demand legislative changes.

As the national movement gained in strength, the early 20th century showed some activity in the legislative field. The plight of widows without any means of their own, depending entirely on the family, led to the passing of the Hindu Women's Rights to Property Act in 1929 followed by another in 1937. These laws, while they made the widow less dependent financially during her lifetime, stopped short of giving her any substantial rights of ownership since her right to property was only for life.

The success of the policy of division can also be seen from the fact that though demands for changes in the Muslim law to improve the position of women were also building up, the reformers of the two communities did not work together. The significant change that was made as a result of all the agitation for improvement among the Muslims was to give the right of divorce to Muslim women in 1939.

A by-product of the policy of non-intervention in family law had been the diversification (due to customs) among the major personal laws in different parts of the country and varied interpretations of the sacred texts. These differences had hardened over the years. Among the Muslim schools of law—there were others besides the Sunnis and Shias. This was partially remedied by the Sharīat Act 1937 which brought all Muslims under the Act and practically abrogated the customary practices which had grown over the years. Among the Hindus where there were two major schools—Mitakshara and Dayabhagi—and other sub-schools, lack of uniformity posed a serious problem.

The demand for major changes, no longer marginal ones, grew as a result of the untiring efforts of Gandhiji, who wanted women to suffer from no social or legal disabilities. The inferior position of women in all matters, guardianship, inheritance and divorce, had an effect on the personality of the women. Under Gandhiji's leadership the demand for improvement and modernisation of the law grew and ultimately the government was compelled to move. A committee was constituted under the chairmanship of Sir B.N. Rau, whose terms of reference included the suggestions for change and the Codification of Hindu Law, so that all Hindus would be governed by the same. Even though the report was ready and Gandhiji's exhortation that 'women must suffer from no disability or discrimination' had influenced India's national leaders, the resistance to change was so great that no effective steps could be taken for a number of years.

Only after independence, under the leadership of Pandit Nehru could this matter be taken up. Even so the law had to be passed piecemeal owing to resistance from those who believed in the *status quo*. It is significant that the same body which, sitting as the Constituent Assembly, adopted the equal rights clauses in the Constitution without any debate, while functioning in its capacity as the Central Legislature, blocked the Hindu

Code Bill which attempted to provide only partial equality to women.

The participation in the freedom movement had greatly helped in the acceptance of the idea of women's equality and the need for their emancipation. As a result, Indian women achieved political and same social rights easily with independence, and did not have to struggle for them as women in many other countries.

But legislation cannot by itself change society. To translate these rights into reality is the task of other agencies. Public opinion has to be moulded to accept these rights. The judiciary and the executive have a major role to play in this. This effort has not always been forthcoming. Sometimes the judiciary has interpreted new legislation strictly and failed to give effect to the principle underlying the legislation, as for example in dealing with cases of bigamy or the right of women to work. The executive branch of the government has seldom made an effort to set up the machinery to educate the people about the socio-economic changes. The mass media used for publicity for certain measures taken by government, has been conspicuously silent about social legislation. If legislation reflects the social values of a country 'the degree of women's emancipation is the natural measure of the general emancipation in any given society'. It is, therefore, necessary not only to legislate but to see that it is implemented. In the following sections an effort has been made to point out the areas where the law is lagging behind the principles which have already been accepted by our Constitution.

I. POLYGAMY

General

Full equality of sexes can hardly be possible in a legal system which permits polygamy and a social system which tolerates it. Though the institution of polygamy has prevailed traditionally in India, in the last five or more decades it is on the wane and most marriages are today monogamous. The spread of

Christianity with its concept of marriage 'as a union for life of one man with one woman' marked the first step towards the legal recognition of the principle monogamy. The advanced communities in the country like the Parsees and the Brahmos opted for the principle. The Parsee Marriage and Divorce Act, 1865 provided that any marriage during the life-time of his or her wife or husband was void. The Indian Christian Marriage Act, 1872 lays down the condition that neither of the persons intending to be married shall have a wife or husband still living. With the enactment of the Hindu Marriage Act, 1955, which lays down the principle of monogamy for all Hindus, 88 per cent of the Indian population are legally governed by the principle of monogamy.

The only personal law, which has remained impervious to the changing trend from polygamy to monogamy, is Muslim Law. Most Muslim countries such as Turkey, Iraq, Iran, Syria, Tunisia, Indonesia, Pakistan (including Bangladesh, which was then a part of Pakistan) have introduced reforms of varying degrees to correct the abuse of polygamy, but no legislative effort has so far been made in India to ameliorate the hardship caused to the Muslim women by the continuance of the institution of polygamy. According to an extract given by a Urdu Editor:

> "...the law of polygamy is not an invention of the Muslims, but a part of the comprehensive religious code granted to them by God. And the Muslims have been exercising this right of theirs since the time of the holy Prophet to this day. To tamper with it would definitely amount to interference in religion. If some Muslim or non-Muslim administration forces monogamy on Muslim, it would be a case of gross injustice; and the Muslims will oppose it as a religious duty."

During its tours, the Committee met with three different types of reaction. In Uttar Pradesh we found a positive hostility to any reform in Muslim Law particularly in the educated middle classes. Among the poorer classes of the same State we found a desire to have monogamous marriages and blunt denunciation of the inequities of polygamy. In Kashmir the women uniformly and emphatically demanded that polygamy must be banned.

The seeming indifference on the part of the government in leaving only one section of the citizens to be governed by a law permitting polygamy and other inequalities was sought to be explained by the Minister for Law and Justice, Gokhale, when he said, "We believe that while we should do everything possible to build up and cultivate the consciousness for reform, the urge and the demand for the reform must come from the community itself."

Standardized Contracts

Marriage is regarded as a contract under Muslim law for the purpose of procreation and legalizing of children. Therefore, some eminent jurists like Fyzee and Danial Latifi advocate the device of standard contract of marriage which would provide *inter alia* for stipulation like, "The husband shall not take a second wife while the first marriage subsists and if the husband has married or gone through a form of marriage with another woman after the date thereof" the wife shall have the power to divorce. As in Islamic Law marriage is regarded as a contract, the prevailing opinion of the jurists is that generally such contracts become enforceable in courts.

Two subsidiary views exists as regards the technique:

(i) to propagate the standard form of contract and leave it to the volition of the parties to enter into such contracts, and

(ii) to provide an amendment to Section 2 A of the Shariat Act *inter alia* that "every contract of marriage shall be deemed to include, unless otherwise expressly provided, the terms set out", which would contain a provision that the husband shall not take a second wife during the subsistence of the marriage.

The critical question for consideration is: What are the consequences of a breach of the contractual stipulation on the part of the husband that he would not contract a second marriage during the subsistence of the prior marriage? Fyzee says that:

(*a*) restitution may be refused to the husband;
(*b*) certain rights as to dower may arise; or
(*c*) the wife may have a right to divorce; or in an extreme case
(*d*) the marriage itself may be dissolved.

Thus the effective right of a Muslim wife having a standard contract is to get the dissolution of marriage or a right to live separately from the husband. This fails to provide a substantive relief to the first wife with children. As the second marriage is not invalidated, the position of the husband is not prejudicially affected but for the financial implications arising out of the step. The deterrence of the criminal sanction when a person intends to contract a second marriage is absent. Further, the solution of standard contracts is ineffective, in cases of fake conversions to Islam from other religions to circumvent the prohibition against bigamy. The remedy is out of step with the position in the other personal laws in India and should be rejected.

Reforms to Correct the Abuse of Polygamy

The first approach to reform Muslim law relating to polygamy is to abolish it altogether. In Turkey polygamy was abolished by law. The Turkish Civil Code lays down that no person shall marry again unless he proves that the former marriage has been dissolved by death, divorce or by a decree of nullity. The Turkish Family Law of Cyprus also provides that a marriage shall be declared invalid where at the date of the marriage one of the parties is already married. The Tunisian Code of Personal Status in Article 18 provides: "Plurality of wives is prohibited. Any person who being already married and before the marriage is lawfully dissolved, marries again, shall be liable to imprisonment for one year or for a fine of 2,40,000 francs or to both even if the second marriage is in violation of any requirements of this law. The Muslims in the U.S.S.R. and the Peoples Republic of China are also governed by the rule of monogamy.

It deserves to be emphasized that in Tunisia the justification for the abolition of polygamy had its basis on a re-evaluation or re-interpretation of Islamic principles. Professor Anderson points out the following distinctive grounds:

> "The first was the broadly based argument that there were certain institutions, such as slavery and polygamy, which were acceptable at a certain stage in human development, but which were repugnant to the civilised conscience today....
> The second argument was...that the "Verse of polygamy" itself allows plurality of wives only on two conditions, one of which is that the would-be polygamist should have no fear whatever of treating them with less than equal justice. But experience, the President said, had proved that no man other than a Prophet was capable of such a feat especially in contemporary conditions".

The second approach is to regulate the husband's right to contract a second marriage by rendering it necessary to obtain judicial or official sanction for a bigamous marriage. In most countries where Muslims constitute a majority of the population this approach, with variations, is favoured. Iran, Iraq, Singapore and Syria provide that the permission of the court is necessary for a bigamous marriage of the husband. The laws provide that in granting the permission the courts should satisfy themselves about the financial capacity of the husband to maintain more than one wife. Some of these laws provide for additional grounds to be fulfilled like the capacity to do equal justice to the co-wives.

On the other hand, Pakistan, Ceylon and Indonesia confer the power to regulate bigamous marriage on institutions other than the regular courts. For example, Section 6 of the Muslim Family Laws Ordinance of Pakistan states that no male can contract another marriage during the subsistence of an existing marriage except with the previous permission of the Arbitration Council. The Arbitration Council may grant the permission if it is satisfied that the proposed marriage is necessary and just.

If a person contracts another marriage without such permission, upon a complaint being made, he is liable for punishment which may extend to one years' simple imprisonment or a fine of Rs. 5000 or both. The legislation in Ceylon prescribes for the prior notice of the intended marriage and the display of the notice in the mosques and at the residence of the parties, that is, the husband, the first wife and the prospective second wife. In Indonesia the Family Law Regulations of 1947 enjoin the marriage officials to clarify and explain the position of a bigamous marriage under Islamic Law and legal conditions and obligations relating to it, to the person intending to contract a bigamous marriage.

David Pearl studied the impact of the Muslim Family Laws Ordinance (1961) in Quetta (Baluchistan), Pakistan. Two points relevant for our consideration emerge from his study. First,

> "many men risk the penalties inherent in Section 6(5) (a) and (b) of the ordinance, and marry a second wife without bothering to apply to arbitration council for its approval."

The second relates to classification of marriages in the Muslim Law. A marriage is valid (*sabih*) if all the conditions and formalities relating to marriage have been properly fulfilled. A valid marriage confers on the wife the right to dower, maintenance etc.; and creates reciprocal rights of inheritance between the husband and wife. Among the Sunnis, a marriage that is not valid may be either void (*batil*) or irregular (*fasid*). A void marriage does not create any rights or obligations among the parties. The children of the union are illegitimate. An irregular marriage has no legal effect before consummation and it can be terminated by words showing intention to separate. The children of the union are legitimate but the irregular marriage does not create mutual rights of inheritance between the husband and wife. Pearl points out that the distinction between valid, void and irregular marriages was not eliminated and, therefore, "it was remarkably easy...for a girl under 16 to be married, or a man to ignore Sections 6 and 7 of the ordinance".

While the desirability of reform in Muslim Law is generally acknowledged, as mentioned, the government has taken no step towards changing the law for over two decades on the view that public opinion in the Muslim community did not favour a change. But this view cannot be reconciled with the declaration of equality and social justice. We are, therefore, of the opinion that ignoring the interest of Muslim women is a denial of social justice. The right to equality, in our view, like the right to free speech, is an individual right.

An Analysis of Polygamous Marriages Among Muslims

An analysis of polygamous marriages among Muslims in India classifies them into four groups:

(*a*) The largest number of cases are of husbands who abandon their wives (and frequently children as well) and go off and marry somebody else. Frequently, the second wife remains ignorant about the earlier marriage and the children;

(*b*) Where the wives, finding the marriage unbearable have left their husbands who, in order to avoid paying the deferred Mahr, refuse to divorce them;

(*c*) Wives who because of economic dependence acquiesce in the second marriage;

(*d*) Where a person of another religious persuasion deliberately adopts Islam to contract a marriage which could not be permitted under his own system of law.

Regulated Bigamy

The adoption of monogamy as a rule among the Hindus under the Hindu Marriage Act, 1955 has been criticised and an opinion has been expressed in favour of "carefully regulated bigamy."

> "It is a serious question whether the sympathy which the public and courts seem to harbour for bigamous unions has not solid basis which we ought to recognise. It is argued that a carefully regulated bigamy *i.e.* popular

> marriages in cases of infertility, mental instability of the wife, and other cases where the good sense and humanity of the husband and his family recoils from divorcing her or annulling the marriage would not only be in accord with traditional Hindu religious sentiment and practice, but also much more realistic. It would savour less of "shop-window-dressing" with which the Hindu Code is charged. There is a small part of India which at present has controlled bigamy for Hindu husbands, namely the former Portuguese India (Goa, Daman & Diu).... This appears to work extremely well, and the Parliament has had the good sense not to interfere with the modified Hindu Law still in force in those territories.... Moreover, it was the opinion of Mahamahopadhyaya Dr. P.V. Kane, that polygamy should be tolerated for some classes on purely economic grounds.... It is the health and happiness of Hindus that counts, and the rash abolition of polygamy in a euphoric moment is not working out satisfactorily."

As this view gives a misleading impression of being in the interests of women and as it is likely to be advanced in the context of Muslim Law also, it needs to be rebutted in full. We are not aware of a sympathy for bigamous unions or an opinion in favour of them in the absence of a systematic survey. A survey made some years ago showed 85 per cent of the men and 96 per cent of the women to be in favour of compulsory monogamy. While judicial decisions have rendered the enforcement of the penal provision against bigamy in Section 17 of the Hindu Marriage Act, 1955, difficult, it would only be fair to say that this stemmed not from a sentiment in favour of bigamy, but from a deep seated judicial attitude that penal provisions should be construed strictly. The 'economic grounds', in our considered view, equate women with beasts of burden and cannot be accepted. It is doubtful whether the advocates of controlled bigamy will also favour controlled polyandry as a general rule on the same grounds.

Long before the passing of the Hindu Marriage Act, monogamy in preference to controlled bigamy existed under the Marumakattayam Law in the State of Tranvancore-Cochin and in the Malabar District of the Madras Province. It was introduced in the province of Bombay in 1946 and in the province of Madras in 1949.

We are of the firm view that there can be no compromise on the basic policy of monogamy being the rule for all communities in India. Any compromise in this regard will only perpetuate the existing inequalities in the Status of women.

Enforcement of Provisions Against Bigamy Under the Hindu Marriage Act

While bigamy has been made an offence and the second marriage should be void, bigamous marriages are still prevalent among Hindus. Apart from the figures available, during its tour in many of the States the Committee came to know of a large number of such marriages. In Manipur even though the women were very bitter about the wide prevalence of this practice, they were compelled to accept it as divorce or prosecution of the husband resulted in social ostracism. The government had failed to enforce the law. Even government servants, who are forbidden under the Government Servants' Conduct Rules, were practising polygamy. The Committee was also informed that a Resolution in the Legislative Assembly calling upon the government to enforce the law had been defeated by an over-whelming majority. It is interesting to note that most women of Manipur earn to support their families. In spite of their economic independence they have been unable to assert their social and legal rights. Quite a few of them were living with their co-wives some had separate establishments but all of them contributed a part of their incomes to their husbands. Little social stigma seemed to be attached to such a situation. In West Bengal a training centre in Sriniketan for promoting self-employment had a number of women discarded by their husbands who had married a second time. We met two co-wives taking the training whose husbands discarded them for a third wife. Similar cases were brought to our notice in some parts of Andhra Pradesh, Bihar, Uttar Pradesh and in the rural areas of Madhya Pradesh.

Under the present law, only an aggrieved person can initiate proceedings for bigamy, which means the husband or the wife. In the case of the wife the complaint may be made on her behalf by one of her family members. Quite often an economically dependent woman who is also uneducated has neither the knowledge nor the means to go to court. Many of them are reluctant to appear in court and face social, criticism as brought out very clearly by Justice Sachar:

> "We also cannot shut our eyes to the practical difficulties and problems faced by an Indian girl.... Instances are numerous where Indian women have gone through a literal misery of marriage for years rather than go to a court of law and expose themselves to public gaze. The attitude of the parents and relations in most of these cases is also un-sympathetic."

Where social customs prevent a woman from appearing in public, the law permits some other person to make the complaint with the permission of the court. The question to be considered is whether the right to initiate prosecution for bigamy should be extended to persons other than the girl's family in all cases, in view of the general reluctance of her family members to lodge a complaint against the son-in-law or brother-in-law. The necessity of obtaining prior permission of the Court would provide adequate safeguard against undue harassment. In small towns and villages a social worker could fulfil this role admirably.

In our opinion such a provision is necessary to prevent the current widespread violation of a most salutary provision of the law which very clearly lays down the social policy of the country.

The existing penal provision against bigamy is further defeated in a considerable number of cases because of a technical construction placed on Section 17 of the Act. The Supreme Court in *Bhaurao vs. State of Maharashtra* held that the offence of bigamy was not proved unless it was established that the second marriage was celebrated with proper ceremonies and due form. This conclusion was arrived at on the basis that the section used the word 'solemnized'. They observe:

> The word 'solemnize' means, in connection with a marriage, 'to celebrate the marriage with proper ceremonies and due form' according to the Shorter Oxford Dictionary. It follows, therfore, that unless the marriage is 'celebrated' or performed with proper ceremonies and due form it cannot be said to be 'solemnized'. It is therefore essential, for the purpose of Sec. 17 of the Act, that the marriage to which Sec. 494, I.P.C. applies on account of the provisions of the Act, should have been celebrated with proper ceremonies and due form.

As the law requires no specific ceremonies but recognises ceremonies of marriage according to custom it becomes extremely difficult to determine which ceremony or ceremonies were really essential. Whether the construction put by the court will subserve the policy and purpose of the Act or the social objectives of the legislation was never in their contemplation.

The result of this interpretation is that a difficult burden is cast on the prosecution to show that the second marriage is performed with all due formalities. This burden in many cases cannot be discharged owing to the fact that second marriages during the subsistence of a prior marriage are seldom performed with the usual pomp and show.

Even if it is not so, this judicial interpretation facilitates widespread evasion of law. As pointed out by Professor Derrett, the existing position will give rise to two types of devices being followed to evade prosecution for bigamy. First, a person intending to take a second wife may deliberately undergo a defective form of marriage, to defend himself against a prosecution launched by the first wife or her relatives. Second, the relatives and friends of the second "wife" may commit perjury and say that the marriage is not properly solemnized and the first wife or her relatives would not be in a position to rebut it.

M.B. Majumdar suggested that the word: "solemnized" may be replaced by the words "contracted". But given the contemporary judicial attitudes, inherited from the English legal system, whereby the policy and purpose of an Act often are sacrificed to a literal construction of the Act, it is doubtful whether the suggested amendment will change the situation materially.

We recommend that the words 'solemnized' should be replaced by the words "goes through a marriage." Further, an explanation should be added to the section that an omission to perform some of the essential ceremonies by parties shall not be construed to mean that the offence of bigamy was not committed, if such a ceremony of marriage gives rise to a *de facto* relationship of husband and wife.

Injunction

As already mentioned there is often an inhibition against prosecuting a husband for his second marriage in the present social context. The easier remedy is to prevent such a marriage taking place, if there is prior knowledge of its impending celebration. The following two cases will show that though bigamy, including the attempt and abetment of it is an offence, the position is not as clear cut as we would like it to be.

In *Sankarappa vs. Basamma* the Mysore High Court held that a Hindu wife is entitled to a perpetual 'injunction restraining her husband from contracting a second marriage; that the suit is clearly permitted by Section 54 of the Specific Relief Act, 1877 (Sec. 38 of the Specific Relief Act, 1963).

On the other hand, a Division Bench of the Patna High Court in *Uma Prasad Singh vs. Smt. Radha Devi* takes the view that a remedy by way of injunction against a second marriage is not available under the provisions of the Hindu Marriage Act.

The case seems to have been argued only on the basis of the Hindu Marriage Act, 1955 and the question of remedy under the Specific Relief Act, 1963 was not referred to by the parties or by the court. "The only point for consideration is...where the suit as framed and filed by opposite party 1, could be maintained under any provision of the Hindu Marriage Act, 1955.

Though the two cases can be clearly distinguished and there is no real conflict, it is desirable to clarify the matter. *We recommend that a provision be introduced in Section 6 of the Hindu Marriage Act to the effect that nothing contained in the Hindu Marriage Act shall prevent a court from granting an injunction against a proposed bigamous marriage under Act or under the provisions of the Specific Relief Act, 1963.*

Laws in Former French and Portuguese Territories

After the merger of the former French and Portuguese colonial possessions with India, the laws in force prior to merger in these territories have not been abrogated and therefore they continue to be in force. A reference will now be made to these laws insofar as they affect the status of women.

A. Laws in Pondicherry

Prior to the merger, three different systems of personal law were applicable in Pondicherry. First, the Hindus Laws and customs applicable to Hindu and native Christians, (other than renoncants). However, in matters relating to marriage, divorce and allied topics the Christians were governed by the French Civil Code. Second, the Muslim Law, which was applied to the people of French origin and *renoncants.*

After the merger with India the categories of laws applicable increased and consequently the applicability of the Hindu Law became complicated. David Annoussamy categorizes the application of Hindu Law thus:

A. Hindu Law prevailing in India applicable to migrants from the rest of India.
B. Hindu Law applicable to Hindus of Pondicherrian origin consisting of Indian statutes Applicable to Hindus.
C. Hindu Law consisting solely of the Hindu local customs adhered to by Hindus who remained French nationals.
D. Hindu Law consisting of customs of Pondicherry except in matters of marriage and divorce. This category has

been further subdivided into two groups, *viz:*

1. Indian Christians who are governed according to their choice in respect of marriage either by the French Civil Code or the Indian Christian Marriage Act and the Indian Divorce Act, and
2. Indian Christians who are exclusively governed by the French Civil Code.

B. Laws in Goa, Daman and Diu

Even though these territories are now a part of India, no effort has far been made to extend the Hindu Marriage Act to them. The result is that a section of Hindus today continues to be governed by a law which permits polygamy.

1. Districts of Goa and Diu

In the districts of Goa, polygamy is permissible among Hindus under the following circumstances:

(i) when the previous wife is childless upto the age of 25 years;

(ii) when there is no male issue from the previous wife till her 30th year or when the previous wife who is below 30 does not conceive for ten years after her past conception;

(iii) in cases of judicial separation by wife and when there is no male issue.

(*Note:* In the case of Goa, previous wife's consent is required for the cases mentioned in *(i)* and *(ii)* above).

2. District of Daman

According to the Code of Customs and Usage of Non-Christian inhabitants of Daman, the male individuals are allowed to have many wives but Bramos of Modd Caste cannot have more than two wives.

However, there is no polygamy among Dhobis, Morai-Machines, Barbers, Capris, Salvia, Betelas, Porobias and Bramos except those belonging to Teloquia and Modd caste.

(*Note*: For an individual to marry or re-marry more than twice—when his previous wives are living, an express previous consent of all of them is required which shall be drawn by the 'Chief of Rancho' or by the Notary Public in the Presence of four witnesses).

Judicial justification of any of the circumstances mentioned above is a condition precedent for polygamy.

In our opinion, the continuation of such diverse Laws contradictory to our social policy, in these territories is totally unjustified. *We recommend therefore, the immediate replacement of these laws by the Hindu Marriage Act, 1955.*

II. AGE OF MARRIAGE

Legal Provisions

Another major social evil which was sought to be curbed by legislation is child marriage. The disastrous effects of such marriages have been discussed already. One of the few areas where our social reformers had taken the initiative, even in the nineteenth century, was to curb this evil by legislation. The first legislation was the Civil Marriage Act which laid down the age of marriage to be 14 years. But as only a very small section of the. people married under this Act, the problem continued.

One of the adverse consequences of child marriage, as realised by the reformers, was early consummation, with disastrous effect on the health of the young wives and their children. An effort was made in 1891 to prevent early consummation by the Age of Consent Act which prohibited consummation before 12 years. Due to lack of publicity and propaganda, there was no impact of this provision. In 1925, the Age of Consent was raised to 13. This was the forerunner of the Sarda Act of 1929.

Perhaps the realisation that legislation, while one of the major instruments of social change, is not sufficient by itself to fight against deep rooted prejudices and traditional practice made the legislators compromise by leaving the validity of child marriage untouched but making such practice a penal offence. Parents of children, those 'performing, conducting or directing' as also the adult bridegroom, were all liable to punishment in varying degrees. The Act was further amended but left untouched the structure of the earlier Act. The impact of this legislation and the present position regarding child marriages have been discussed already.

Apart from the Sarda Act, the various personal laws have their own minimum age of marriage. Not only do they vary in regard to the minimum age but also in the consequences of violation of the law.

The Hindu Marriage Act lays down as one of the conditions the completion of 18 years and 15 years by the bridegroom and the bride respectively. Though passed in the post-independence era, the Act remains silent about the effect on the marriage and continues the earlier penal policy in cases of violation. Most writers hold the view that the validity of the marriage is not affected and this is also supported by judicial decisions.

The Parsi Marriage and Divorce Act, 1936 on the other hand lays down that no suit shall be brought to enforce a marriage between two Parsees or any contract connected with the marriage if at the date of the institution of the suit the husband has not completed age of 16 years and the wife 14 years. The Christian Marriage Act, 1872 provides that for a valid marriage under the Act, the age of the male shall exceed 16 years and that of the female 13 years. For a valid marriage under the classical Muslim Law the parties should not be minors, this is, the parties should have attained puberty. Puberty is presumed in the absence of evidence to the contrary, at 15 and 19 in the case of girls and boys respectively.

Only the Special Marriage Act, 1954, a post-independence legislation which provides for a secular marriage irrespective of the religious affiliation of the parties, contemplates the solemnisation of marriage between adults under its provisions, as it fixes the minimum age at 21 and 18 for males and females respectively.

The legal position noted above brings forth an important feature, namely, a lesser age of marriage is prescribed in the case of girls. No doubt throughout the world, the laws generally provide for a lesser age in case of girls. For example, in the

U.S.A. only eleven States prescribed the same minimum age for boys and girls. The remaining thirty-nine states permit girls to be married at a lower age than boys. As pointed out by Konowitz: "It (early marriage for women) can lead to premature removal from socially productive enterprise or lost opportunities."

When the legal age of marriage in case of a female is below the age of discretion she cannot be expected to form an intelligent opinion about her partner in life. The policy of law which permits the marriage of a girl before she is physically and mentally mature is open to serious question. As reported by the Pushpaben Committee, child marriage is one of the significant factors leading to the high incidence of suicide among young married women in India. Therefore, increasing the marriage age of girls to eighteen years is desirable.

In this context it is necessary to point out an anachronism that exists in the Muslim Law that governs some sects. After attaining puberty, a Muslim male in all sects and a Muslim female belonging to the Hanafi and Ithana Ashari Shiite sects can marry without a guardian. But "a Maliki, Shafi, or Daudi or Sulaymani Bohra virgin cannot marry without a guardian and her only remedy is to change over to the Hanafi School and marry according to its tenets."

In two recent decisions, *viz. Muhammad Hazi Kammu vs. Ethiyumma and K. Abubukker vs. Marakkar* (The Kerala High Court) struck a different note which mitigates this hardship. The parties in both cases were Shafis. In *Abubukker's* case, the mother who was divorced, sought the consent of her ex-husband to the daughters' marriage which he refused. On the marriage being solemnized, the fathei filed a suit for a declaration that the marriage was invalid as his consent was not obtained. The lower Court declared the marriage to be invalid even though the girl was already pregnant. Reversing the decision of the lower Court, Justice Pillai stated that under the Maliki and Shafi law the marriage of an adult girl is not valid unless her consent is obtained, and communicated through a legally authorised *wali* (guardian). As the father refused his consent, she could constitute any other relation or Kazi (in this case the Kazi) to act as her agent. *In our opinion a change in the law to remove the existing disability in these sub-schools and to bring them in conformity with the Hanafi law is necessary.*

Aspects Relating to Prevention of Child Marriages

As mentioned earlier the policy of the Child Marriage Restraint Act or other statutes is not to invalidate child marriages but to punish their solemnization. The offences under the Act are, however, non-cognizable, and no woman is punishable with imprisonment.

There are large scale violations of the Act particularly in the rural areas. The non-cognizable character of the offence is a serious hindrance to the effective enforcement of this law. The State of Gujarat amended the Child Marriage Restraint Act by making it a cognizable offence. Provisions have also been made for the appointment of a Child Marriage Prevention Officer. These changes have been welcomed by the Pushpaben Committee. *We recommend that all offences under the Child Marriage Restraint Act should be made cognizable, and special officers appointed to enforce the law.*

Another effective approach to this problem is to render such marriage void. But in the present social and economic conditions such a rigorous measure may create more problems than it seeks to solve. We suggest, that it should be envisaged as a future goal.

As immediate measures to deter child marriages and to alleviate their consequences we suggest the following:

(a) to provide the girl the right to repudiate the marriage on attaining majority on lines similar to the "option of puberty" under Muslim Law;
Note: A Muslim girl married during her minority is entitled to a dissolution of marriage if the following facts are established:
- *(i)* that she was given in marriage by her father or other guardian before she attained the age of 15;
- *(ii)* that she repudiated the marriage before she attained the age of 18;

(*iii*) that the marriage was not consummated.

In our view the right to repudiate the marriage on attaining majority should be made available to girls in all communities whether the marriage was consummated or not.

(*b*) A general legal provision analogous to section 38 of the Parsi Marriage and Divorce Act, 1865 which provides that "no suit shall be brought in any court to enforce any marriage between Parsees, or any contract connected with or arising out of any such marriage, if, at the date of the institution of the suit, the husband shall not have completed the age of 16 years, or the wife shall not have completed the age of 14 years." Under the Egyptian Civil Code, a marriage in contravention of the rule relating to age of the parties (completion of 18 years and 15 years in case of males and females respectively) though not invalid *per se* will not be registered. Under Article 99 of the Code such a marriage will not be recognised by the Court for the purpose of granting any relief, except a claim relating to legitimacy of issues.

We recommend legislation prohibiting courts from granting any relief in respect of a marriage solemnized in violation of the age requirements prescribed by law unless both the parties have completed the age of 18 years.

Compulsory Registration of Marriages

Compulsory registration of marriages operates as an effective check on child and bigamous marriages and also offers reliable proof of marriage. It ensures the legitimacy and inheritance rights of children. Section 8 of the Hindu Marriage Act, 1955, enables the State Governments to provide for compulsory registration of marriages, and any person contravening the rule may be punished with a fine which may extent to twenty-five rupees. However it has been stated that failure to register a marriage will not affect its validity. Laws which provide for the voluntary registration of Muslim marriages are in force in the States of Assam, Bihar, Orissa and Bengal.

Among the Parsees and Indian Christians the registration of marriages is compulsory. Registration is also compulsory for marriages solemnised under the Special Marriages Act, 1954. Section 16 of this Act permits voluntary registration of marriages celebrated under other laws. The figures given below illustrate that the appeal of this secular law, though it ensures better legal protection to all parties, is still limited to a very small minority. Neither has the permission for voluntary registration attracted much response.

Number of Marriages Registered Under the Special Marriages Act of 1954

	Bombay	*Rajasthan*	*Delhi*
1968	601	11	148
1969	621	8	194
1970	766	13	229
1971	705	11	235
1972	816	6	212

Number of marriages celebrated under other laws but subsequently registered under Section 16 of the Special Marriages Act, Bombay

1968	19
1969	18
1970	43
1971	36
1972	26

The ultimate object should be to recognise registration as the sole and conclusive proof of marriage, irrespective of the religious rites under which it was solemnised. It may be mentioned here that India has neither signed nor ratified the United Nations Convention on Consent to Marriage, Minimum Age for Marriage and Registration of Marriage. Explaining the position of India on ratification, the Indian delegate stated "the Convention would impose an obligation to introduce legislation, and since that might not be feasible at the present time he must reserve his government's position on the question of ratification."

We regret that for over a decade no attempt has been made to introduce legislation to implement the objects of the U.N. Convention. This attitude indicates a casualness and lack of concern on matters affecting the status of women. *We recommend that registration should be made compulsory for all marriages.* We have a clear precedent for a uniform measure in the Registration of Births and Deaths Act.

III. DOWRY

The dimension and ramifications of the dowry system in its present form have been discussed in numerous studies.

We are compelled to record our finding that the Dowry Prohibition Act 1961, passed with the ostensible purpose of curbing this evil, if not of eradicating it, has signally failed to achieve its purpose. In spite of the rapid growth of this practice there are practically no cases reported under the Act. During its tours of all the States, the Committee was informed of only one case that was pending before the court in Kerala, in which the father had filed the complaint only because of the ill-treatment meted out to his daughter.

During the debate on the Dowry Prohibition Bill, one MP observed, "But I feel the whole problem will be solved—very easily and more quickly, not by legislation, but by rousing social conscience. As soon as our women get economic opportunities and economic freedom, as soon as avenues of employment and other opportunities are opened to them, as soon as they become independent of their families, possibly there would not be any occasion for this law to operate."

The eradication of this evil by rousing social conscience is seemingly an attractive approach. The Committee's findings, however, indicate that there is hardly any evidence of social conscience in the country today. In Indore, at a fairly large meeting, the Committee was told of the case of a girl who was burnt in the legs and in the back by her in-laws as she had not brought an adequate dowry. The acceptance of this situation was indicative of society's indifference to this social evil. No onc at the meeting mentioned the need to report the case to the police or even of socially boycotting the family. Many such cases were brought to our notice, but nowhere did we hear of any social censure being exercised.

An increase in economic freedom and job opportunities for women, to the extent that the practice of dowry becomes obsolete, under the existing economic conditions, will be a very long process. The educated youth is grossly insensitive to the evil and un-ashamedly contributes to its perpetuation. In our opinion, therefore, a stringent enforcement of the policy and purpose of Act may serve to educate public opinion better. *A very small but significant step could be taken by the government, by declaring the taking or giving of dowry to be against the Government Servants Conduct Rules.* Such a lead was given earlier to prevent bigamous marriages and giving or taking of dowry should be similarly dealt with.

The major cause for the failure of the Dowry Prohibition Act, 1961 is that an infringement of the provisions of the Act is not made a cognizable offence. That the offences under the Act should be made cognizable was in fact suggested during the debate in Lok Sabha.

But the offence was not made cognizable, as it was apprehended that this might result in the harassment of citizens by the police and lead also to undue invasion of the individual's right of privacy.

In our opinion the policy of making the offence non-cognizable completely nullifies the purpose of the Act as it is unrealistic to think that the father of a girl who had paid the dowry (and who alone is in a position to adduce evidence of the fact that dowry was stipulated and given) would prefer a complaint against the interests of his daughter after her marriage. *We recommend, therefore, that the offences, under the Act, should be made cognizable.* We are fortified in our conclusion by the recommendation of the Pushpaben Committee. To overcome the fears regarding harassment by the police and encroachment on the right of privacy; *it is suggested that the enforcement of social laws like the Dowry Prohibition Act, the Child Marriage*

Restraint Act, should be entrusted to a separate administration with which social workers and enlightened members of the community should be associated.

In addition, two ancillary provisions should be incorporated in the Dowry Prohibition Act, 1961. It has been pointed out that one of the 'major loopholes' in the existing legislation is that anything is allowed in the name of gifts and presents.

Therefore, *any gifts made to the bridegroom or his parents in excess of Rs. 500 or which can be so used as to reduce his own financial liability should be made punishable.*

The practice of displaying the dowry by parents of the bride or the bridegroom, as discussed earlier, is prevalent in some parts of India. This naturally tends to perpetuate the practice as others follow suit. To curb this evil we recommend legislation on the lines of the West Pakistan Dowry (Prohibition of Display) Act, 1967 which penalises such display.

We suggest that *an evaluation of the impact of the amended Dowry Prohibition Act should be made after five years.* It will help in plugging loopholes which facilitate the evasion of this law. *The next step should be to set a ceiling even on the gifts that may be made to the bride.* This will help to improve the situation further because we have found that gifts given to the bride are often only a guise for dowry since generally she has little or no control over them.

IV. DIVORCE

A monogamous marriage without the right of divorce would cause great hardship to both parties to the marriage. The concept of 'union for life' or the sacramental nature of the marriage which renders the marriage indissoluble has gradually been eroded and through legislation the right of diverce has been introduced in all legal systems in India, but the same various and unequal treatment of sexes characterises this branch of law also.

According to the Census of 1971, the total number of divorced or separated women in the country is estimated to be 8,17,700; of which 7,43,200 are in the rural areas and 1,27,500 in urban areas. The ratio of divorced or separated women is

1,630 per thousand males. The table below indicates the relative percentage of divorced or separated men and women to the total male and female population in 1961 and 1971. It is clear that the proportion of women who remain in this state is higher than men, in both rural and urban areas.

Percentage of Divorced and Separated Persons

	1961			*1971*		
	Rural	*Urban*	*Total*	*Rural*	*Urban*	*Total*
Males	0.43	0.22	0.39	0.21	0.12	0.19
Females	0.53	0.43	0.51	0.35	0.25	0.33

Source: Country Statement—submitted to the World Population Conference, Bucharest (Rumania) 19-30 August 1947—Government of India, 1974.

Note: 1971 figures are based on 1 per cent sample data.

A survey undertaken by the Census in 1961 in 587 selected villages with a sample of 1,33,775 marriages covering a period of 50 years, had indicated wide acceptance of divorce by the village community and some variations of incidence among the religious communities. Incidence of divorce was highest among Muslims (6.06%), followed by Hindus (3.21%). Among the Buddhists it was 3.07, among the Jains 1.68% and among Sikhs 0.91%. The incidence of divorce among Christians was considerably lower (0.41%). The causes for divorce show that adultery and barrenness are the commonest grounds for divorce in most of the villages studied. Extreme poverty is also found to be cause for divorce. In Rajasthan: sexual incompatibility and incapacity are recognised as grounds for divorce.

Hindu Law

According to traditionalists, divorce was unknown in Hindu Law. Even today divorce is not a socially accepted norm among many sections.

> "We can take judicial notice of the fact that even today considerable sections of the Hindu society look with disfavour on the idea of dissolving a marriage."

Polygamy, without the right of divorce, caused, in many cases, tremendous hardship.

Customary Divorce: Contrary to the general notion regarding the indissolubility of Hindu marriages, a large section of Hindus among the lower castes have traditionally practised divorce. These customary forms of divorce were recognised, both socially and judicially. The usual customary forms are:

(a) by mutual consent;
(b) unilaterally—at the pleasure of the husband or by the abandonment of the wife;
(c) by deed of divorce (*Char—chitti*);

(a) *By Mutual Consent:* The custom of obtaining divorce by mutual consent is prevalent among certain castes in Bombay, Madras, Mysore and Kerala. In Madhya Pradesh it has been held that divorce by mutual consent is a valid custom among the Patwas of that State. A customary form of divorce by agreement (*chuttam-chutta*) amongst the Barai Chaurasiyas of Uttar Pradesh has been declared valid by the Allahabad High Court. These are only a few illustrations to indicate the existence of divorce by mutual consent.

(b) *Unilateral Divorce:* According to the custom prevailing in Manipur (Khaniaba), it has been stated that a husband can dissolve the marriage without any reason or at his pleasure. Among the Rajpur Gujaratis in Khandesh, and in the Pakhali Community marriage is dissolved if the husband abandons or deserts the wife. Among the Vaishyas of Gorakhpur in Uttar Pradesh a husband may abandon or desert his wife, and dissolution takes place even without reference to the caste tribunal.

(c) *Divorce by Deed:* This form is prevalent among certain castes in South India, also in Himachal Pradesh and the Jat community. Recently the Supreme Court has

upheld a deed executed by the husband divorcing his wife.

Usually customary divorces are through the intervention of the traditional Panchayats of caste tribunals. Therefore, in States where this has not been customary, the courts have not permitted Panchayats to take upon themselves the right to dissolve a marriage. Once the custom is proved, however, the courts will not interfere.

The courts have exercised a lot of judicial scrutiny and discretion in upholding or rejecting such customary divorce practices. In doing so they have applied the strict test for the validity of such customs. When the existence of a custom was not proved, or where the custom could be regarded as running counter to the spirit of Hindu Law, or was against public policy or morality, courts have declared such customary forms of divorce as invalid.

Under customary law there is no waiting period after divorce to remarry. But if divorce is obtained under the Hindu Marriage Act, then either party to the marriage can lawfully remarry only after a lapse of one year after the decree of divorce (Sec. 15). Retention of customary forms of divorce under the Hindu Marriage Act is advantageous because this process of dissolving the marriage saves time and money in litigations. The only difficulty that may arise is if the divorce according to customary law is brought at some stage to the notice of the court and the latter decrees that particular form of divorce to be against public policy or morality. If one or both parties have remarried, such a marriage will be void and the status of the children will be affected. To minimise this, it has been suggested that the Ministry of Law should prepare an exhaustive record of customs relating to divorce found in different States and set up a panel of socio-legal experts to determine if any of these customs are invalid. Copies of the record should be made freely and easily available to the people and the Panchayats.

With the enactment of the Hindu Marriage Act of 1955, divorce became a part of the law governing all Hindus. The ground for this had been already prepared by the passing of the Hindu Women's Right to Separate Residence and Maintenance Act in 1946, which *inter alia* permitted the wife to separate from her husband on the ground that he had married again. Following this, some of the States took the initiative and as with monogamy, legislated to permit divorce for Hindus.

Divorce Under the Hindu Marriage Act, 1955

The various grounds on which a husband or a wife can obtain divorce are:

- *(a)* living in adultery,
- *(b)* conversion to other religion,
- *(c)* insanity,
- *(d)* incurable form of leprosy,
- *(e)* venereal disease,
- *(f)* renunciation,
- *(g)* where the respondent has not been heard of as being alive for a period of seven years or more by persons who would naturally have heard of it,
- *(h)* failure to resume cohabitation for a period of 2 years after the decree of judicial separation, and
- *(i)* failure to comply with a decree for restitution of conjugal rights.

Two additional grounds have been given to the wife:

- *(i)* to obtain a divorce if the husband has more than one wife living, and
- *(ii)* if he has been guilty of rape, sodomy or bestiality.

The former has a retrospective effect in the sense that when the marriages took place (*i.e.* before the Act), polygamy was legally permissible. This right can be exercised by either of the wives, and has obviously been provided to strengthen the social policy of monogamy. From the cases reported, it appears that many women have benefited from this provision.

Adultery: Since adultery is a very grave matrimonial offence, a very high degree or standard of proof is required. The

Courts have insisted that the offence of adultery should be proved beyond reasonable doubt. A husband or wife can ask for divorce only if at the time of filing the suit, the other party 'is living in adultery'. A single act of extramarital intercourse in not sufficient to dissolve the marriage, thought it is sufficient for a decree of judicial separation. The Bombay High Court, therefor, rejected the petition of a husband as at the time of the petition there was no evidence that the wife was leading an adulterous life, though there was evidence that she had done so earlier.

Refusal to resume cohabitation: Another provision of the Act which is often taken advantage of is non-compliance with a decree restituting conjugal rights for two years or the lapse of the same period after a decree of judicial separation. One of the grounds for judicial separation is desertion provided it is 'without reasonable cause'. In interpreting 'reasonable cause', the judiciary has often exhibited their inability to appreciate the socio-economic changes and the Constitutional right to equality.

Whenever conjugal rights have come into open conflict with the woman's right of equal opportunity in education or employment, the attitude of the judiciary has often been rather ambiguous. Instead of guiding the conflicting parties towards a rational adjustment to the process of social change, the judiciary has either evaded the issue or thrown its weight on the side of the traditional view of the husband's authority. Two illustrations will suffice to demonstrate this tendency:

(a) A husband's demand for his wife to resign her job as a teacher in a city away from his place of employment, to join him, was upheld by the Punjab High Court, which ruled that it was the duty of the wife to remain under the 'roof and protection and submit obediently' to the authority of the husband.

(b) In a similar case, the Allahabad High Court took a step forward by opining that the concepts of protection and society are "inelastic and rigid rules which cannot be interpreted in the context of present day conditions and needs of society.... In view of the altered social

and economic conditions both husband and wife may think it necessary to work and contribute to the family chest". The Court, therefore, conceded the right of deciding the question to the wife where "in cases of economic stress...for the sake of the family and children" the wife genuinely thinks it is necessary for her to work. The judgement, while conceding the right in cases of genuine economic necessity, totally evades the issue of the individual woman's right to decide whether to work or not.

We are of the opinion that difference in the place of work should not be regarded as a ground for a case of desertion or restitution of conjugal rights.

Cruelty and Desertion: Cruelty and desertion have not been made grounds for divorce though they are recognised as grounds for a judicial separation. It, therefore, follows that in these cases the innocent party to the marriage, against whom there has been cruelty, or who has been deserted, has to wait for two years before he or she can get a divorce. Uttar Pradesh has given the lead in this and amended their law to make these grounds for divorce. *In our opinion these should be added as grounds for divorce in the Hindu Marriage Act so that persons are not compelled to follow the present circuitous route and undergo the expense of going to court twice.*

Muslim Law

Under Muslim Law a husband has an absolute and unlimited right to repudiate the marriage at his will. This is known as *Talaq*. A Muslim wife has no such right to dissolve her marriage. Unwritten and traditional law tried to ameliorate her position by permitting her to seek dissolution under the following form:

(a) *Talaqi Tafwid:* This is a form of delegated divorce. According to this the husband delegates his right of divorce in a marriage contract which may stipulate that *inter-alia* on his taking another wife the first wife has the right to divorce him. The courts have upheld these

pre-nuptial and post-nuptial agreements as not opposed to public nor against the spirit of Muslim Law. The Assam High Court has strengthened this right by declaring that such a power of *Talaq* given to the wife is irrevocable.

(b) *Khul:* This is a dissolution by an agreement between the parties to the marriage, on the wife's giving some consideration to the husband for her release from the marriage tie. The terms are a matter of bargain and usually takes the form of the wife giving up her dower.

(c) *Mubarrat:* This is divorce by mutual consent.

According to Hanafi Law the inability of the husband to maintain his wife does not give her the right to dissolve the marriage. Following the Hanafi Law the court in India had refused the wife the right to dissolve her marriage on the ground of non-payment of maintenance. The Shafi and the Maliki Laws, however, allowed the wife to obtain divorce on this ground.

Dissolution at Muslim Marriages Act, 1939: This Act took advantage of the law as enunciated by the Maliki and Shafi Schools and recognised the right of a wife to dissolve the marriage on the following grounds:

(i) that the whereabouts of the husband have not been known for a period of four years;

(ii) that the husband has neglected or has failed to provide for her maintenance for a period of two years;

(iii) that the husband has been sentenced to imprisonment for a period of seven years or upwards;

(iv) that the husband has failed to perform, without reasonable cause, his marital obligations for a period of three years;

(v) that the husband was impotent at the time of marriage and continues to be so;

(vi) that the husband has been insane for a period of two years or is suffering from leprosy or a virulent venereal disease;

(vii) that she, having been given in marriage by her father or other guardian before she attained the age mof fifteen years, repudiated the marriage before attaining the age

of eighteen years; provided that marriage has not been consummated;

(viii) that the husband treats her with cruelty...

(ix) on any other ground which is recognised as valid for the dissolution of marriage under Muslim Law.

Muslim women have benefited by the Act. The provisions that have been resorted to most frequently are the 'option of puberty' and failure to provide maintenance by the husband.

Option of Puberty: According to traditional Muslim Law, when a minor girl had been given in marriage by the father or the father's father, the marriage was valid. She could, however, repudiate the marriage if she could show that the guardian had acted negligently or fraudulently. But if the minor had been given in marriage by any other guardian, she had the right to repudiate the marriage on attaining puberty. The present Act has modified the traditional law permitting her to exercise the right irrespective of who was the guardian who gave her in marriage. The courts in India have interpreted this right very liberally, often invoking the principles of equity and justice in favour of the girl. They have not rigidly applied the letter of the law in regard to the time when this right could be exercised. It has been held that a minor wife did not lose her right to repudiate the marriage within a reasonable time after she came to know of her right and not necessarily when she attained puberty. In such cases they have even waived the condition of non-consummation when such consummation was by force or before she attained the age of 15.

Right of the wife to dissolve the marriage on ground of failure to maintain: This right has been interpreted in two ways. One group of decisions, basing itself on the traditional 'fault theory', has denied the right to a wife to divorce where her conduct was such as to absolve the husband from his duty to provide maintenance. The other group has tended to uphold the right, irrespective of the wife's conduct.

These two groups of decision clearly indicate that legislation alone cannot eliminate rigid traditionalism, with its desire to preserve the *status quo*. Without supporting judicial interpretation, even the policy of the law is negated. The decision of Justice

Krishna Iyer is, therefore, significant as he has focussed his observation on the right of the Muslim wife to divorce when her husband has failed to provide her maintenance for two years. He has used his erudition to support the theory of dissolution when the marriage has broken down, irrespective of the relative faults of the parties.

> "There is no merit in preserving intact the tie of marriage when the parties are not able to and fail to live within the bonds of Allah, that is to fulfil their mutual marital obligations, and there is no desecration involved in dissolving a marriage which has failed. The entire emphasis is on making the marital union a reality and when this is not possible..., the Quran enjoins a dissolution.... This secular and pragmatic approach on Muslim law of divorce happily harmonises with contemporary concepts in advanced countries."

We recommend that the right of the wife to divorce, on the failure of the husband to maintain her, irrespective of her conduct which may be the main or contributory cause, should be clearly spelt out.

Muslim Law had always recognised that in some cases the wife may be able to get a divorce. To the uncodified law the Dissolution of Muslim Marriages Act, 1939 has added further grounds. But the power of the husband to pronounce *talaq* unilaterally remains, and has is no way been curtailed either judicially or through legislation. As long as this absolute and unlimited right remains, the position of the Muslim wife will remain insecure and her status cannot be raised. We totally disagree with the view that with Justic Krishna Iyer's judgement and her right to obtain divorce by *Khul*, a Muslim women's rights "are brought into approximation with those of the man." While the judgement is undoubtedly a great step forward, it has to be remembered that she still has to wait for two years without maintenance before getting her release. Also, a right to buy her release, as provided in the Koran can hardly be regarded as approximating the unilateral right of the man.

Legislation is the only instrument which can bring the Muslim divorce law into line with not only the needs of society but with the prevailing law in other Muslim countries. Turkey and Cyprus have completely prohibited unilateral divorce, while in Tunisia, Algeria, Iraq and Iran the husband has to apply to a court. In Pakistan Legislation has restrained the freedom of the husband to divorce his wife. He has to inform the Arbitration Council which will try and bring about a reconciliation. The husband's pronouncement of 'talaq' without informing the Arbitration Council has been declared to be an offence.

We recommend immediate legislation to eliminate the unilateral right of divorce and to introduce parity of rights for both partners regarding grounds for seeking dissolution of a marriage.

Christian Law

All Christians are governed by the Indian Divorce Act, 1869. Under the Act both husband and wife can obtain a divorce, but there is a great difference between the rights of the husband and the wife. The husband can obtain a divorce if the wife has committed adultery. The wife can seek a divorce on the following grounds:

- *(a)* husband's conversion from Christianity and marriage another woman.
- *(b)* incestuous adultery.
- *(c)* bigamy with adultery.
- *(d)* marriage with another women with adultery.
- *(e)* rape; sodomy or bestiality.
- *(f)* adultery with cruelty.
- *(g)* adultery with desertion.

Thus the wife has to prove two offences by the husband before she can obtain a divorce.

The law is so outdated that the need for revision has been felt for quite some time. The government, realising the need for reform, referred the matter to the Law Commission in

1960. The Commission prepared a Draft Bill. The Christian Marriage and Matrimonial Causes Bill, 1960, contains almost all the grounds included for divorce under the Special Marriage Act, 1954, such as desertion, cruelty, adultery, leprosy, venereal disease, conversion to another religion, and willful refusal to consummate the marriage. Further, either party to a marriage can also obtain a decree of judicial separation on any of the grounds mentioned for divorce.

We regret that in spite of these preparatory steps, no action to enact this measure has been by the government so far and *recommend that no further time be lost to reform and amend this law on the lines suggested by the Law Commission.*

Parsee Law

The Parsees are governed by the Parsee Marriage and Divorce Act, 1936. Both the parties to the marriage can initiate divorce proceeding on the following grounds:

(a) continuous absence for 7 years without information to those persons who would naturally have heard of him or her.
(b) non-consummation.
(c) insanity.
(d) adultery, bigamy, rape or an unnatural offence.
(e) causing grievous hurt or venereal disease.
(f) imprisonment for 7 years or more.
(g) desertion for three years.
(h) non-resumption of co-habitation following a decree of judicial separation or restitution of conjugal rights.
(i) conversion.

(In addition to these common grounds, the wife can obtain a divorce if she has been compelled by her husband to prostitution. The husband has the right to dissolve the marriage if the wife was pregnant by some other person at the time of marriage).

Jewish Law

The Jews in India are not governed by statutory law but by their customary law. Originally, the *ghet* was the only form of divorce. In India, however, dissolution of the marriage can be done through the court on grounds of adultery or cruelty. The marriages are generally monogamous excepting in certain specific cases. Because they are a small minority, no effort has been made to codify or reform this law. *We feel that this should be undertaken now and the principle of monogamy as well as the normal grounds for divorce as provided in the Special Marriage Act should be adopted for the community also.*

Special Marriage Act, 1954: This Act provides for a secular form of marriage which can be taken advantage of by all persons in India irrespective of their religious faith. Persons who marry under this Act will be governed by the provisions of the Act and not by their own personal law, with respect to their matrimonial rights and remedies.

The grounds on which divorce can be obtained by either party to marriage are adultery, desertion for a period of three years, cruelty, unsound mind for 3 years, leprosy, venereal disease, continuous absence for 7 years without information to those persons who would naturally have heard of him or her, non-resumption of co-habitation for 1 year following a decree of judicial separation or restitution of conjugal rights. In addition to these, the wife can obtain divorce on the ground of rape, sodomy or bestiality. A special feature of this act is that the parties can also dissolve the marriage by mutual consent. All that the parties need do in order to obtain divorce under this provision is to present a petition to the court that they have been living separately for a period of one year or more and that they have not been able to live together and that they have mutually agreed to dissolve the marriage.

Conversion as a ground for divorce: In the field of personal law and particularly in divorce, the existence of various legal systems create a peculiar situation. The Constitution recognises the right freely to profess, practise and propagate religion. Conversion, therefore, from one faith to another is an individual's right and the motive for the conversion is or should be beyond judicial scrutiny. But when such conversion impinges on the right of another person, the question poses a problem. In India today as a legacy of the multiple systems, a person by his or her conversion also acquires the right to be governed by a different set of laws. Even after the Constitution, the codified Hindu Marriage Act has mentioned conversion as a ground for divorce. Is conversion then to be treated as a matrimonial wrong? Under statutory Muslim Law a woman converted to a faith other than Islam or renouncing Islam has only the right to divorce if the husband has committed a matrimonial wrong—conversion *per se* does not affect the validity of the marriage and is in no way a bar to its continuance. On the other hand, a man converted to Islam from another religion has the right to be governed by his new personal law, including the right to marry more than once. This is so even when his first marriage was a monogamous marriage. He is also entitled to claim that his new faith does not permit him to remain married to a Hindu and he can, therefore, proceed to divorce her by uttering *talaq* three times. The Indian Divorce Act does not recognise conversion as affecting the validity of the marriage unless it is followed by the marriage of the husband to another woman. The Converts' Dissolution Act permits the convert to Christianity to dissolve the marriage provided the marriage has in-effect broken down as a result of the conversion. It requires to be proved clearly that cohabitation has been discontinued because of the conversion. Under the Parsee Law, conversion is a ground for divorce provided the suit is brought within 2 years. This thorny question is dealt with in many ways, but the problem remains of reconciling the right to freedom of religion with the possible impact of conversion on marriages. It has been suggested that the question of marital rights on conversion should be governed by principles of equality, justice and good conscience. The other is that no converted person can, for a period of two years at least, be able to affect any marital rights by resorting to the new religion. While the second suggestion has the merit of deterring people from easy conversion to solve their matrimonial problems, *in our opinion conversion should not be a ground for divorce as it offers an easy way of evading matrimonial obligations.*

Divorce by mutual consent: Our review of the different laws governing divorce indicates that both customary laws and the secular law, *i.e.* the Special Marriage Act, 1954 recognise mutual consent as a ground for divorce, but this conspicuous by its absence in any of the statutory laws governing different communities. On the other hand, the religious laws and judicial interpretations of them have generally tended to emphasise the fault theory, being particular to prevent the party guilty of a matrimonial wrong from obtaining a dissolution of the marriage. This leads often to the use of perjured evidence. As there is even today an indirect way of getting divorce by mutual consent, by registering one's marriage under the Special Marriage Act, after celebration according to religious rites, *we recommend that this ground should be recognised in all the personal laws so that two adults whose marriage has, in fact, broken down can get it dissolved honourably.*

Prostitution as a ground for divorce: The provision in the Parsee Marriage and Divorce Act, 1936 which enables a wife to obtain a divorce if her husband has compelled her to prostitution, in our view, is a very desirable protection. *We recommend inclusion of this provision in all other Personal laws.*

As a general principle, we recommend parity of rights regarding grounds for both husband and wife: This already exists in some of the personal laws, and in our view is essential to guarantee equality of status for both partners. It may be noted that the findings of our survey on this question shows an overwhelming opinion in favour of parity. 74 per cent of the respondents (72.9 per cent males and 74.37 per cent females) have stated that the grounds for divorce should be the same for both husband and wife.

V. ADOPTION

"Adoption is the institutionalised practice through which an individual belonging by birth to one kinship ties that are socially defined as equivalent to the congenital ties. These new ties supersede the old ones either wholly or in part". It is the act of a person who takes upon himself the position of a parent to a child who is not in law his own child.

The origin of the custom of adoption is lost in antiquity. It has, however, been recognised in India for centuries and is also recognised in other South Asian countries, such as Burma and Thailand. Adoption forms the subject matter of personal law. In India the only personal law which recognises adoption in the true sense of the term is Hindu Law which regarded adoption as the 'taking of a son as a substitute' in case there is no male issue.

Muslim Law

Even though Muslim Law does not recognise adoption, in India previously the law had permitted this right to Hindu converts to Islam, who had enjoyed this right prior to their conversion. This customary right was, however, partially abrogated by the Shariat Act under which a Muslim could make a declaration that he and his sons would in future give up all customary rights including that of adoption and be governed by the Act.

But the custom of adopting sons was in vogue in Arabia at the time of the Prophet Mohammad. The word adia used in the Holy Quran means adopted sons. Justice Ameer Ali held that a family Waqf could be made not only for the benefit of descendants of the founder but also of dependents, which would include an adopted child who has resided with the settler as a dependent relation. The Lahore High Court held the word 'family' to include an adopted child who had resided with the settler as a dependent relation. All these clearly indicate that adoption was not unknown among Indian Muslims.

Islam never gave any special significance to an adopted son, as it does not to a natural son. Islamic religion, unlike the Hindu one, does not associate a son, or any other relative, with the performance of the last rites of a deceased Muslim whether male or female. It, therefore, does not recommend adoption of a son or a daughter for a person dying issueless, nor does it absolutely prohibit it. The Quranic verses having a bearing on adoption did not lay down a specific negative rule.

Parsee Law

For the Parsees, there is no law of adoption as such or is adoption recognised by custom. However, the widow of a Parsee dying issueless can adopt a *Palak* on the 4th day of the deceased's death, for the *ad hoc* purpose of performing certain religious rites for the deceased. This adoption is only for a limited purpose and does not confer any proprietary rights on the *Palak*.

4

Transnational Application: Divorce Laws and Customs

Irrevocable and Revocable Divorce: Triple Repudiation

An irrevocable (*bā'in*) divorce becomes operative immediately with all the legal effects attendant on the dissolution of a marriage with regard to matrimonial and financial rights. After divorcing the wife for the first and the second time, the husband may take her back by means of a new marriage and a new dower. A revocable (*raj'i*) divorce becomes operative only after the expiration of the waiting-period; within that period, the husband may take the wife back without her consent and without a new marriage, by express declaration or significant conduct, provided the marriage had been consummated; he may take her back to this way after the first and the second divorce. If the husband does not take the wife back within the waiting-period, the divorce becomes irrevocable, and if he subsequently wishes to take her back, it has to be by means of a new marriage and a new dower. After the third divorce, the wife is not permitted to return to the husband either during the waiting-period or by means of a new marriage until she has been married to another man, the new marriage has been consummated and she has been divorced by the other man in good faith. The purpose of this harsh provision, the *taḥlil* introduced by Muḥammad, is to prevent ill-usage of the wife by unlimited alternate divorce and reinstatement (without a new marriage), in other words, to deter the husband from such a divorce by creating a formidable obstacle to his taking back the wife after she has been divorced for the third time. This provision was stultified by all the orthodox schools, which permit divorcing one's wife in one session by, the use of an expression known as triple repudiation, which has the effect of three separate divorces, although they deprecate this form of divorce as *ṭalāq al-bid'a* (in contrast to the various forms of *ṭalāq al-sunna,* recommended by them).[1] Muḥammad's provision thus did not achieve its purpose and may even have aggravated the position from the point of view of both spouses.

The various kinds of divorce take effect through explicit (*ṣariḥ*) or metaphorical (*kināya*) *ṭalāq* expressions and differ from one another as to the formula, the degree of finality and the element of the husband's intent (*niyya*). The Ottoman legislator, although recognizing both explicitly and metaphorically pronounced divorces, laid down that the meaning of the expression used must be known and clear; if it is not, the divorce is valid only after the husband's intention to divorce the wife has been proven.[2]

The *sijills* contain a variety of triple repudiation formulas, including some combining triple repudiation with archaic expressions, such as *ilā* and *zihār.*[3] About 90% of *ṭalāq* divorces were single, irrevocable ones.[4] In fewer than 10% of divorces other than by judicial proceedings, the wife was divorced three times. This was almost always done in one session by triple repudiation; only rarely was the wife divorced by three separate acts.[5] Almost three-quarters of the triple repudiations were *ṭalāq* divorces performed unilaterally by the husband, as against about one-quarter which were by mutual agreement. Triple repudiations constitute about one-quarter of *ṭalāq* divorces other than by agreement. Triple repudiation was particularly frequent under the following circumstances: a fit of anger, or provocation by the wife[6]; an affront to the husband's honour, disgraceful misconduct of the wife, such as adultery[7]; serious disputes between the spouses or their families[8]; suspended repudiation intended to make the wife obey the husband by the threat of the ultimate sanction, or a vow of divorce intended to demonstrate serious intention or firm belief regarding a matter not necessarily connected with the wife (more than one-third of suspended repudiations were by triple repudiation[9]); in the case of exchange marriages, triple repudiation of one of the wives, which leads to triple repudiation of the other[10]; in the case of childlessness or a cousin marriage, where the spouses wish to demonstrate that they do not intend to restore their marriage in the future[11]; the husband's wish to grant the wife maximum freedom in return for renunciation of matrimonial rights[12]; and the intention to take another wife in place of the divorced one.[13]

The *sijills* do not to a significant extent reflect the grave human problems likely to arise from the desire of the spouses to restore their marriage legally after a triple divorce. The author came across only one instance of an intermediate marriage, and this was undoubtedly a fictitious marriage contracted specifically *biqaṣd al-taḥlil,* in order that the wife might again be permitted to return to her first husband, in express contradiction to the *sharī'a* (as propounded by some schools of law). The second "husband" told the court ingenuously that he had contracted the marriage as a *muḥallil min al-ṭalāq,* one who causes the wife to be again permitted to her first husband, from whom she has been separated by triple repudiation. He swore that he had consummated the marriage. Thereupon the wife was divorced, at her request, on agreed terms of renunciation; the *qāḍī* confirmed the divorce and instructed her to observe the *'idda* before remarrying. The ease with which this divorce was performed and confirmed may indicate that this was a customary way of circumventing the intermediate-marriage provision.[14] Another method was referred to in a case in which the wife alleged that the husband had divorced her some years previously by triple repudiation and had remarried her a year later without her having been married to another man.[15] There can be no doubt that such things actually happened, and if they are not reflected in the *sijills,* it is because neither of the spouses was anxious to raise problems.[16] The author came across only a limited number of cases in which the wife denied or objected to a triple repudiation,[17] and not one case in which she tried to soften the blow by claiming there had only been a single repudiation. Moreover, in a not inconsiderable number of cases, the wife applied to the court on her own initiative for registration of a triple repudiation,[18] and sometimes she demanded that the husband perform such a repudiation in return for her renouncing various matrimonial rights or paying him compensation.[19]

Revocable divorce was not widely practised: according to the *sijills,* it represents about 3% of all divorces other than judicial. The real figure is probably higher because there is evidence that the husband who divorced his wife and then took her back during the waiting-period sometimes did not trouble to register the divorce.[20] This can also be inferred from the fact that the *qāḍī,* when called on to confirm the divorce and the wife's reinstatement, sometimes asked the parties to declare any divorce that might have preceded the divorce in question or decided that the husband might take back or remarry the wife if the quota of three divorces had not been filled.[21] In other words, the courts had no way of keeping track of the matter.

It seems that revocable divorce achieved its original purpose in the sense that the husband, regretting his rash act, took back the wife before the end of the waiting-period. He sometimes did so at the very time the divorce was registered,[22] and sometimes he used go-betweens, *ahl al-khayr,* for the purpose.[23] He might ask the court to regard the divorce as revocable so that he could take the wife back; this request was occasionally backed up by the plea that the divorce was pronounced in a fit of anger.[24] Sometimes in the case of an irrevocable divorce a husband asked a religious functionary or *qāḍī* for a legal opinion, (*fatwā*) enabling him to take the wife back without a new marriage.[25] In a few cases the wife was not taken back during the waiting-period and the divorce became irrevocable.[26]

Revocable divorce might be combined with suspended

repudiation. This combination was apparently intended to ensure the wife's obedience by deterrence while giving her two chances before the final dissolution of the marriage. If she failed to obey and the condition was thus fulfilled, she became revocably divorced, but if she persisted in her disobedience during the waiting-period, the husband might not take her back and the divorce would then become irrevocable. Also, in this manner, the husband reserved to himself the option to preserve the marriage and take the wife back during the waiting-period.[27] Moreover, on reinstatement of the wife during the waiting-period, the question of divorce against the wife's will was no longer of real concern although the divorce was still counted as one of the three permitted by the *sharī'a*. At the same time, there is evidence that the question of the wife's consent arose also in the case of revocable divorce.[28] In several cases in which a suspended repudiation was to give added weight to some pronouncement of the husband totally unconnected with the wife, the husband asked that the divorce be regarded as revocable when the pronouncement had proved wrong.[29] In other cases, the wife was revocably divorced under an agreement between the parties according to which she renounced various matrimonial rights.[30] It seems that the husband wished to retain an option to take the wife back while restoring the rights she had renounced.[31]

From the wife's point of view, revocable divorce was advantageous or disadvantageous according to the circumstances of the case: where she did not want a divorce, she hoped that the husband would exercise his right to take her back during the waiting-period; where she wanted a divorce, she feared that he would exercise this right. Both cases involved an intermediate state of uncertainty and insecurity for the wife: she might be for many months in a limbo between marriage and a divorce.[32] This situation is perhaps the most unpleasant manifestation of the freedom of *ṭalāq* vested in the husband by Islamic law. The author came across some cases in which the husband divorced his wife, took her back, divorced her again, took her back again and then divorced her a third time.[33] The outrage was still greater in the case of an exchange marriage, where the alternate divorce and reinstatement of one wife automatically entailed a similar treatment of her *badila.*[34] On the other hand, where the wife was not interested in the marriage, she might claim that she had been revocably divorced, that the waiting-period had passed without her being reinstated and that the divorce had thus become irrevocable; or she might contend that she had been irrevocably or triply divorced in the first place whereas the husband might deny having divorced her at all or admit only to a revocable divorce or ask that the divorce be regarded as revocable.[35] In one case, the wife said that the husband had taken her back against her will by having intercourse with her by force and threats, and that she still did not want ever to be his wife again.[36] In sum, it may be said that Muslims are not strict with regard to *ṭalāq al-sunna* and *ṭalāq al-bid'a.* Revocable divorce, which is the type most recommended by all the schools, was rather rare, while divorce by triple repudiation, which is the most frowned on, was rather frequent.

Maintenance During the Waiting-Period

A divorced woman is entitled to maintenance during the waiting-period (*idda*), provided she is not rebellious. The waiting-period is usually three menstruations if the marriage has been consummated or *khalwa* (privacy of husband and wife) has taken place.[37] If the divorced woman is pregnant, she is entitled to maintenance until delivery.[38] The rate of maintenance is fixed by mutual agreement or, in the absence of agreement, by experts (*mukhbirūn*). The *sijills* show fewer than 50 claims for maintenance during the *'idda* although about 1,900 divorces of all kinds were confirmed and registered by the courts. There are several reasons for the small number of maintenance claims: about three-quarters of the different kinds of *ṭalāq* divorces are, as stated, by agreement between the parties, and such divorces usually involve renunciation of maintenance during the *'idda*; the spouses may on divorce determine the wife's rights by agreement, so that the wife need not file a claim for maintenance; if maintenance is not claimed within the waiting-period, the right to it lapses.[39] Only in one case did the husband agree to pay maintenance although the waiting-period had expired.[40] Rebelliousness of the wife at the time of the divorce was a (rare) ground for loss of the right to maintenance.[41]

From the evidence, it appears that the wife did not usually enjoy her right to maintenance during the *'idda,* just as she did not enjoy her right to deferred dower—this, too, because she renounced the right on divorce by agreement. On the other hand, as set out above, a revolutionary change in the matter of ensuring the divorced woman's subsistence was the practice of paying her maintenance beyond the waiting-period: for life, until remarriage, or until she became entitled to a National Insurance pension.

DECLINE OF THE DIVORCE RATE

The divorce rate in Israeli Muslim society has considerably declined since the end of the Mandate. It dropped sharply until the middle 1960s and stabilized only by the late 1960s: it was 1.7 per thousand persons in 1946, 1.2 in 1953, 0.6 in 1960 and 0.4 in 1965 and 1968.[42] In other words, since the middle 1960s the rate has been about one-quarter of what it was at the end of the Mandate. These data should be treated with some caution for a number of reasons: official statistics, based on divorce certificates issued by the *shari'a* courts,[43] are underestimates because in Muslim society, for reasons extensively discussed above,[44] the registration of divorces is not complete. This is true especially for divorces followed by reinstatement of the wife before the end of the *'idda* and for arbitrary *ṭalāq* divorces. Moreover, a divorce is sometimes registered many years after the event. The data of the Central Bureau of Statistics reflect the dates of registration and not the dates of the divorces themselves. Legal statistics of divorces[45] have similar defects and thus do not reflect the divorce rate accurately. Besides, the subject-matter of the claim is not necessarily identical with the final judicial award. Thus, for instance, many claims for maintenance, obedience and so forth ended in divorce, and on the other hand, many actions for the confirmation of divorces were dismissed. These shortcomings existed also during the Mandate, but in Israel, although data collection procedures in vital statistics have greatly improved, there is a further motive for abstention from registration of divorces, *viz.*, the wish to conceal infringements of the ban on divorce against the wife's will.

It can therefore safely be assumed that the real divorce rate was higher than that reflected in official statistics. At the same time, it seems that this does not basically affect the conclusion that the divorce rate in Israeli Muslim society was low.[46] A Muslim did not hasten to exercise his right of *ṭalāq* despite the ease of divorce in Islam. The divorce rate has dropped significantly since the time of the Mandate. The traditional factors likely to deter from divorce are the prospect of having to discharge the attendant obligations, especially to pay the deferred dower; the possible deterioration of relations with the wife's family or *ḥamūla*; the expenditure involved in taking another wife (prompt dower, celebration of the marriage, gifts) etc.[47] The importance of some of the traditional factors seems to have increased in Israel, and some new ones have been added. The respective weight of the different factors cannot be ascertained, but they can be divided into two groups: factors accounting for the decline of the divorce rate compared with the closing period of the Mandate and factors likely to account for its decline in Israel. Within the latter group, one may distinguish between those operative in the early years of the State and those operative at a later period.

One of the chief factors in the decline of the divorce rate as against the Mandate period has been the decline in the Muslim urban population. The divorce rate in towns is higher than in rural areas.[48] There is a striking difference in Israel between the respective rates of Muslim divorces in mixed towns and in Arab villages and towns: 0.9-1.0 as against 0.3 (1967), respectively; among the Beduin, the rate is 0.4-0.5.[49] The high rates in mixed towns are certainly due to the influence of norms prevailing in Israeli society. Some villages, especially in the Little Triangle, are not inferior in economic, social and cultural respects to Nazareth or Shafā Amr. The data on Beduin should be treated with caution, although it is usually assumed that divorce is frequent among them.[50]

Another factor involved was the youthful age-structure of the Muslim population in Israel compared with that during the Mandate. Also of account in considering the declining divorce rate was the solution during the early years of the State, either by divorce or reunion, of the problem of families separated as a result of the 1948 War. The enormous increase in the amount of dower from the late 1950s, and the necessity to pay compensation, or provide maintenance (including a dwelling) for life or until remarriage in return for the wife's consent to the divorce, also mitigated against divorce. As stated, this custom, sometimes involving an outlay of thousands of pounds, was prevalent in the prosperous Little Triangle villages yet rare elsewhere. The increased expenditure involved in a new marriage as a result of a rise in economic expectations, the standard of housing and the standard of living, must also have had an effect.

It is difficult to assess to what extent the decline of the divorce rate is attributable to the Knesset's ban on divorce against the wife's will. Although there are signs of a deterrent effect of the penal sanction, the main result of the ban, as stated, may simply have been avoidance of registration. Moreover, divorce against the wife's will was still frequent and the ban was circumvented by various devices. As stated above, the divorce rate also decreased in the Jewish sector of the population from 2.6 per thousand persons in 1946 to 1.8 in 1951 and 0.9 in 1968,[51] *i.e.*, to one-third of the figure at the end of the Mandate, although the ban on divorce against the wife's will was almost without significance for this sector.[52] The decline of the divorce rate must therefore be mainly attributed to other factors: demographic, social and economic, rather than to Knesset legislation—as is also the case with the rise in the age of marriage.[53] In fact, Israeli legislation has, in another way, led to an increase of the divorce rate. As has been shown, the Knesset's ban on polygamy was one of the most frequent causes of divorce.[54] If the increase in the divorce rate from this cause is not reflected in statistics, this is, apparently, because it was offset by other factors making for a decline.

THE *QĀḌĪS* AND DIVORCE

Establishment of Peace Between the Parties

The *qāḍīs* held that the primary task of the *sharī'a* courts is to establish peace between the spouses and to preserve the marriage intact. Thus, Shaykh Ḥasan Amīn al-Ḥabash suggested that the courts should make it standard practice not to register a divorce before its efforts to reconcile the estranged spouses had failed,[55] and Shaykh Ḥusnī al-Zu'bī considered that even where there was a legal ground for dissolution the *qāḍī* should not dissolve the marriage before all avenues to the restoration of domestic peace had been exhausted.[56] The comparison of the *qāḍī* to a family doctor was very frequent and is of special significance in this context.[57] The *sijills* contain many instances of *qāḍīs* using their judicial and personal authority in order to smooth out differences between spouses with a view to preventing dissolution. The judgment frequently notes that the *qāḍī* "strove with all his might" for a reconciliation and compromise settlement[58]; he sometimes adjourned the case in the hope that meanwhile tempers would cool and peace be restored[59]; occasionally he used intermediaries (*ahl al-khayr, ahl al-wāsiṭa*), who were to try to bring the parties closer again[60]; or he might dismiss one party's action for dissolution and direct the other to adopt a conciliatory attitude.[61] But in almost all cases, "the court's efforts were in vain": it was not able to avoid dissolution of the marriage.[62]

As has previously been mentioned, the conciliatory role of the *qāḍīs* is in keeping with a basic attitude long observed in them, *viz.*, a desire to avoid, as far as possible, the rendering of judgment and the application of the *sharī'a,* for fear of perverting the latter, and a striving to get the spouses to settle their dispute by agreement.[63] An institutionalized manifestation of this attitude is the "family council" of arbitrators with the meaning of article 130 of the Family Rights Law. All the *qāḍīs* believed that the main function of the arbitrators is to effect a compromise and reconciliation between the spouses or, as Shaykh Tawfīq 'Asaliyya put it, "to save the marriage from dissolution."[64] Some *qāḍīs,* especially Shaykh Ṭāhir Ḥamād and Shaykh Ḥusnī al-Zu'bī, appointed arbitrators on their own initiative.[65]

Divorce on the Husband's Initiative

(a) The Freedom of Ṭalāq

The *qāḍīs* condemned arbitrary *ṭalāq,* stressing, in accordance with the orthodox Islamic view expressed in a saying attributed to the Prophet, that "of all permitted things, the most hateful to God is *ṭalāq*" (*abghaḍ al-ḥalāl ilā Allāh al-ṭalāq*). At the same time, different nuances can be discerned in their attitudes. Shaykh Ḥasan Amīn al-Ḥabash said that "*ṭalāq* is an institution of Islamic law resorted to when necessary, when the marriage cannot be preserved," that *ṭalāq* "is a necessity making the forbidden permissible" (*al ḍarūrāt tubiḥ al-maḥzūrāt*) and that "the *qāḍī* only orders a divorce for a compelling reason," whence the legal distinction between *ṭalāq al-sunna,* which is recommended and *ṭalāq al-bid'a,* which is deprecated. Although marriage in Islam is not a religious act but a civil contract, he called it a "sacred union" (*'aqdmuqaddas*) and stressed that Islam had "sanctified woman." But beyond the religious argumentation, a progressive social philosophy is recognizable in Shaykh Ḥasan. According to him, divorce, even if based on *shar'i* grounds, destroys the family and harms especially the wife and the young children. He saw a great danger to society in the high divorce rate prevailing in the Little Triangle villages.[66]

Shaykh Tawfīq 'Asaliyya likewise combined religious with social arguments. He condemned *ṭalāq* as hateful to Allāh and stressed the importance of the happiness of the family, as the basic social cell, to the welfare of the *umma* and civilization. Since "women are the natural source of the *umma's* existence," Islam shows great solicitude for them; it enjoins men to provide for their subsistence and to treat them gently so as to enable them to "fulfil their destination in the best and most perfect manner," for the "supreme goal of marriage is offspring." But marriage, like every other human relationship, sometimes runs into difficulties that make life unbearable, so that there is no way out but dissolution (which in itself is "a crime against the children"); for this purpose, Islam has devised the differnt forms of *ṭalāq*.[67]

Shaykh Ḥusnī al-Zu'bī stressed that the *sharī'a* advocates the stability of marriage, an institution "vital to the survival of the human race." Divorce without reason or necessity is foolish and impious as well as injurious to the wife and children[68] Shaykh Amīn Qāsim Mudlij said that the exercise of the right of *ṭalāq* in an unjust and aggressive manner, without a legal ground, was the most hateful way of using a permission granted. Shaykh Ṭāhir Ḥamād treated *ṭalāq* as a necessary evil which had to be endured. "Divorce in Islamic law is not a custom (*āda*) but is [unavoidable] on accumulation of tension between the spouses."[69]

Despite the condemnation of *ṭalāq* by all the *qāḍīs*, they hardly ever challenged the actual system which grants the husband a unilateral right of divorce. They accepted the inequality of the sexes and sometimes even found justification for it in nature. Shaykh Ḥusnī al-Zu'bī thought that *ṭalāq* was given to the husband because there were natural differences in the qualities of men and women: "God has entrusted *ṭalāq* to the husband because patience, determination, foresight and the faculty of soberly weighing up benefit and damage are usually male qualities, and He has not entrusted *ṭalāq* to the woman because she is quick-tempered, excitable, impressionable and emotional. Dissolution of the marriage [even] on her initiative is entrusted solely to the husband, who may effect it at will, or to the *qāḍī*." On the other hand, the financial consequences of divorce are borne by the husband.[70]

The motif of the natural inequality between the sexes is found also with other *qāḍīs*. Shaykh Tawfīq 'Asaliyya said that the *sharī'a* was designed to regulate what he called the "natural relationship" of the spouses while preserving the equilibrium between the rights and duties of each party in accordance with his or her natural status.[71] Shaykh Amīn Qāsim Mudlij said that Allāh had given the husband a "natural right" to dissolve the marriage unilaterally and that he might exercise this right at any time and place.[72] Shaykh Ṭāhir al-Ṭabarī and Shaykh

Mūsā al-Ṭabarī stressed time and again when confirming divorces that according to the *sharī'a ṭalāq* is the husband's exclusive right.[73]

Shaykh Ḥasan Amīn al-Ḥabash indeed maintained that according to the *sharī'a* there is full equality between man and woman, but he probably meant equality in the religious sense, equality before the Creator, for immediately afterward he said that there were material differences between them originating in nature. Thus, woman's task was to bear and bring up children, whereas man's task was to provide the family's living.[74] At the same time, he was undoubtedly unique among the *qāḍīs* in his professed attitude toward *ṭalāq* as a legal and social problem, although he was fettered by inhibitions originating in adherence to the Ḥanafī school. In his opinion, the husband's right of *ṭalāq* ought to be restricted, though he dared not actually restrict it in view of an express provision of the *sharī'a* in this matter. "*Ṭalāq* of any kind pronounced by the crowds in coffee-houses, alleyways, etc., is vanity and vexation of spirit; it carries no more weight than the gossip they utter most, if not all, of their lives; and *shar'i* law must not be applied to such a divorce[!]." The children of the couple, Shaykh Ḥasan said, were likely to be abandoned; the wife's and her family's honour would be defiled though she had had no part in bringing about the divorce; and her home would be in ruins. *Ṭalāq* was valid he thought, where the spouses, or the husband alone, appeared in court, explained the reasons which led to the divorce and convinced the court of their justness but only when the court had failed to effect a reconciliation should the divorce be officially registered. This is no other than a bold attempt to turn *ṭalāq* into a judicial divorce. But Shaykh Ḥasan added regretfully that this reform had no basis in the *sharī'a,* which recognizes even a divorce pronounced by a man in jest (*hāzil*), thus lacking the element of intent. He wished that the *qāḍīs* and *'ulamā* might find elements in the rich Islamic legal heritage that would allow a compromise between the orthodox point of view and the requirements of society.[75] He said so even before the Knesset's ban on divorce against the wife's will. In fact, he tried, by means of a religious-legal device, to achieve the same object as the Knesset had set itself, *viz.*, to compel the husband to have recourse to the court and give the *qāḍī* wide discretion to examine in each case whether, under the circumstances, a divorce was justified.

(b) Suspended Repudiation

The declared position of some *qāḍīs* as to suspended repudiation is represented by their comments on the Egyptian Personal Status Bill of 1966, which, if enacted, would have lain down that deferred divorce and suspended repudiation were invalid. According to the majority of the *qāḍīs* the proposed reform was contrary to the provisions of the *'sharī'a,* to the position of all the orthodox schools and to the Ottoman Family Rights Law, and according to Shaykh Ṭāhir Ḥamād, it was contrary also to customary practice (*al-isti māl al-urfī*). Shaykh Tawfīq 'Asaliyya feared that the reform might lead to infringements of prohibitions and, in consequence, to acts of apostasy. Shaykh Ḥusnī al-Zu'bī opposed the reform, but conceded that its adoption would have solved many problems. Only Shaykh Amīn Qāsim Mudlij agreed to the reform; he said that his decisions were conceived in the same reformist spirit, in reliance on the teachings of the Ḥanafī school.[76]

Until the early 1960s, the general attitude of the *qāḍīs* to suspended repudiation was formalistic and rigid. No account was taken of the intention (*niyya*) of the husband who resorted to this mechanism,[77] of the contents of the condition or of the circumstances under which it was fulfilled. When the fulfilment of the condition had been proven, the *qāḍī* immediately decided that the divorce was effective. Thus, in the case of a man who had sworn to divorce his wife although he "had not intended to forbid her to himself but only to humour his father," Shaykh Ṭāhir Ḥamād said: "Since our faith is based on linguistic expressions (*alfāz*) and constructions (*mabān*) and not on intentions (*maqāṣid*) and meanings (*ma'ān*) . . . . he must be judged according to his oath and admission, and no importance attaches to his intention (*walā 'ibra liniyyatihi*) that his wife should not be under prohibition (*taḥrīm*) [to him]"; and he decided that the divorce was effective.[78]

A surprising change in the position of the *qāḍīs* as to this question became apparent at their 1963 conference. This conference resolved, *inter alia,* that whenever a divorce due to the wife's fulfilment of a condition was referred to the court, the *qāḍī* should examine the circumstances of the fulfilment, and if he reached the conclusion that it had been unavoidable, compelled by circumstances (*iḍṭirāriyya*), he should decide that the divorce was not effective.[79] This resolution, the legal basis of which was not indicated, gives the *qāḍī* wide discretion to rely on social considerations. In other words, what is involved here is an application of the principle of *ḍarūra* (necessity), which is a form of *maṣlaḥa* (public interest).[80] This resolution curtails the husband's unilateral right of *ṭalāq*.

The *qāḍīs'* resolution was put into practice shortly afterward. A husband had made the divorce of his wife conditional on her leaving the house without his permission. The wife contended that she had been compelled to fulfil the condition by most vital necessity (*ḍarūra*) in that the husband had deserted her and she had had to go to the court-house to claim maintenance for herself and her starving children, and that the divorce was therefore not effective. The wife's attorney, Advocate S. Darwish, sought support for this contention in Muḥammad Zayd al-Abayānī's modern commentary, which states that a suspended repudiation becomes an effective divorce if the wife is not under compulsion (*muḍṭarra*), for example, in danger of being burned or drowned.[81] The wife's going to the courthouse to claim maintenance for her children was, he argued, immeasurably more a matter of compulsion than escaping death by fire or water. Shaykh Ḥusnī al-Zu'bī accepted this contention and decided that the divorce was not effective. The husband resorted to the *Sharī'a* Court of Appeal, whose members were divided on the issue. Shaykh Amīn Qāsim Mudlij accepted the plea that fulfilment of the condition under compulsion did not count relying on the view of the three orthodox Sunnī schools, as against that of the Ḥanafī school, that "a sin is not imputed to him who is forced to transgress"; he also stressed the social aspect: divorce was a very serious matter, hurting the whole family, and especially the innocent children. Shaykh Ḥasan Amīn al-Ḥabash, a staunch adherent of the Ḥanafī school, allowed the appeal, stating that the plea that the condition had been fulfilled under compulsion was not one of the *shar'ī* grounds on which the effectiveness of the divorce might be denied.[82]

(c) Divorce Pronounced in a State of Intoxication

It seems that the *qāḍīs* accepted the Ottoman legislator's precept that a divorce pronounced in a state of intoxication shall not be valid. In one case, Shaykh Ṭāhir Ḥamād set aside a judgment for divorce after the husband had proved that the wife had extorted a *ṭalāq* from him by provocation when he was drunk, and Shaykh Mūsā al-Ṭabarī dismissed a husband's application to set aside a judgment for divorce because his witnesses did not confirm his plea that he had been drunk at the time of the divorce.[83] Shaykh Tawfīq 'Asaliyya, Shaykh Amīn Qāsim Mudlij and Shaykh Ḥusnī al-Zu'bī agreed to a provision in the Egyptian Personal Status Bill of 1966 invalidating divorce pronounced in a state of intoxication on the ground that it was in conformity with the Ottoman Family Rights Law,[84] which deviates from the Ḥanafī school in this matter.

The Ban on Divorce Against the Wife's Will

(a) The Knesset's Restriction on the Freedom of Ṭalāq

The declared position of the *qāḍīs* was, with immaterial differences in wording and style, that they did not object to the Knesset's intervention as far as it was of a penal or procedural character; on the other hand, they objected most vigorously to reforms derogating from substantive provisions of Islamic law even if enacted by the parliaments of Arab states. Shaykh Ṭāhir Ḥamād said that Israeli legislation in the matter of divorce against the wife's will and other matters not only did not abolish religious law but heightened its effectiveness by means of the criminal sanction. Islam, too, condemns the practices in question, but its ethical sanctions (*al-'iqāb al-ukhrawiyy*) are not effective deterrents. At the same time, Shaykh Ṭāhir was at pains to emphasize that "the [secular] law is designed to preserve the existing rightful order" and that "Qurānic legislation fits every time and place."[85]

Shaykh Ḥasan Amīn al-Ḥabash not only did not oppose secular legislation on divorce but welcomed further reforms of a procedural or penal character, as will be seen below. Shaykh Tawfīq 'Asaliyya condemned the ban on divorce against the wife's will and other enactments of the Knesset, but was careful to note that they were introduced "whilst preserving the validity of religious law."[86] Most of the *qāḍīs* who commented on the Egyptian Personal Status Bill of 1966 strongly opposed any curtailment of the husband's right of *ṭalāq*.[87]

(b) The Wife's Consent to the Divorce

The question of consent in cases where the wife was unilaterally divorced did not usually concern the *qāḍīs,* and even where it was referred to it is not always certain that this was done under the influence of Israeli legislation, for the subject was known even before the enactment of the Women's Equal Rights Law and the wife's consent usually related to the settlement of matrimonial rights. A clear indication of such influence exists only in cases where the *qāḍī* took the trouble to ascertain, himself or through an agent, whether the wife had agreed to the divorce.[88]

A more meaningful conception of the *qāḍīs'* stand on the ban on divorce against the wife's will may be obtained from those cases in which the wife contested the divorce. Here can be distinguished two diametrically opposed approaches. One, which was common to Shaykhs Ṭāhir al-Ṭabarī, Ḥasan Amīn al-Ḥabash, Tawfīq 'Asaliyya and Ḥusnī al-Zu'bī, conformed with the Knesset's intention. In dozens of judgments given by them, it was found, with differences in wording and style, that the *qāḍī* warned the husband not to divorce the wife against her will and drew his attention to the penal sanction; when the wife had been divorced against her will, the *qāḍī* confirmed the divorce, sometimes explaining that it was valid according to religious law, registered it and, if the wife was not in court, directed that she be notified[89]; occasionally he noted that the wife did not consent to the divorce or, if she was absent, that it was not known whether she consented or objected to it[90]; he might also add that the court had not given permission for the divorce, as required in the absence of the wife's consent.[91] In some cases, the judgment notes that if the competent authority found that an offense had been committed the husband should be punished in accordance with law.[92] Moreover, in most cases, the *qāḍīs* stepped outside their own province by stating expressly that the husband had violated the secular law.[93] Shaykh Ḥasan went so far as to draw the wife's attention to the fact that she could file a criminal charge with the competent authority,[94] and Shaykh Tawfīq directed that those of his decisions which indicated that the wife had been divorced against her will and without the husband having obtained in advance permission of the court for divorce, be communicated to the Attorney-General or the Ministry of Religious affairs for appropriate action against the husband.[95]

The second approach is marked by indifference to the significance of divorce against the wife's will from the point of view of secular law. The emphasis is on its significance from the point of view of religious law. The chief exponent of this approach was Shaykh Ṭāhir Ḥamād. In his judgments, he pointed out that the wife's consent was not essential to the validity of the divorce and that it was the duty of the court to confirm it even if it was against the wife's will because the validity of *ṭalāq* was recognized by secular law. The wife's consent was only required as a defense against the penal sanction. But Shaykh Ṭāhir himself did not trouble in his *ṭalāq* judgments to refer to the criminality of divorce against the wife's will. Only in one case did he note that the wife had the right to bring a criminal action in a civil court because she had been divorced under these circumstances, but in this case he apparently made an exception because the wife had threatened to have him (and the husband) jailed if he confirmed the divorce.[96] Shaykh Mūsā al-Ṭabarī and Shaykh Amīn Qāsim Mudlij also did not refer in their judgments to infringements of the ban on divorce against the wife's will, although there must have been some in their areas of jurisdiction. This may in part be due to their attitude regarding permission for divorce.[97] Shaykh

Tawfīq ʻAsaliyya was not strict about the wife's consent in the case of divorces performed in East Jerusalem.[98]

The question of the wife's consent to the divorce and the criminality of divorce against the wife's will did not concern the *qāḍīs* in the case of revocable divorce, barring exceptional instances. This was probably because in most cases revocable divorce ended in reinstatement of the wife and there was no reason, as far as the *qāḍī* was concerned, to raise problems likely to exacerbate relations between the spouses. A particularly striking example is the attitude of Shaykh Ḥasan Amīn al-Ḥabash. In all the cases in which the divorce ended in reinstatement of the wife, he completely ignored the question of her consent, whereas in the only case in which the divorce became irrevocable because the wife had not been reinstated during the *ʻidda* he decided that the divorce was valid and, as was his wont, advised her to take legal steps against the husband.[99]

(c) Suspended Repudiation as a Means to Circumvent the Penal Sanction

It has been shown that suspended repudiation served as a device to circumvent the ban on divorce against the wife's will.[100] The *qāḍīs* were divided as to the criminality of this mode of dissolution. Shaykh Ḥasan Amīn al-Ḥabash said that a suspended repudiation was like an ordinary divorce from the point of view of the general law; a husband who pronounced it against the wife's will before obtaining the permission of the court did commit a criminal offense; although the divorce was valid according to religious law and the husband was exercising a *sharʻi* right, it was forbidden by secular law. Shaykh Ḥasan, therefore, confirmed and registered such a divorce rather reluctantly,[101] and if he was satisfied that the wife opposed the divorce, he advised her to apply to the appropriate authorities for prosecution of the husband.[102] Moreover, it seems that he spared no effort to place procedural and other difficulties in the way of husbands wishing to dissolve their marriages by suspended repudiation.[103] Out of concern for the preservation of the marriage, he dismissed applications for the confirmation of divorces by husbands trying to use suspended repudiation as a means to evade the penal sanction. He also dismissed such applications by wives seeking to avail themselves of that mechanism in order to obtain their freedom.[104] In one case, Shaykh Tawfīq Maḥmūd 'Asaliyya decided that the wife's admission of the fulfilment of the condition "makes it necessary to declare that the divorce is valid according to *shar'i* law"; but he added that since it had not been definitely proven that the wife consented to the divorce, or rather, since the wife had clearly stated that she did not consent, he left the matter to be decided by the "competent agencies."[105]

A different approach to the question can be found with other *qāḍīs* especially with Shaykh Ṭāhir Ḥamād. He was not only unwilling to admit any restriction on the husband's unilateral right of *ṭalāq* as being without foundation in religious law, but helped, directly and indirectly, to turn suspended repudiation into an efficient means to circumvent the penal sanction. In one case, a husband wished to have the divorce of his wife confirmed because she had fulfilled one of the stipulated conditions, and contended that she had "divorced herself voluntarily and by her own choice." The wife's representative, on the other hand, contended that the divorce had been against her will; he told the *qāḍī* that the court's duty was not to help the husband to commit a criminal offense, but "to help the law and censure him who broke it." The *qāḍī* replied that the husband's action was not contrary to Section 181A of the Criminal Code Ordinance because "the wife was not divorced against her will; the husband did not divorce her but made the divorce conditional on a certain occurrence . . . and left the matter in her hands" (*faja' ala al-amr biyadihā*).[106] This latter expression is, as stated, typical of the phraseology of delegated repudiation (*tafwīḍ al-ṭalāq*) and its use and that of similar expressions permits the assumption that in this case there was a conscious, systematic attempt to circumvent the ban on divorce against the wife's will without becoming guilty of a criminal offense. Shaykh Ṭāhir admitted to Advocate S. Darwish that he had been in the habit of advising husbands who wished to divorce their wives without becoming guilty of a criminal offense to use the mechanism of suspended repudiation. Moreover, in one of these cases, the *qāḍī* himself had been called by the husband to testify in court that suspended repudiation had been pronounced and that he, the *qāḍī,* had seen the wife leaving the house and thus fulfilling its condition. The husband declared in court that she "had opted for *ṭalāq* for herself."[107] The attempt to treat suspended repudiation as similar to or even identical with delegated repudiation is, of course, unwarranted and misleading. Although the two mechanisms are similar in that it is the wife who fixes the time at which the divorce becomes complete and effective, there is a fundamental, undeniable difference; while the power to divorce herself is delegated to the wife and used by her at her discretion, suspended repudiation is forced on her arbitrarily by the husband.

Shaykh Ḥusnī al-Zu'bī and Shaykh Amīn Qāsim Mudlij also considered that suspended repudiation did not involve a criminal offence. Referring to the wife's contention that the divorce was contrary to law, they decided, as members of a Court of Appeal (under the chairmanship of Shaykh Ṭāhir Ḥamād), that "the court does not think so and holds that there is nothing contrary to law in this pronouncement [of suspended repudiation] because of the wife's opting for *ṭalāq* for herself by leaving the house."[108] Shaykh Ṭāhir al-Ṭabarī confirmed a suspended repudiation in several cases under circumstances raising a suspicion of a circumvention of the penal sanction without touching at all on the question of the wife's consent[109]; in the cases in which the question of the criminality of suspended repudiation came up, it was not the *qāḍī* but one of the parties who raised it.[110]

(d) Confirmation and Registration of Divorce

As stated, the ban on divorce against the wife's will without permission from the court does not invalidate unilateral divorce as far as it is valid according to the *sharī'a.* Most *qāḍīs* were alive to the fact that the Knesset's intervention was of no substantive significance. They explained to the parties on several occasions that non-registration of the divorce did not affect its validity.[111] The registration of divorces is not a *shar'i* but a civil obligation, and most *qāḍīs* regarded it as a requirement of good order which should be fulfilled in the public interest; they usually did not connect it with the question of the ban. Thus, for instance, Shaykh Ṭāhir Ḥamād, even before the enactment of the Women's Equal Rights Law, suggested that divorces should be registered "for fear of disavowal" of the divorce by the husband. After the prohibition of divorce against the wife's will by the Knesset, he said that secular law recognized *ṭalāq* divorces, whether they had been pronounced with or without the wife's consent, in her presence or in her absence in or out of court, but that the infringer of the ban was liable to a penal sanction; in his opinion, it was the *qāḍī's* duty to register the divorce although it was contrary to secular law, and then hand over the offender to the competent authority for punishment.[112] Shaykh Mūsā al-Ṭabarī, in 1950, directed all *ma'dhūns* and *imāms* in his area of jurisdiction to prepare an exact record of every divorce in the village and have it signed by the witnesses who heard the divorce; thereafter the husband was to be summoned to the court for the divorce to be registered and the marriage to be dissolved in accordance with law. Shaykh Mūsā believed that the requirement of registration was likely to prevent hasty divorces.[113]

Shaykh Ḥasan Amīn al-Ḥabash was an exception among the *qāḍīs* as regards his attitude toward the confirmation and registration of divorces. Before the enactment of the Women's Equal Rights Law, there was, in his opinion, no choice but to confirm arbitrarily *ṭalāq* divorces. After the prohibition of divorce against the wife's will, and especially since the amendment of that prohibition in 1959, he considered that the *qāḍī* was not doing justice to all parties if the divorce of a wife who did not consent to it was registered automatically, before the husband had obtained a judgment permitting it. The husband's punishment was no remedy to the wife's position, for "what benefit," he asked, "does a murdered man, who has breathed his last, derive from the punishment of the murderer?" In his opinion, it was pointless to explain to the divorced wife that she was entitled to bring a criminal action against the husband. Such advice was belated. Since the wife did not know her rights and was unfamiliar with legal proceedings, the filing of a criminal action against the husband involved costs and advocate's fees. Under these circumstances, the wife would forgo the action and the husband would escape the penal sanction provided for by law. The solution at first suggested by Shaykh Ḥasan was that the court should refrain from registering the divorce. He said that he, for one, did not automatically confirm every divorce brought before him; if he did not use his discretion he would be turning the court into "a dwelling-place of lovers of *ṭalāq*"; in many cases, stratagems (*ḥiyal*) were applied to circumvent the provisions of both the *sharī'a* and secular law.

Shaykh Ḥasan thought that in this way he was carrying out the Knesset's intention as to divorce against the wife's will. He ingeniously believed for some time that the court should refrain from registering a divorce when it had been performed in contravention of the criminal law; a conflict thus seemed to have arisen in his mind between secular law and the *sharī'a,* which latter requires the confirmation of valid divorces. He declared, though not with a light heart, that in the event of such a conflict the *qāḍī* must follow the secular law. "What is the court to do under such circumstances?" he asked rhetorically. Is it to register the divorce and ignore the law which forbids divorce without permission from the court, especially the amended version of 1959? His reply was that the *sharī'a* courts were integrated in the State and duty-bound to apply its laws. He also maintained that there was no express provision in either Islamic or secular law requiring the court to register a divorce, whether lawfully performed or not.[114] He did not, he asserted, by taking the said attitude, permit anything Allāh forbade or forbid anything He permitted. He found support for this view in the sources: God "deters [from transgression] through the ruler what He has not deterred through the Qur'ān." But he soon realized that this remedy was illusory—that the *qāḍī* had no choice but to register the divorce if its validity according to the *sharī'a* had been proven. He then suggested reframing the section concerning divorce against the wife's will so as to make it more procedural and technical: a man who divorced his wife out of court or before obtaining permission from the court should be liable to heavy punishment. He also suggested that the divorce should only be registered by the court after the offender had been punished.[115] In one case, he refrained from registering a divorce on the ground that an action had first to be filed with the court and the wife summoned to the hearing. The husband refused, submitted there and then a letter to the effect that the wife had already been divorced, and asked that the divorce be registered. The *qāḍī* decided that the divorce was valid "only after the requirements of the existing law had been fulfilled."[116]

In fact, as far as appears from the *sijills,* the *qāḍī's* function in *ṭalāq* divorces was essentially technical and hardly ever involved discretion. He was seldom asked to permit the divorce when the wife opposed it. He was usually confronted with an accomplished fact: the divorce was performed and completed out of court or in his presence without his being able to prevent it. For, the *ṭalāq is a unilateral act of the husband, the court having no standing in it,* and therefore nothing remained for him but to confirm it as far as its validity had been proven to his satisfaction, and to register it.[117] The husband's admission (*iqrār, i tirāf*) that he had divorced the wife was usually sufficient to satisfy the *qāḍī.*[118] If the wife denied the divorce, the testimony of two persons who were present was required, but the *qāḍīs* were not always very strict on this point. Thus, Shaykh Tawfīq 'Asaliyya confirmed a divorce in a case where the witnesses, as usual among Beduin, did not know the wife and were unable to give her name.[119] Where a doubt arose as to the divorce, the husband sometimes repeated it in the presence of the *qāḍī* "to make sure" (*ziyāda fi al-ta 'akkud, al-istithāq*).[120]

The *qāḍīs'* main concern was that the divorcing husband should be in fit condition for divorce: deliberate, calm (not angry), in control of his nerves and mental faculties, not insane, not drunk not bewildered (*madhūsh*), not disconcerted, clear-headed, and whatever else is required for the divorce to be valid.[121] In one case, Shaykh Tawfīq 'Asaliyya set aside a judgment for divorce (triple repudiation) on the basis of the husband's plea that he had pronounced the divorce in a fit of anger without understanding the meaning of his act. The *qāḍī* explained his decision by arguing that *ṭalāq* was "conditional on intactness of the mental powers."[122]

In many cases, the husband divorced the wife in her absence, but the *qāḍī* confirmed the divorce without hesitation.[123] The question of the wife's presence at the divorce did not trouble the *qāḍīs*; it was not relevant to the validity of the divorce. The same is true of the question of where it was performed—whether in or out of court. These remarks apply especially to Shaykh Ṭāhir Ḥamād. He felt no concern about criminal offenses being committed by divorces against the wife's will. He confirmed almost mechanically every divorce brought before him, whether the wife was present in court or not, whether the divorce was performed out of court or in court in the presence of the *qāḍī* and also when the wife had not been asked to consent to the divorce or had expressly opposed it. In one case, a man was unable to prove that he had divorced his wife by suspended repudiation. When the wife had left the court, relieved that her husband's design had failed, the husband declared before the *qāḍī* that he was under no circumstances willing to accept "that this one should be my wife" and divorced her in the *qāḍī's* presence, and the *qāḍī* confirmed the divorce there and then in the wife's absence, in the certain knowledge that she did not want the divorce and had not consented to it; and he did not trouble to point out to the husband that he had committed a criminal offence. In another case, a husband wanted to divorce his wife outside Shaykh Ṭāhir Ḥamād's house, and the *qāḍī* advised him to do so in court[124]; he held that if the divorce was valid on the sole admission of the husband, it was the more so if pronounced in court.[125]

Under these circumstances, it is not surprising that a civil court should have expressed the view that such an interpretation of the ban on divorce against the wife's will made a mockery of the law. It suggested that the legislator reformulate the relevant section so as to make it more rigorous in procedure. It also expressed the wish that Israeli *qāḍīs* might follow reformist *ulamā* and jurists who advocated a renewed *ijtihād* ("effort," the use of individual reasoning) to adapt Islamic law to the requirements of modern life.[126] In one case, the Supreme Court reduced the sentence of a man who had divorced his wife without her consent in view of the fact that he had followed the instructions of Shaykh Ṭāhir Ḥamād, who had advised him, because of the wife's opposition to the divorce, to divorce her first and then to obtain confirmation from him that she was divorced. In another case, that *qāḍī* was convicted and fined by the district court for drawing up a divorce agreement fraudulently. The wife had not consented to the divorce and had not been present in court when it was pronounced, and her signature to the record had been forged with the knowledge of the *qāḍī*.[127] Other *qāḍīs,* too, confirmed and registered almost blindly every *ṭalāq* divorce brought before them, though the author did not get the impression that they treated the retroactive confirmation of divorce as a device for circumventing the ban on divorce against the wife's will. They proceeded in this matter as the *sharī'a* courts had done before the enactment of the Women's Equal Rights Law.

(e) Permission for Divorce Granted by the Court

How did the *qāḍīs* exercise the wide discretion granted them by the Knesset in dealing with husbands' applications for permission to divorce their wives? Most of them were aware of the need for such permission where the wife did not agree to the divorce, but some did not interpret this need correctly. Thus, in some cases, Shaykh Mūsā al-Ṭabarī and Shaykh Amīn Qāsim Mudlij granted permission only when the wife had consented to the divorce,[128] and thereby restricted the husband's right of *ṭalāq* to an unprecedented degree. Still, barring a few exceptions, the *qāḍīs* granted permission because they thought that the circumstances afforded legitimate grounds for divorce according to the customary and *shar'i* norms. Such grounds were the wife's absence, departure from Israel, barrenness, or inability to fulfil her domestic duties toward her husband and family by reason of illness or age. The principal arguments in all these cases were that the husband needed another wife to look after the children and the household and that "the legal purpose of marriage is the production of offspring and the continuance of the family line."[129] Shaykh Ḥasan Amīn al-

Ḥabash permitted a man to divorce his barren wife after 25 years of marriage in order to take another wife, and Shaykh Mūsā al-Ṭabarī granted permission to divorce an incurably insane wife on the ground that she was "unfit for marital life."[130] Sometimes the impression is given that permission was granted solely because the wife, though summoned, had not appeared at the hearing of the court and not for any substantive reason.[131] In fact, for some decisions no reason at all was given, so that it seems—and this goes especially for the judgments of Shaykh Ṭāhir Ḥamād and Shaykh Mūsā al-Ṭabarī—that the response to the application for dissolution was automatic or, in other words, that this was no more than an *ex post facto* confirmation and registration of a *ṭalāq* divorce.[132]

Perhaps more significant in this context is the question of the extent to which the *qāḍīs* refused to permit a divorce where in their opinion there was no justification for it. In only one or two cases did a *qāḍī* expressly refuse permission. In one case, the husband applied for permission on the ground that the wife had borne him no children after 15 years of marriage and that "he lived with her compulsorily." The wife opposed the divorce vehemently, declaring that she preferred death. Shaykh Ḥasan Amīn al-Ḥabash dismissed the application.[133] He was probably influenced by the wife's desperate resistance, for, as has been seen, he, too, regarded barrenness as a ground for dissolution. At any rate, the dismissal of the application in this case was, in the author's opinion, the boldest instance of the exercise of discretion by a *qāḍī* in Israel in accordance with a norm set by the Knesset and not rooted in Islamic law. At the 1963 *qāḍīs'* conference, this *qāḍī* stated that he knew from judicial experience that not every man applying for permission for divorce was an aggrieved person deserving legal relief; in fact, it was mostly the other way round, so that, in the words of a popular saying, it was a case of "he hits, and then cries and goes to complain."[134] Yūsuf Dasūqī, Secretary of the *Sharī'a* Court of Ṭayyiba, attested that it was very difficult to obtain permission for divorce from Shaykh Ḥasan.[135]

In another case, Shaykh Amīn Qāsim Mudlij refused to permit a wife to be divorced on the ground that she was mentally ill. More exactly, the husband applied for the marriage to be dissolved under Article 123 of the Family Rights Law. The *qāḍī* declared that even if *ṭalāq* were intended he would dismiss the application because, in his opinion, *ṭalāq* required the consent of both spouses (and the wife was unable to consent owing to her mental condition).[136] In other words, permission was withheld not because the *qāḍī* did not think the wife's illness a ground for divorcing her against her will but owing to an incorrect interpretation of the law.

It is true that in several cases there are indications that Shaykh Ṭāhir Ḥamād opposed the divorce and tried to dissuade the husband from performing it. In one decision such an attitude is suggested by the statement that the husband "insisted" on divorcing the wife and in fact carried out his intention and that the *qāḍī* had no choice but to confirm and register the divorce.[137] But in other cases it appears that this *qāḍī*'s intervention under such circumstances was not guided by the Knesset's legislation but by the court's custom of seeking to reconcile the spouses.[138] Moreover, when despairing of his efforts to restore domestic peace, he sometimes decided on divorce even though no initiative for it had come from the parties themselves.[139] This enforcement of divorce on the spouses is, of course, another form of interference with the husband's freedom of *ṭalāq* (although it was he, the husband, who actually performed the divorce).

Dissolution on the Wife's Initiative

(a) Ṭalāq Divorces

It has been shown that the wife sometimes played an active part in the dissolution of the marriage and that she pursued this object in various ways. To what extent did the *qāḍīs* assist her efforts to obtain her freedom? The matter hardly troubled them with regard to *ṭalāq* divorces because in their view the wife was a passive party to them. In some cases, they dismissed the wife's demand that the husband should divorce her or that the court should compel him to do so on the formal ground that the court could not force a divorce on the husband or dissolve the marriage judicially in the absence of a legal ground.[140] The *qāḍīs* confirmed the different kinds of *ṭalāq* divorces on the wife's application as far as their validity had been proven to their satisfaction. The question of initiative or of the exploitation of weak spots in the *ṭalāq* mechanism by the wife, as in the case of suspended divorces, did not trouble them.

(i) Delegated Repudiation

As regards delegated repudiation (*tafwiḍ al-ṭalāq*), which, as stated, is the most striking manifestation of the wife's freedom of divorce, the *qāḍīs* did not depart from the formal conception that this sophisticated type of divorce is a form of *ṭalāq* not impairing the husband's sovereignty. They seemed to think that it was a legitimate device and that all that was required of the wife in order for her to obtain her freedom by it was to prove that she had indeed been delegated the power to divorce herself, either in the marriage contract or in a special agreement subsequent to the marriage, that the husband had fulfilled the condition of the conditional delegation (and thereby given her the right to divorce herself), and lastly, that she had divorced herself in the manner required by law.

Shaykh Ṭāhir Ḥamād sometimes encouraged the estranged spouses to use the mechanism of delegated repudiation, probably as a last resort short of actual divorce.[141] At the same time the author did not encounter an instance of a *qāḍī* encouraging the wife, through the *ma'dhūn* or otherwise, to assure herself freedom of divorce by a stipulation in the marriage contract.

(ii) "Renunciation Divorces" and "Compensation Divorces"

It seems that dissolution by agreement between the parties was the type of divorce most acceptable and convenient to the *qāḍīs*. *Ṭalāq* under these circumstances was not arbitrary; it did not involve any infringement of the ban on divorce against the wife's will and thus did not embarrass the *qāḍī* by a conflict between the religious-legal and the secular-legal norms; it did not require him to exercise his discretion as to whether to permit or prohibit the divorce. All that was really required of him was to give an official stamp in the shape of a judgment to the agreement reached by the parties or to certify that the divorce was operative when the agreed condition of suspended repudiation had been fulfilled.[142] As regards the mechanism, it is little more than a kind of agreement for arbitration concerning the dissolution of the marriage. This mechanism was very much to the liking of the *qāḍīs,* who refrained as far as possible from applying the law. The *qāḍīs'* influence on the contents of the agreement seems to have been limited. The spouses usually came to court after agreeing on the terms; they sometimes brought a text properly drawn up and signed. In one case, it was agreed between the parties that the wife, after marrying another man, should compensate the former husband. Although this was a departure from the *shar'i khul,* Shaykh Tawfīq 'Asaliyya held that "mutual agreement is stronger than the *qāḍī" (al-tarāḍī yaghlib al-qāḍī).*[143]

(b) Judicial Dissolution

Only in judicial dissolutions did the *qāḍīs* refer to the question of dissolution on the wife's initiative. Considerable importance attaches to the manner in which they interpreted the grounds (widely or narrowly), and different attitudes were indeed adopted by them as to some of the new grounds provided by the Ottoman legislator (but not as to Knesset legislation). Their attitudes in this matter were determined by religious-legal reasoning, school affiliation, and by social factors.

(i) Defects and Diseases of the Husband

The main difficulty in applying grounds of disease or defect in the husband seems to lie in the fact that they are based on provisions not emanating from the Ḥanafī school. Shaykh Ḥasan Amīn al-Ḥabash dismissed, for various reasons, all suits women filed with him for dissolution of their marriages on these grounds.[144] These dismissals were probably due to opposition in principle. The *Sharī'a* Court of Appeal intervened several times in Shaykh Ḥasan's decisions concerning the application of the aforesaid grounds. Thus, in one case, it pointed out to him that he should have applied Article 123 of the Family Rights Law, which deals expressly with mental illness, and not

Article 120, which deals with defects in a general way. It is difficult to assume that the *qāḍī* had overlooked Article 123. It seems more likely that he applied Article 120 because its provisions conform with the view of the Ḥanafī school, which does not count the husband's mental illness among the grounds for dissolution.[145]

Shaykh Mūsā al-Ṭabarī was willing to consider the wife's suit for dissolution on one of the said grounds, but he frequently proceeded in accordance with the teachings of the Ḥanafī school. Thus, for instance, he did not trouble to examine beforehand, as required by Article 121, whether the husband's impotence was temporary, curable, or permanent. In all cases of this kind that were brought before him he gave the husband a year's respite in the hope that the defect would disappear.[146] On the other hand, as regards mental illness, he strictly followed the provisions of Article 123.[147]

Shaykh Ḥusnī al-Zu'bī carefully observed the provisions of the Family Rights Law, uninhibited by the teachings of any school.[148] In one case, he indeed deviated from the provisions of Article 121, but not for any religious-legal reason. The wife had charged the husband with impotence after she had borne him one child; the husband was given respite three times at his request. The *qāḍī* gave effect to an agreement reached between the parties on the intervention of village notables that the wife should return to the husband's home "for the last time" for three months, and if there was no improvement in his performance during that period the marriage should be dissolved by the court. A medical institution found that his condition was incurable, and the *qāḍī* dissolved the marriage.[149] This deviation from the provisions of Article 121 is another indication that the *sharī'a* courts were disinclined to apply the full force of the law when the dispute could be settled by agreement between the parties.

Shaykh Ḥusnī al-Zu'bī and also Shaykhs Amīn Qāsim Mudlij and Tawfīq Maḥmūd 'Asaliyya recognized the husband's mental illness as a ground for dissolution, as provided in Article 123 of the Family Rights Law.[150] Shaykh Amīn expressly recognized the wife's right to dissolve the marriage where the husband suffered from an illness likely to cause injury (*ḍarar*) to her; he probably had in mind Article 122. He took the trouble to add that this right was granted her by the *sharī'a,* quoting the modern legal commentator al-Abayānī in evidence. The same *qāḍī* dismissed a husband's application for dissolution on the ground of mental illness of the wife with the argument that the grounds provided by the Family Rights Law were intended for the protection of the wife only, since the husband was able to protect himself by *ṭalāq.*[151]

(ii) Dissolution of Marriage to an Absent Husband

The *qāḍīs* were divided as to the dissolution of the marriage of the wife of an absent husband. Some were loath to apply Articles 126 and 127 for religious-legal, technical-procedural and other reasons, some applied them unhesitatingly and some even stretched the grounds provided by them far beyond their original meaning. The question of the wives of absent husbands was discussed as early on as the first *qāḍīs'* conference in 1950, when it was decided to adjourn the discussion until the Muslim Division of the Ministry of Religious Affairs had clarified how information as to the whereabouts of the husbands might be obtained from Arab governments.[152] The *qāḍīs* again discussed the matter on July 18, 1951, when it was decided that the court should dissolve the marriage of a wife left without maintenance after the following procedure; the court, through the Muslim Division, should forward a notice of the wife's application for dissolution to the Red Cross, which should see that it was transmitted to the husband; and if within three months from the delivery of the notice to the Red Cross the husband did not provide maintenance to the wife—himself or through another—the court would regard this as evidence of "inability to obtain maintenance from him . . . after making the necessary inquiries," within the meaning of Article 126 of the Family Rights Law.[153] This decision was ilberal from the point of view of the wife. It emphasized non-provision of maintenance in the spirit of the Ottoman reform.

The arrangement with the Red Cross did not work. An attempt to transmit the notices to the husbands *via* the mixed armistice commissions also failed. Except for isolated cases, the members of the Arab delegations refused to co-operate.[154] The problem soon arose again, this time in all its poignancy. The reason was seemingly a technical-procedural one, but behind it were fundamental differences between the *qāḍīs*. On the strength of a custom dating from the Ottoman period (the legal basis for which had lapsed since the establishment of the *Sharī'a* Court of Appeal during the Mandate), the head of the *Sharī'a* Court of Appeal, Shaykh Ṭāhir al-Ṭabarī, directed that every judgment for divorce under Article 126 of the Family Rights Law should be referred to the *Sharī'a* Court in Jerusalem for confirmation prior to execution. This direction was issued following a series of such judgments by the *Sharī'a* Court of Jaffa. The *Sharī'a* Court of Appeal set aside one of those judgments and declared that Article 126 required the court to conduct the necessary inquiries about the absent husband itself and not to content itself with the publication of a notice of the legal proceedings in the Israeli Press, because, under existing circumstances, while the country was at war, the husband was unable to appear in court and answer the wife's contentions. Shaykh Ṭāhir al-Ṭabarī held that Article 126 of the Family Rights Law was applicable only during a period of peace and voluntary absence of the husband, but not during a period of war, armistice or forced absence, when it was impossible to make the necessary inquiries as to the husband's whereabouts. As for the absent man's wife, he suggested that she earn her own living or ask assistance from welfare institutions.[155]

Shaykh Ḥasan Amīn al-Ḥabash also opposed application of Articles 126 and 127. Although he was a party to the abovementioned *qāḍīs'* decision of July 18, 1951, he somehow always dismissed applications for dissolution on formal or technical grounds, such as inability to give notice (*tabligh*) to the husband in an Arab country.[156] In one case, a woman whose husband had been absent for many years asked for dissolution in reliance on the closing passage of Article 127. She contended that more than a year had passed since the signing of the armistice agreement and that the fighters and prisoners of war were supposed to have returned home. The *qāḍī* dismissed the suit on the ground that "the Arabs of Palestine, in addition to the Arab countries, are still fighting both in practice and theory and have not returned to their homeland, which is under Israeli rule, and peace has not been concluded, an armistice not being peace . . ." and in reliance on the aforesaid judgment of the *Sharīʻa* Court of Appeal.[157] It seems that all the technical reasons for the dismissal of the suits were merely intended to cover up opposition in principle to the application of provisions contrary to the view of the Ḥanafī school. As for the wife, Shaykh Ḥasan suggested that she join the husband or ask for his admission to Israel under the family reunion scheme.[158]

Shaykh Mūsā al-Ṭabarī at first held that Articles 126 and 127 could not be applied because of the state of war between Israel and its neighbours, and in any case he believed that there were no laws in Israel allowing the dissolution of the marriage of a deserted wife. Referring to Shaykh Ṭāhir Ḥamād's dissolution decisions, he complained that the laws of the *sharīʻa* were transgressed and that some of the women added sin to transgression by living maritally with men other than their husbands (*i.e.*, remarried after the first marriage had been dissolved), whereas chaste women "expect early salvation from God. . . ."[159] In one case, he decided that if the absent husband was found he would have to divorce the wife at her request, and in another case he held that the husband would have to pay maintenance to the wife, and if he was unable to do so, divorce her.[160] On the other hand, in judgments rendered a few years later, this *qāḍī* did not hesitate to dissolve the marriage of the wives of absent husbands.[161]

Shaykh Ṭāhir Ḥamād and Shaykh Ḥusnī al-Zuʻbī showed exceptional liberalism toward the wife in that they were inclined to widen the ground for dissolution under Article 126 by the inclusion of new elements. Shaykh Ṭāhir held that the court should grant full relief to the wife. He said that although the article was contrary to the teaching of the Ḥanafī school, the court should apply it because it was in the nature of a Sulṭānic decree, which must be obeyed by order of the *fuqahā'* (specialists in the science of the *sharīʻa*).[162] The wife, he thought, was not required to join the husband because there was more than *masāfat al-qaṣr* between them, and moreover, if she did so she would be liable to hardship and humiliation. He also dismissed the contention that Article 126 was inapplicable in wartime because the *tabligh* could not be effected then. He said that the principal element in that article was non-provision of maintenance and that the wife could not be expected to support herself or to ask assistance from welfare institutions. The distinction between peacetime and voluntary absence on the one hand and war, armistice or forced absence on the other was irrelevant. Lastly, Shaykh Ṭahīr rejected as without legal foundation the practice of referring the dissolution of marriages of deserted wives to the *Sharī'a* Court of Appeal for confirmation.[163] This liberal attitude was also reflected in his judgments.[164] In fact, he recognized non-provision of maintenance as a ground for dissolution even when the husband had been located and negotiations had been conducted with him but it had been proven to the *qāḍī*'s satisfaction that he had no property in Israel. The reasons Shaykh Ṭahīr gave for this decision were that maintenance judgments of Israeli courts were unenforceable in Arab countries and that the state of war between Israel and its neighbours did not permit the husband either to come to Israel to pay maintenance or to legally send maintenance payments to Israel.[165]

For some time, Shaykh Ṭahīr followed the directives contained in the *qāḍīs'* resolution of July 18, 1951, whereby, in his opinion, he was fulfilling his obligation to "carry out the necessary inquiries" within the meaning of Article 126.[166] He said that the government had done all it could in the matter; he put the blame on the Arab members of the armistice commissions, who had refused to co-operate.[167] But he soon ceased trying to send notices to the husbands through these bodies and contended himself with publishing notices in the local Press; and when the husband did not appear in court within 30 days to answer the claim he pronounced the dissolution of the marriage.[168] At a later period he did not even publish a notice but contented himself with the wife's statement on oath and confirming testimonies that the husband had gone abroad without leaving her maintenance.[169] It is probably no accident that more than half of the judgments of *sharī'a* courts dissolving the marriages of wives of absent husbands were given by Shaykh Ṭahir. It seems that he acquired a reputation for leniency in this domain as against the more severe attitude of other *qāḍīs;* in fact, women from the areas of jurisdiction of other *sharī'a* courts would apply to him in such matters.[170] Not a single application to him for dissolution of a marriage to an absent husband was refused.

Shaykh Ḥusnī al-Zu'bī also granted almost every application of this kind. He was not punctilious as to the "necessary inquiries" concerning the husband's whereabouts, and performed this obligation by publishing a notice in the local Press. Although he was usually careful to note in his judgments that it had proven impossible to collect maintenance from the husband, he seemed to think that the injury (*ḍarar*) caused to the wife by the husband's absence was a more, or at any rate not less, important element of the ground for dissolution under Article 126 than non-provision of maintenance.[171] In one case, the allegation of injury arose in connection with the husband's imprisonment. After dissolution under Article 126, it suddenly appeared that the husband was in prison in Israel, and the *qāḍī* rescinded the dissolution at his request. The wife again applied for dissolution, this time on the grounds of non-provision of maintenance and injury caused during the husband's absence in an Arab country and during his imprisonment. Shaykh Ḥusnī granted the application, holding that the husband's imprisonment was tantamount to absence without providing maintenance within the meaning of Article 126. The wife was also, in his opinion, entitled to dissolution if the husband had been absent for over a year even if he had left property for her upkeep, because the wife's being alone for such a long time was contrary to human nature and intolerable.[172] In sum, Shaykh Ṭāhir Ḥamād and Shaykh Ḥusnī al-Zu'bī, by their liberal interpretations, gave a wider meaning to the ground for dissolution under Article 126. Whereas the Ottoman legislator had meant only non-provision of maintenance to the wife of an absent husband, they had included new elements: non-provision of maintenance in cases where the husband had been traced and contacted in another country, and injury caused to the wife by the husband's absence and imprisonment. These elements are unknown to the Ḥanafī school, but are each recognized as an independent ground for dissolution in the modern legislation of several Muslim states.[173]

Shaykh Tawfīq 'Asaliyya and Shaykh Amīn Qāsim Mudlij applied Article 126 without any inhibitions, religious-legal or other, though not in quite the same way. The former insisted on fulfilment of all the conditions imposed by that article,[174] while the latter did not exert himself unduly making inquiries about the husband's whereabouts; he generally contented himself with the wife's testimony and the oaths of witnesses as proof of the husband's absence and of the non-provision of maintenance.[175] It is true that in more recent years, Shaykh Amīn was accustomed to certify to the wife that she was a *mahjūra* (deserted wife) and that this status did not involve a dissolution of her marriage, but he did so at the wife's request.

The differences between the *qāḍīs* as to the interpretation and application of Article 126 remained unsettled. The opposition of some *qāḍīs* to its application was probably due to their zealous adherence to the Ḥanafī school. In the absence of a supreme *shar'ia* authority in Israel there was no-one who might have been asked to decide the matter. Following the setting aside by the *Sharī'a* Court of Appeal of a judgment of Shaykh Ṭāhir Ḥamād dissolving a marriage to an absent husband, there were several inquiries to the President of the Jordanian *Sharī'a* Court of Appeal, *inter alia*, as to whether there was a legal basis for the direction forbidding *sharī'a* courts to apply Article 126 on the ground that it was impossible to make the "necessary inquiries" in wartime; whether the criterion of dissolution was the making of the necessary inquiries (as asserted by the *Sharī'a* Court of Appeal) or the impossibility of obtaining maintenance (as held by Shaykh Ṭāhir Ḥamād); and what was the procedure in Jordan concerning the dissolution of a marriage to an absent husband on the ground of impossibility of obtaining maintenance. Shaykh Mūsā al-Ṭabarī asked that the Jordanian Law of Family Rights be adopted so that *sharī'a* courts in Israel might apply it in regard to wives of absent husbands. No reply to those and other questions has yet been received from Jordan.[176]

The *Sharī'a* Court of Appeal had another opportunity to deal with the issue in 1958. Shaykh Ḥasan Amīn al-Ḥabash dismissed the wife's action for dissolution in reliance on previous decisions of the Court of Appeal, while Shaykh Ṭāhir Ḥamād held that there was no legal obligation at all to refer the judgment to the Court of Appeal for confirmation.[177] The question was thus not decided. Since then, the *qāḍīs* practically ceased to refer their judgments in matters of marriages to absent husbands to the Court of Appeal. Every *qāḍī* dealt with the matter in accordance with his social and religious philosophy, and, as has been seen, the legal consequences of the case depended on the venue.

A problem also arose over the divorce of wives who had gone to an Arab country and could not be served with the notice (*tabligh*) of divorce. This question occupied the *qāḍīs* especially in the early years of the state. Shaykh Ḥasan Amīn al-Ḥabash held that *tabligh* was essential to the completeness of the divorce.[178] Shaykh Ṭāhir Ḥamād and Shaykh Mūsā al-Ṭabarī decided that the divorce should be registered whether or not *tabligh* was possible; a circular to this effect was issued by the Muslim Division, ordering that the certificate of divorce be kept by the court "until required"; the *qāḍīs* acted accordingly.[179]

(iii) Discord and Incompatibility

As to the application of Article 130 of the Family Rights Law, the *qāḍīs* were at variance on two basic points: the power of the arbitrators to dissolve the marriage and the circumstances under which a family council might be established. Some *qāḍīs* were unwilling to apply the article properly, apparently because of their adherence to the Ḥanafī school, whereas others applied it unhesitatingly in accordance with the conception of the Mālikī school. Shaykh Ṭāhir al-Ṭabarī and Shaykh Ḥasan Amīn al-Ḥabash confirmed dissolution by arbitrators only if effected in the way determined by the Ḥanafī school, *i.e.,* if the spouses had empowered the arbitrators in advance to perform it.[180] Shaykh Ḥasan held that Article 130 was not applied by the *sharī'a* courts during the Mandate and that its application by the courts in Israel was unwarranted. In one case, he stopped arbitration proceedings because, in his opinion, the arbitrators had strayed "from the ancient path," and ordered obedience, probably for fear that they might decide on dissolution.[181] In another case, the *Sharī'a* Court of Appeal set aside his judgment dismissing the wife's demand for arbitration.[182]

Shaykh Amīn Qāsim Mudlij expressly declared that a condition for dissolution by arbitrators was that the husband empower the arbitrator serving on his behalf to pronounce *ṭalāq* or *khul* if efforts at reconciliation should fail and that the wife empower the arbitrator serving on her behalf to pay the husband monetary compensation in that event. In one case, he ordered obedience because the wife refused to appoint a family council "for purposes of reconciliation." On another occasion, he expressed the view that where reconciliation was impossible the Ḥanafī school saw no need to appoint arbitrators because the *qāḍīs* themselves acted in that capacity before giving judgment.[183] Shaykh Mūsā al-Ṭabarī changed his attitude in this matter in the course of time. He at first adopted the mechanism devised by the Ḥanafī school and afterward applied Article 130 properly.[184] But other *qāḍīs* were not inhibited by adherence to a particular school of law from applying Article 130. Most noteworthy in this respect was Shaykh Ṭāhir Ḥamād. He considered that in cases of discord and incompatibility the provisions of this article should be followed and not those of Article 210 of Qadri's collection, which is based on the Ḥanafī school. He argued that "the Sulṭān of the Muslims chose and confirmed it [the article] because it agrees with one of the four schools, and directed that judgment should be given in accordance with it; and obedience to his command is a *shar'i* duty, as explained by Ibn Ābidīn; and judgments in accordance with other provisions, prescribed by other schools, are contrary to *shar'i* duty." In one judgment, he remarked incidentally in this connection that "the [Ottoman] legislator did not transgress the bounds of the Muslim *sharī'a*."[185] In other words, he suggested that the four orthodox schools had equal standing and that inter-school mobility of the *qāḍī* was permitted and even required by virtue of the *siyāsa* (policy) principle.

Shaykh Ḥusnī al-Zu'bī also did not shrink from resorting to the mechanism of arbitration created by Article 130. He was accustomed to confirm the arbitrators' awards, whether the result was *tafriq* or something else[186]; when sitting in appeals, he did not hesitate to set aside judgments of other *qṭḍīs* which deviated from the provisions of Article 130 or to dismiss appeals against *tafriq* judgments validly given.[187] Nor did the judgments of Shaykh Tawfīq 'Asaliyya suggest in any way that dissolution required advanced authorization by the parties. He instructed the arbitrators to settle the dispute between the parties "peacefully or by *tafriq*."[188] The circumstances of "discord and incompatibility" (*nizā' washiqāq*) in which arbitration may be applied tended to be defined by most of the *qāḍīs* within the limited framework of the matrimonial obligations and rights of the spouses. Thus, Shaykh Amīn Qāsim Mudlij held that where the spouses fulfilled their mutual matrimonial duties there was no basis at all for arbitration. Where the wife refused without just cause to live with the husband she not only could not invoke Article 130 but was considered rebellious; she could not contend that the husband had quarrelled with her since he was not a party to the dispute; the husband, on other hand, might demand a judgment for obedience. Again, Shaykh Amīn said that where the wife fulfilled all her matrimonial duties toward the husband, his demand for application of Article 130 was disregarded and he was considered a rebel against her rights and ordered to pay maintenance. In Shaykh Amīn's opinion, Article 130 could only be applied where the wife refused to comply with an order for obedience and might be declared rebellious, or where the husband refused to comply with an order for maintenance and the wife was in danger of incurring injury (*ḍarar*).[189] The restriction of the possibility of dissolution to cases in which the defendant did not fulfil his or her obligations to the plaintiff and the orthodox legal remedies had been exhausted, had no basis in Article 130.

Shaykh Ḥasan Amīn al-Ḥabash decided in an appeal that there had been no basis for appointing arbitrators and that the matter before the court of first instance had not been a dispute between the parties but a question of maintenance. He set aside the judgment for dissolution and returned the case to the lower court for further consideration of the maintenance claim although that court had held that there was a serious dispute between the spouses which required arbitration.[190]

Shaykh Ḥusnī al-Zu'bī and Shaykh Tawfīq 'Asaliyya also tended to interpret the term "discord" in the limited context of matrimonial rights.[191] At the same time, the former sometimes departed from this line when he was convinced that there was no point in preserving the marriage. Thus, in one case, when the wife sued for maintenance and the husband for obedience, he reached the conclusion that the rift between the spouses was fundamental and could not be healed, and appointed a family council on his own initiative. In another case, when the wife sued for maintenance and the husband rejected the claim and applied for the appointment of a council of arbitrators, he granted the husband's application.[192]

Shaykh Ṭāhir Ḥamād was the only *qāḍī* who gave a wide interpretation of the circumstances under which the mechanism of arbitration might be applied. He held that "discord" was not necessarily a *mutual* action or attitude of the spouses. In his opinion, a hostile attitude of one spouse toward the other was sufficient to warrant resort to arbitration, and the attempt to interpret "discord" within the narrow context of matrimonial rights contradicted the general meaning of the term. Moreover, he held that Article 130 gave the *qāḍī* absolute discretion to appoint arbitrators even where only one of the spouses wished it.[193] This approach was reflected in many judgments for dissolution in reliance on Article 130.[194] In almost all cases, Shaykh Ṭāhir appointed arbitrators when his attempts at reconciliation had failed.[195] He sometimes appointed arbitrators on his own initiative.[196] In appeals, he would set aside judgments of courts of first instance which deviated in the matter of arbitration from the provisions of Article 130 as he interpreted them.[197] By this attitude, he consciously or unconsciously helped to turn arbitration into a refined instrument of dissolution by the wife in cases of cruelty and injury to her non-provision of maintenance to her and the children, disputes in consequence of exchange marriages, social or cultural incompatibility between the spouses, and so forth. As stated, some of these achievements were recently recognized by parliamentary legislation of several Arab countries as new grounds for judicial dissolution.

(iv) Dissolution of the Marriage of a Girl Under 17

It seems that the *qāḍīs,* contrary to the expectations of the Knesset, were unwilling to recognize the bride's being under 17 as a ground for dissolution, seeing that it was not so recognized by Islamic law. On the other hand, they did not oppose the application of the penal sanction attached to contraventions of the Age of Marriage Law. The first *qaḍīs'* conference in 1950 resolved unanimously that dissolution by the court must be based on "express religious-legal law laid down by the Ḥanafī school save in so far as it conflicts with [secular] law." Shaykh Ṭahīr Ḥamād expressed the opinion that a marriage must not be dissolved on this ground because this was contrary to Islamic law and also because it was likely to cause damage. He suggested upholding the validity of the marriage and replacing dissolution with the imposition of blood-money (*diya*) or a substitute payment (*badal*); this would leave both the marriage and the law intact. Shaykh Tawfīq Mahmūd 'Asaliyya declared that he tried as hard as he could to avoid dissolving marriages of girls under 17 "with a view to protecting the offspring." In doing so; he acted, in his opinion, in accordance with the spirit of both the *sharī'a* and the secular legislator, since the parties were liable to the penal sanction prescribed by law.[198] The attitude of the *qāḍīs* is not reflected in judgments, which means that the matter was of no practical concern to them.[199]

(v) Termination of Irregular or Void Marriage

The *qāḍīs* were not always alive to the reforms introduced by the Family Rights Law in the classification of irregular and void marriages and continued to follow the rigorous precepts of the Ḥanafī school in this matter. Thus, in one case, Shaykh Ṭāhir Ḥamād decided that the "marriage" of a woman already married to another man was void, although according to the Ottoman legislator it was merely irregular.[200] Such deviations are, of course, significant as to the legal consequences for the woman and her children.

Effects of Divorce

(a) Triple Repudiation and Revocable Divorce

The declared position of the *qāḍīs* as to triple repudiation is indicated by their attitude toward the Egyptian Personal Status Bill of 1966, which would have provided that successive repudiation, *i.e.,* repudiation pronounced in one session with the force of two or three separate repudiations, should be considered a single repudiation. Shaykh Ṭāhir Ḥamād and Shaykh Tawfīq 'Asaliyya opposed the suggested reform in reliance on the various sources of religious law. Shaykh Ḥusnī al-Zu'bī and Shaykh Amīn Qāsim Mudlij welcomed it and found support for it in the teachings of non-Ḥanafī schools and in other sources.[201] Anyhow, the *qāḍīs'* attitude in this matter as displayed in practice was generally orthodox traditional. They blindly confirmed every triple repudiation that came their way.[202] They did not refer in any manner to the damage likely to be caused by this kind of divorce to the wife, the family and even the husband. They admitted no normative difference between three repudiations pronounced separately and a triple repudiation, pronounced on a single occasion. Their distinction between these two was purely technical in the case of separate repudiations they counted the times that the wife had already been repudiated and noted how many repudiations the husband still had left, and when three had been performed, they noted this fact and drew the couple's attention to the requirement of an intermediate marriage.[203] They did not try to influence the definition of the type of divorce or to mitigate the legal consequences.

Only once did one of the *qāḍīs,* Shaykh Tawfīq 'Asaliyya, make an exception in order to accommodate a couple who asked for a triple repudiation to be annulled on the plea that it had been performed in a fit of anger. He granted the application, *inter alia,* on the ground that "*ṭalāq* requires soundness of the mental faculties, and the continuance of married life is better than its discontinuance . . . and the *ṭalāq* was performed at a single session, contrary to what should be the practice according to the *sharī'a,* and there is someone who says that three repudiations performed at one and the same time have the effect of a single repudiation. . . ."[204] In other words, the *qāḍī*'s decision was based on legal and social grounds. This was, in fact, a bold attempt to rely on the opinion of an individual Islamic jurist who, contrary to the orthodox schools, did not recognize the validity of triple repudiation.

The *qāḍīs'* indifference to triple repudiation is particularly surprising in view of the pains they sometimes took to prevent ordinary divorce. They possibly did not treat triple repudiation very severely because the requirement of an intermediate marriage was usually circumvented by a fictitious marriage or some other device. In fact, at least Shaykh Mūsā al-Ṭabarī lent his hand to such a circumvention. The case has been described of a fictitious intermediate marriage obviously designed to permit the woman to her first husband; surprisingly enough, this *qāḍī* did not reject outright the woman's attempt to get round the legal requirement although the stratagem was quite transparent. He confirmed dissolution of the intermediate marriage, acquiescing in the ruse.[205] In other words, an important contribution of the *qāḍīs* in the matter of triple repudiation may consist, not in their having denied its validity or mitigated its legal consequences, but in having helped to circumvent the requirement of an intermediate marriage through conscious or unconscious disregard of the fiction involved.

Revocable divorce did not often occupy the *qāḍīs,* and its handling did not as a rule deviate from orthodox doctrine.[206] Still, their attitude was less formal to it than to triple repudiation; they sometimes made an effort to mitigate the consequences of the divorce and to help the couple to rebuild their marriage, provided the husband regretted his hasty action. This is seen especially in cases where the husband contended that he had divorced the wife in a fit of anger.[207] In one case, the husband had used a formula particularly expressive of finality: "You are divorced; no Ḥanafī, no Shāfi'i, no Mālikī and no Ḥanbalī, no demon and no devil shall bring you back." He claimed that he had said this in a very angry mood, and Shaykh Ṭāhir Ḥamād decided that the wife was revocably divorced; he added that that formula was "foolishness, not to be taken seriously from a *shar'i* point of view.[208]

In many cases in which a marriage to an absent husband was dissolved by reason of non-provision of maintenance, the *qāḍīs,* and especially Shaykh Ṭāhir Ḥamād, decided that the dissolution was equivalent to a revocable divorce.[209] This was in deviance from the provisions of Article 131 of the Family Rights Law, which provides that judicial dissolution is to be treated as irrevocable divorce. The Mālikī school recognizes non-provision of maintenance as a ground for dissolution equivalent to revocable divorce: the husband may have the wife back if during the *'idda* he proves to the satisfaction of the court that he is able and willing to support her.[210]

(b) Maintenance During the Waiting-Period and Compensation to Divorced Women

The *shar'i* law of maintenance is adapted to the structure of the patriarchal family, in which a woman is completely exempt from the care for her own maintenance. After a divorce, she returns to her father's or brother's house or remarries as soon as possible, so that the responsibility for her livelihood passes to other men.[211] Maintenance during the waiting-period (*'idda*) is without functional significance; unlike, for instance, deferred dower, it is not designed to afford economic security to the divorced wife or to act as a deterrent to divorce. The waiting-period has two purposes: to provide certainty as to the identity of the natural father in the event of pregnancy and to enable the revocably divorced wife to be reinstated without need for the contraction of a new marriage, the payment of dower, etc.; and as the wife remains in the husband's house during the waiting-period, he meanwhile continues in any case to be responsible for her maintenance. But in view of the changes in the structure of the family and the social status of women in recent times, when a divorced wife does not necessarily return to her father's house or remarry and her upkeep becomes more and more her own affair, maintenance begins to be appreciated in economic terms: it now has functional significance as a means to secure her economic position. It follows that maintenance for three months, which is generally the waiting-period of a non-pregnant woman, does not ensure a decent living to a divorced wife who wishes to be independent or who has no relatives required or able to provide for her.

To what extent were the *qāḍīs* alive to this problem and did they give their minds to improving the position of divorced women? The attitude of Shaykah Ḥasan Amīn al-Ḥabash and Shaykh Ḥusnī al-Zu'bī in this matter was radical to the point of explicit deviation from religious law. As against this, the other *qāḍīs* did not deviate from the traditional religious-legal conception. At a *qāḍīs'* conference in 1963, measures were discussed to ensure the position and rights of the divorced woman. Shaykh Ḥasan Amīn al-Ḥabash expressed the view that it was the court's "most sacred duty" to protect her rights. In his opinion, the problem was not her right to maintenance during the waiting-period but how to ensure to her "a decent life until her death or until God prescribed a way for her," *i.e.,* until she remarried.[212] He recently expressed the belief that the problem required a radical solution by Knesset legislation: a man who divorced his wife should not only be liable to the penal sanction but should be *ordered* to compensate her rather than left to do so voluntarily. He did not regard compensation to a divorced wife as conflicting with religious law since in his opinion there was no express provision in the *sharī'a* forbidding it. He considered that the provision prescribing compensation should be treated as based on the doctrine of *siyāsa* (policy), as a provision of state law intended to supplement the *sharī'a.*[213] Shaykh Ḥusnī al-Zu'bī suggested specifically that a provision should be enacted, by an amendment to Section 7 of the Penal Law Amendment (Bigamy) Law, 5719-1959, or to the Criminal Code Ordinance to the effect that a man must compensate his divorced wife in accordance with the circumstances of the case or until she remarries.[214]

Shaykh Ṭāhir Ḥamād and Shaykh Amīn Qāsim Mudlij, on the other hand, were strongly opposed to any deviation from the duty of maintenance imposed on the husband by Islamic law. They rejected the proposal to require him to pay the wife maintenance until she remarried on the ground that it was contrary to the *sharī'a*. Shaykh Ṭāhir held that Islamic law "has left nothing, great or small, without an express provision (*naṣṣ*) for it in the law books." There was no need, in his opinion, to change the law of maintenance because "Qur'ānic legislation is suitable for every time and place." He saw only one way to increase the amount of maintenance to a divorced woman, *viz.*, by agreement between the parties. Moreover, he insisted that if the wife neglected to file a claim for maintenance before the expiration of the waiting-period she would lose her right to it, as prescribed by Islamic law.

Shaykh Amīn Qāsim Mudlij's attitude to the question of the maintenance of a divorced woman was rooted in the traditional view that there is a close connection between maintenance and the existence of the marriage. On the expiration of the waiting-period, the wife leaves the husband's *'isma* completely and there is no longer any reason to require him to pay maintenance. He saw this view confirmed by the absence of maintenance out of the estate in Islamic law, that is to say, in the fact that a widow is not entitled to obtain maintenance out of the husband's estate. Another argument advanced by him was that "by the nature of things, when her *'idda* is over, she passes to another husband, who will provide her maintenance." On the other hand, a man should not, in Shaykh Amīn's opinion, be ordered to pay maintenance to his divorced wife until she remarries because this may take 20 years and he may thus suffer damage. He suggested referring the question of the divorced woman's maintenance to the court, which was to proceed in accordance with the principles of dissolution by arbitration, that is to say, the rights of the parties were to be determined by distinguishing between the party responsible for the dissolution and the injured party. He said that the courts were accustomed to settle the question of maintenance before deciding on divorce and to delay judgment until the parties had reached agreement as to the amount of maintenance or the latter had been fixed by experts. At a *qaḍīs'* conference in 1963, it was in fact decided that on giving a judgment for *talāq* the court might adjudicate the rights of the divorced woman in accordance with an agreement between the parties or [in the absence of such an agreement] "at the court's discretion in accordance with the circumstances of the case," and that the court should remind the *ma'dhūns* to clearly indicate in the marriage contract the stipulations ensuring the wife's rights, such as compensation (*ta'wīḍ*) on divorce in accordance with the circumstances of the case or as fixed by the court.[215] Wide discretion of the *qāḍī* as to the divorced woman's rights permits him to award maintenance or fix compensation over and above maintenance for the waiting-period, and he is in fact guided in this matter, consciously or unconsciously, by his social philosophy.

From the evidence of the *qāḍīs* it is doubtful whether, in introducing such a radical reform, the *shar'i* basis of which is slight, in the status of women, the *qāḍīs* actually drew encouragement from the fact that a similar reform had been introduced in several Arab countries by way of secular legislation.[216] Their decision was probably intended to confirm a social custom established in several areas, especially in the Little Triangle villages, of compensating a divorced woman. Shaykh Ḥusnī al-Zu'bī explained that the idea was that the court should be competent, when confirming a divorce, to adjudicate the rights of the woman and that the rate of maintenance should, in the absence of agreement between the parties, be fixed by experts "having regard to the interest of the woman and to every other right arising out of the divorce in the circumstances of the case (in accordance with my basic proposal)," with a view to doing justice to the woman.[217] He did not make it clear to what "basic proposal" he was referring, but, as stated, above he was credited with two proposals in this connection: compensation to the woman by the enactment of a binding provision of secular law and assurance of maintenance to her until her remarriage. Both proposals deviate from the religious law of maintenance. Shaykh Ḥasan Amīn al-Ḥabash gave to understand that the decision was intended to enable the *qāḍī*, in the absence of agreement between the parties, to pronounce on the wife's rights when confirming the divorce, whereas until then the wife had in this case been compelled to file a separate claim for her rights.[218] At a *qāḍīs'* conference in 1966, it was decided to make provision, when drawing up the marriage contract, for deferred dower in addition to prompt dower so that it might serve as security to the wife in the event of divorce or widowhood and as a deterrent to hasty divorce by the husband.[219]

A *qāḍīs'* conference is not a statutory institution competent to decide questions of the material law applicable to *sharī'a* courts or to enact religious-legal provisions. Nor have its decisions the effect of religious-legal opinions in the orthodox sense of this term, and if the *qāḍīs* took it on themselves to act in accordance with them, they did so voluntarily. In fact, these decisions are meaningful to the extent that they were applied in judgments. Moreover, the decisions concerning the rights of divorced women left wide discretion to the *qāḍīs* to adjudicate "in accordance with the circumstances of the case" as each of them understood them. In other words, each *qāḍī* was guided by his religious-legal and social philosophies.

The *sijills* indeed reveal two diametrically opposed attitudes in this matter, one conservative-formalistic, the other liberal-reformist. The exponents of the former, who were the majority of the *qāḍīs,* insisted on the wife's right to maintenance during the *'idda,* but not beyond it, in strict adherence to religious law. For this very reason, it may be assumed, Shaykh Ṭāhir Ḥamād ordered a man to pay maintenance to his divorced wife although she admitted having been the principal supporter of the family, including her jobless husband.[220] Moreover, they did not shrink from denying a divorced woman's right to maintenance during the *'idda* on some technical *shar'i* ground. Thus, for example, Shaykh Ṭāhir al-Ṭabarī and Shaykh Ṭāhir Ḥamād in some cases dismissed a divorced woman's application for such maintenance for the sole reason that it had been filed after the expiration of the waiting-period, and Shaykh Ṭāhir Ḥamād denied a divorced woman's right because she had left the *bayt al-'idda* and refused to return there.[221] It might happen that a woman at the time of her divorce renounced her right to maintenance for her children and undertook to support them "with her own money," but after a time found herself unable to do so and asked the court to order the father of the children to pay maintenance for them. In all the cases brought before Shaykh Ṭāhir Ḥamād and Shaykh Mūsā al-Ṭabarī, the wife's application was dismissed although she pleaded that she was in distress or had become impoverished after her divorce.[222]

As mentioned, the number of cases when maintenance was awarded to a divorced woman beyond the waiting-period—for life, until remarriage, etc.—was rather limited. It is characteristic that the *qāḍīs* were careful to point out in these circumstances that the husband undertook to pay such maintenance "of his own free will," so as to make it clear that the court did not impose a maintenance arrangement deviating from religious law. This scrupulous observance of the *sharī'a* is particularly noticeable in the judgments of Shaykh Ṭāhir Ḥamād, Shaykh Mūsā al-Ṭabarī and Shaykh Amīn Qāsim Mudlij.[223]

The radical views of Shaykh Ḥasan Amīn al-Ḥabash and Shaykh Ḥusnī al-Zu'bī as to safeguarding the subsistence of divorced women are apparent also in their judgments, although they showed some embarrassment when they awarded benefits beyond those due under religious law. They usually sought to get around this difficulty by various means: in many cases, they represented compensation as a substitute (*badal*) for maintenance for the waiting-period, "whatever its amount may be"; sometimes they added the words "and the other rights connected with the marriage" which were vested in the wife in advance "in a final manner."[224] They might add that the amounts of money to be paid to the wife were "in accordance with our position and that of those like us."[225] This formula is customary in fixing maintenance and denotes that it benefits the economic position of the spouses. But the attempt to equate compensation with maintenance for the waiting-period is out of place since there was often a wide gap between the amount of the latter, which was at most a few hundred Israeli pounds, and that of the former, which sometimes ran to several thousands; the same is the case where property given as compensation included several dunams of land, buildings and the like, the value of which exceeded the usual amount of maintenance.[226]

Moreover, compensation was occasionally equated with maintenance for the waiting-period even where the wife was not entitled to the latter, as where the marriage had not been consummated.[227] The *qāḍīs* seemed to feel uncomfortable when representing compensation as maintenance for the waiting-period, and this is probably why they often made a point of noting that those large amounts were paid "of my own volition and at my own free choice."[228] It indeed seems that in all the cases when a woman received compensation or was assured maintenance beyond the waiting-period this was by mutual agreement without the intervention of the *qāḍī,* who only gave the arrangement the force of a judgment.[229] At the same time, there can be no doubt that the *qāḍīs* were aware of the difference between maintenance for the waiting-period and compensation. They sometimes said that the husband had to pay two amounts: one as maintenance for the waiting-period and the other, larger one, for another purpose, which was really compensation[230] and which now and then they did not hesitate to call by this name without attempting to disguise it.[231] Under these circumstances, compensation was frequently explained as redress for the injury (*ḍarar*) caused to the wife by the divorce.[232] Although the relevant utterances were in the first person, there can be no doubt that Shaykh Ḥasan Amīn al-Ḥabash had a hand in formulating them, and they may represent an attempt to provide a *shar'i* legitimation for a social practice increasingly adopted in the Little Triangle villages.

From this it is clear that the decisions of the *qāḍīs'* conference of 1963 were implemented only in part and only by some of the *qāḍīs.* The author found no confirmation in the *sijills* of Shaykh Amīn Qāsim Mudlij's assertion that the *sharī'a* courts pronounced on the rights of the divorced woman at the same time as they gave judgment concerning the divorce itself. On the contrary, in one case, when the wife claimed various rights at the time the judgment for divorce was given, that *qāḍī* directed her to file a separate action for these rights.[233] The interpretation of the 1963 decision as meaning that the *qāḍī's* discretion is not confined to the wife's *shar'i* rights was applied to a considerable extent by Shaykh Ḥasan Amīn al-Ḥabash only and only in part by other *qāḍīs* and found its expression in compensation to the wife and maintenance beyond the waiting-period. Shaykh Ḥusnī al-Zu'bī declared that compensation and maintenance beyond the waiting-period were assured in advance by stipulations in the marriage contract,[234] but there is no evidence of this in either the *sijills* or in the registers of marriage contracts of the years 1962 and 1968.

Notes and References

1. See Linant de Bellefonds, pp. 321 *seq;* Amīn, pp. 149 *seq.*
2. *FRL,* art. 109, 111-18; *ENFRL;* Qadrī, arts. 226-50, 263. See Linant de Bellefonds, pp. 365 *seq.*, 395 *seq.*; Schacht, pp. 163-4; Anderson, *Islamic Law,* p. 42; Coulson, *History,* pp. 111-12; Levy, p. 121; Goitein and Ben-Shemesh, pp. 136-8, 227-8; Fyzee, pp. 143-51.
3. *E.g.*, "you are thrice divorced from me according to all the schools; neither a shāfi'i nor a Ḥanafī nor another shall bring you back to me"; "*'alayya al-ṭalāq* from you threefold, whenever a Shaykh permits you, a Shaykh shall prohibit you"; "be divorced sixty- and seventyfold"; "be divorced; whenever you are permitted, you shall be prohibited like my sister, according to the four schools of the Muslims"; "you shall never be permitted to me by any school and shall be like my mother and my sister"; "you shall be to me, absolutely, like my mother's back . . ."; "*'alayya al-ḥarām* . . .". See, *e.g.*, *JfQ1*, p. 30: no. 50-f.8/52, p. 53: no. 82-f.54/52; p. 99: no. 159-f.35/53, p. 112: no. 190-f.52/53, p. 247: no. 384-f.17/56; *JfQ3*, p. 5: no. 9-f.88/63, p. 206: no. 339-f.27/66; *JfQ4*, p. 58: no. 54-f.155/67; *ṬbI1*, p. 14: no. 1/16-f.34/50, p. 116: no. 5-f.2/58, p. 131: no. 20-f.26/58, p. 220: no. 15-f.13/63; *NzḤ*15, p. 114; no. 11/166; *NzḤ*20, p. 7: no. 10/101: *NzI4*, p. 51: no. 4/14-f.20/49, p. 156: no. 1/3-f.8/54; *AcṬ2*, p. 68: *AcṬ4*, p. 39: f.4/66. Cf. Granqvist, vol. 2, pp. 273, 275, 279; al-Ārif, p. 133. See Ibn Ābidīn, p. 600; Schacht, pp. 164-5; Fyzee, pp. 154-5.
4. Judicial dissolution has the effect of one irrevocable divorce. See *FRL,* art. 131.
5. See, *e.g.*, *NzI4*, p. 156: no. 1/3-f.8/54; *AcI2*, p. 17: no. 14.
6. See, *e.g.*, *JfQ1*, p.97: no. 155-f.28/53; *JfQ2*, p. 412: no. 579-f.53/59; *ṬbḤ1*, p. 102: no. 1/61; *NzḤI7*, p. 215: no. 16/396; *NzI4*, p. 207: no. 4/7-f.98/60; *AcT3*, p. 237: f.?/62.
7. *JfQ1*, p. 275: no. 424-f.29/57; *JfQ2*, p. 399: no. 559-f.47/59; *NzḤ20*, p. 72: no. 1/63.

8. See, *e.g.*, *JfQ1*, p. 144: no. 243-f.50/54; *ṬbI1*, p. 108: no. 15-f.31/57; *NzḤ18*, p. 253: no. 6/86; *NzI4*, p. 51: no. 4/14-f.20/49, p. 156: no. 1/3-f.8/54.
9. See, *e.g.*, *JfQ2*, p. 426: no. 413-f.79/59; *JfQ4*, p. 147: no. 176-f.118/68; *ṬbI1*, p. 14: no. 1/16-f.34/50, p. 87: no. 6-f.15/56, p. 275: no. 23-f.36/64; *NzḤ*18, p. 182: no. 11/294, p. 190: no. 8/8; *AcI1*, p. 1: no. 1; *AcṬ4*, p. 34: f.25/65.
10. See, *e.g.*, *JfQ4*, p. 165: no. 203-f.49/69; *JfQ5*, p. 102: no. 171-f.258/69; *AcṬ2*, p. 43.
11. See, *e.g.*, *JfQ2*, p. 323: no. 505-f.53/58 (the spouses, "not content with a single divorce, wanted a triple repudiation"); *JfQ3*, p. 306: no. 446-f.144/66, p. 343: no. 480-f.51/67; *AcṬ3*, p. 204: f.8/61; *ṬbḤ2*, p. 53: no. 19; *ṬbI1*, p. 14: no. 1/16-f.34/50.
12. See, *e.g.*, *JfQ2*, p. 527: no. 508-f.62/61; *AcṬ2*, p. 253: f.15/63.
13. *ṬbI1*, p. 116: no. 5-f.2/58.
14. *AcṬ1*, pp. 27-8. There were probably more such cases, which, however, the author was unable to discern because the motive for the divorce (or marriage) was not indicated as it was in this particular case. Cf. Goitein and Ben-Shemesh, p. 137; Granqvist, vol. 2, pp. 281-2; Anderson, *Islamic Law,* pp. 42-3.
15. *NzI4*, p. 54: no. 3/18-f.29/49.
16. Cf. Granqvist, vol. 2, p. 276, and the sources indicated there; Anderson, *Africa,* pp. 167, 213-14, 232, 260, 272, 292.
17. See, *e.g.*, *ṬbI1*, p. 108: no. 15-f.31/57, p. 116: no. 5-f.2/58; *JfQ3*, p. 5: no. 9-f.88/63, p. 11: no. 19-f.77/63; *JfQ4*, p. 67: no. 63-f.17/68 (the couple applied for the triple repudiation to be annulled); *NzI̦I*18, p. 20: no. 21/84; *NzI4*, p. 156: no. 1/3-f.8/54.
18. See, *e.g.*, *JfQ1*, p. 133: no. 224-f.33/54, p. 134: no. 225-f.37/54, p. 247: no. 384-f.17/56, p. 275: no. 424-f.29/57; *NzI4*, p. 52: no. 2/14-f.23/49, p. 125: no. 2/22-f.95/52, p. 147: no. 2/13-f.39/53; *AcṬ4*, p. 1: f.1/64, p. 13: f.26/64, p. 39: f.4/66.
19. See, *e.g.*, *JfQ4*, p. 17: no. 17-f.67/67, *NzḤ*21, p. 173: no. 2/44-f.63/62.
20. See, *e.g.*, *NzḤ*14, p. 18: no. 71; *NzI4*, p. 48: no. 4/6-f.8/49. Cf. Rosenfeld, *Peasants,* p. 129; Anderson, *Africa,* p. 244.
21. See, *e.g.*, *NzḤ*15, p. 127: no. 5/181; *NzḤ*20, p. 24: no. 11/125.
22. *ṬbḤ1*, p. 184: no. 15; *ṬbI1*, p. 130: no. 18-f.14/58.
23. See, *e.g.*, *JfQ3*, p. 358: no. 500-f.71/67; *JfQ5*, p. 96: no. 161-f.246/69.
24. See, *e.g.*, *JfQ1*, p.18: no. 30, p. 54: no. 84-f.62/52; *ṬbḤ*4, p. 259: no. 30-f.55/66; *ṬbI1*, p. 130: no. 18-f.14/58.
25. *ṬbI1*, p. 11: no. 2/12-f.26/50; *NzḤ*14, p. 18: no. 71; *NzI4*, p. 58: no. 3/24-f.40/49; *AcṬ2*, pp. 156, 159. Cf. Rosenfeld, *Peasants,* p. 129; Granqvist, vol. 2, p. 266.

26. See, *e.g.*, *JfQ4*, p. 142: no. 170-f.4/69; *JfQ5*, p. 49: no. 85-f.89/69; *ṬbI1*, p. 218: no. 13-f.10/62; *NzḤ19*, p. 2: no. 7/117, p. 5: no. 3/120; *AcI2*, p. 28: f.41/51; *AcṬ3*, p. 267: f.35/63.
27. See, *e.g.*, *ṬbI1*, p. 130: no. 18-f.14/54, p. 177: no. 18-f.32/60, p. 178: no. 26-f.32/58.
28. See, *e.g.*, *AcṬ3*, p. 254: f.15/63.
29. *ṬbḤ1*, p. 184: no. 15; *ṬbḤ2*, p. 101: no. 11; *NzI4*, p. 23: no. 37-f.44/47.
30. *JfQ2*, p. 445: no. 463-f.65/60; *JfQ3*, p. 350: no. 492-f.59/67.
31. *JfQ1*, p. 104: no. 165-f.26/53.
32. *JfQ5*, p. 49: no. 85-f.89/69 (the waiting-period was seven months because the woman was "perplexed as to her menstruation"), p. 96: no. 161-f.246/69.
33. *ṬbI1*, p. 177: no. 18-f.22/60 and p. 181: no. 2-f.8/61; *NzḤ*17, p. 108: no. 17/251; *NzḤ*20, p. 44: no. 1/26 (the second divorce was irrevocable).
34. See, *e.g.*, *ṬbI1*, p. 31: no. 16-f.38/51.
35. *NzI4*, p. 23: no. 37-f.44/47, p. 36: no. 52-f.108/47, p. 285: no. 1/8-f.8/66; *ṬbI1*, p. 14: no. 1/16-f.34/50; *AcI3*, p. 100: no. 130-f.116/58.
36. *NzI4*, p. 101: no. 1/13-f.40/51.
37. *FRL*, arts. 139-47, 150-1; Qadrī, arts. 315, 324-8. See Eisenman, p. 127.
38. *FRL*, art. 144. See, *e.g.*, *JfQ1*, p. 101: no. 163-fs.63/52, 12/53; *JfQ4*, p. 162: no. 199-f.25/69; *AcI2*, p. 32: f.77/51.
39. See, *e.g.*, *JfQ1*, p. 64: no. 102-f.16/52; *NzI4*, p. 90: no. 1/1-f.2/51.
40. *ṬbI1*, p. 64: no. 1-f.37/54.
41. *JfQ4*, p. 162: no. 199-f.25/69; *JfQ1*, p. 116: no. 198-f.62/53. See Qadrī, art. 326.
42. *GMBCS*, 1948, p. 82; *SAI*, 1969, No. 20, p. 60; *Society*, 1960, p. 60.
43. *SAI*, 1969, No. 20, p. 53.
44. See above, pp. 135-6.
45. Legal statistics of personal status matters dealt with by the *sharī'a* courts are regularly published in *AI*. Those for 1969 appeared in vol. 12 (1970), Nos. 1-2, p. 53.
46. See Rosenfeld, *Peasants*, pp. 128-9. Granqvist, vol. 2, pp. 268, 284-5.
47. See Rosenfeld, *Peasants*, pp. 130-1; Baer, p. 36; Shaykh Husnī al-Zu'bī, *AI*, vol. 8 (1963), Nos. 3-4, p. 4.
48. Cf. Baer, pp. 36-7.
49. *SAI*, 1969, No. 20, p. 64.
50. Marx, *Social Structure*, p. 5. Cf. al-Ārif, p. 133.

51. *GMBCS*, 1948, p. 82; *SAI*, 1969, No. 20, p. 58.
52. Owing to Rabbenu Gershom's Ban. See Schereschewsky, pp. 298-300.
53. See the chapter "Age of Marriage," pp. 22 *seq*. But cf. Ben Amram.
54. Rosenfeld, too, believed that the divorce rate was rising in consequence of the ban on polygamy (interview with him).
55. *AI*, vol. 1 (1950), No. 8, pp. 7-8. He stressed the *qāḍī's* function in establishing domestic peace between the spouses (at interviews).
56. *AI*, vol. 8 (1963), Nos. 3-4, p. 4; *AI*, vol. 9 (1964), Nos. 1-2, p. 6.
57. See Layish, *Qādīs*, p. 304.
58. See, *e.g.*, *JfQ1*, p. 79: no. 124-f.100/52; *JfQ2*, p. 410: no. 576-f.70/59 (Shaykh Ṭāhir Ḥamād); *JfQ4*, p. 53: no. 49-f.153/67 (Shaykh Tawfīq 'Asaliyya), p. 104: no. 117-f.75/68 (the same *qāḍī* tried "to give the matter a different turn acceptable to Allāh"); *ṬbI1*, p. 120: no. 9-f.13/58 (Shaykh Ḥasan Amīn al-Ḥabash).
59. See, *e.g.*, *AcṬ3*, p. 261: f.22/63 (Shaykh Amīn Qāsim Mudlij); *JfQ2*, p. 430: no. 415-f.58/59 (Shaykh Ṭāhir Ḥamād), p. 542: no. 536-f.33/62.
60. See, *e.g.*, *JfQ3*, p. 70: no. 109-f.100/63 (Shaykh Ṭāhir Ḥamād), p. 294: no. 434-f.131/66 (Shaykh Tawfīq 'Asaliyya); *NzI4*, p. 362: no. 3/26-f.70/68 (Shaykh Ḥusnī al-Zu'bī).
61. See, *e.g.*, *NzI4*, p. 206: no. 9/61 (Shaykh Mūsā al-Ṭabarī).
62. See, *e.g.*; *JfQ1*, p. 79: no. 124-f.100/52; *JfQ2*, p. 410: no. 576-f.70/59, p. 492: no. 445-f.80/61; *AcṬ3*, p. 237: f.14/62.
63. See Goitein and Ben-Shemesh, pp. 39-40. See also the chapter "Maintenance and Obedience," p. 106.
64. *AI*, vol. 5 (1957), No. 4, pp. 19-21. See also Shaykh Amīn Qāsim Mudlij, *AI*, vol. 9 (1964), Nos. 3-4, p. 5.
65. See, *e.g.*, *JfQ2*, p. 417: no. 586-f.57/59; *JfQ3*, p. 63: no. 97-f.177/63; *NzI4*, p. 301: no. 2/28-f.188/65.
66. *AI*, vol. 8 (1962), Nos. 1-2, p. 37; *AI*, vol. 9 (1964), Nos. 1-2, pp. 3-4. Interview with Shaykh Ḥasan Amīn al-Ḥabash. See Coulson, *Conflicts*, pp. 84, 92; Schacht, p. 161; Fyzee, pp. 144-7.
67. *AI*, vol. 5 (1957), No. 4, pp. 19-21.
68. *AI*, vol. 8 (1963), Nos. 3-4, pp. 2-3; *AI*, vol. 9 (1964), Nos. 1-2, p. 6.
69. *AI*, vol. 10 (1967), Nos. 3-4, p. 10; *AI*, vol. 9 (1964), Nos. 1-2, p. 9.
70. *AI*, vol. 8 (1963), Nos. 3-4, pp. 2-4; *AI*, vol. 9 (1964), Nos. 1-2, p. 6.
71. *AI*, vol. 10 (1967), Nos. 3-4, pp. 1, 16-18. See also *AI*, vol. 5 (1957), No. 4, p. 19; *JfQ3*, p. 338: no. 478-f.44/67; *JfQ4*, p. 5: no. 5-f.98/67; *JfQ5*, p. 55: no. 92-f.150/69.

72. *AI*, vol. 10 (1967), Nos. 3-4, p. 20.
73. See, *e.g.*, *NzḤ18*, p. 253: no. 6/86, p. 257: no. 5/91, p. 257: no. 6/92; *NzḤ19*, p. 200: no. 8/8; *NzḤ21*, p. 50: no. 13/20-f.25/60, p. 58: no. 1/32-f.48/60.
74. Interview with Shaykh Ḥasan Amīn al-Ḥabash. He also spoke in terms of the natural inequality of the sexes.
75. *AI*, vol. 1 (1950), No. 8, pp. 7-8.
76. *AI*, vol. 10 (1967), Nos. 3-4, pp. 5, 14, 18-20, 22.
77. Modern legislation in Arab countries confines the validity of suspended repudiation to cases in which the husband *intends* to divorce the wife. For more particulars see Layish, *Qāḍīs*, pp. 295-6, 298, and the sources indicated there.
78. *JfQ1*, p. 53: no. 82-f.54/52. See also *NzḤ15*, p. 114: no. 11/166; *NzḤ16*, p. 23: no. 41/242; *NzḤ18*, p. 199: no. 8/8, *NzI4*, p. 31: no. 45-f.87/47.
79. *AI*, vol. 9 (1964), Nos. 1-2, p. 11.
80. See Linant de Bellefonds, pp. 389-90; Kerr, p. 90 *seq.*
81. al-Abayānī, p. 260.
82. *NzI4*, p. 237: no. 1/4-f.4/64; *Apl*, pp. 71-2: f.23/64. See also *Ṭb11*, p. 242: no. 30-f.34/63.
83. *JfQ2*, p. 539: no. 529-f.64/62; and *AcI2*, p. 30 [40]: f.134/51, respectively.
84. *AI*, vol. 10 (1967), Nos. 3-4, pp. 8, 15 and 19, respectively.
85. *AI*, vol. 1 (1950), No. 8, p. 7; *AI*, vol. 8 (1963), Nos. 1-2, pp. 1-2; *AI*, vol. 9 (1964), Nos. 1-2, p. 9.
86. *AI*, vol. 9 (1964), Nos. 1-2, pp. 4-5; and *AI*, vol. 11 (1968), Nos. 1-2, pp. 10-12, respectively.
87. *AI*, vol. 10 (1967), Nos. 3-4, pp. 1, 5, 8, 10, 15-20.
88. See, *e.g.*, *JfQ4*, p. 142: no. 169-f.2/69, p. 230: no. 369-f.50/66; *NzḤ19*, p. 179: no. 4/71; *AcṬ2*, p. 48; *AcṬ3*, p. 91: f.23/58; *AcṬ4*, p. 1: f.2/64, p. 13: f.26/64. At a court session in the Little Triangle on May 26, 1971 (attended by the author), Shaykh Ḥasan Amīn al-Ḥabash asked the wife whether she consented to the divorce and whether she had not been pressed by her father (who was present) or others to consent.
89. See, *e.g.*, *JfQ3*, p. 313: no. 452-f.4/67, p. 338: no. 478-f.44/67; *JfQ4*, p. 11: no. 11-f.109/67, p. 12: no. 12-f.108/67, p. 58: no. 54-f.155/67; *NzḤ*18, p. 257: no. 5/91; *NzḤ19*, p. 200: no. 8/8.
90. See, *e.g.*, *JfQ4*, p. 57: no. 53-f.150/67; *JfQ5*, p. 55: no. 92-f.150/69 (the husband submitted the wife's written consent to the divorce, but Shaykh Tawfīq 'Asaliyya left it to the competent authority to determine whether she had in fact consented because the consent had not been given in court), p. 98: no. 84-f.191/69.

91. See, *e.g.*, *ṬbI1*, p. 131: no. 20-f.26/58.
92. See, *e.g.*, *JfQ4*, p. 11: f.109/67, p. 12: f.108/67; *JfQ5*, p. 69: no. 118-f.230/69; *NzḤ18*, p. 253: no. 6/86.
93. *JfQ4*, p. 126: no. 146-f.119/68 (Shaykh Tawfīq 'Asaliyya noted that the divorce "is in conformity with the *sharī'a* but contrary to secular law . . ."), p. 172: no. 215-f.63/69; *NzḤ19*, p. 17: no. 4/12, p. 27: no. 2/23; *NzḤ18*, p. 20: no. 21/84; *NzḤ19*, p. 200: no. 8/8; *NzḤ22*, p. 47: no. 11/36-f.55/63.
94. *ṬbI1*, p. 108: no. 15-f.31/57, p. 116: no. 5-f.2/58, p. 120: no. 9-f.13/58, p. 124: no. 12-f.18/58, p. 131: no. 20-f.26/58.
95. *JfQ4*, p. 126: no. 146-f.119/68; *JfQ5*, p. 98: no. 84-f.191/69.
96. *JfQ3*, p. 5: no. 9-f.88/63, p. 13: no. 22-f.81/63.
97. See p. 195. The fact that Shaykh Ḥusnī al-Zu'bī referred in only one judgment to the question of the criminality of divorce against the wife's will was due to the almost complete absence of such divorces during his tenure.
98. *JfQ4*, p. 142: no. 170-f.4/69.
99. *ṬbI1*, p. 218: no. 13-f.10/62.
100. See above, pp. 141-2.
101. *AI*, vol. 8 (1962), nos. 1-2, pp. 37-8; *AI*, vol. 9 (1964), Nos. 1-2, p. 10; *ṬbI1*, p. 218: no. 13-f.10/62, p. 220: no. 15-f.13/63.
102. *ṬbI1*, p. 146: no. 9-f.16/59, p. 218: no. 13-f.10/62, p. 220: no. 15-f.13/63.
103. See, *e.g.*, *ṬbI1*, p. 242: no. 29-f.28/62, p. 263: no. 16-f.28/62, p. 242: no. 30-f.34/63; *Apl*, f.81/64; *ṬbI1*, p. 268: no. 18-f.34/63.
104. *NzI4*, p. 58: no. 3/24-f.40/49.
105. *JfQ4*, p. 147: no. 176-f.118/68.
106. *JfQ2*, p. 426: no. 413-f.79/59.
107. *NzI4*, p. 237: no. 1/4-f.4/64.
108. *Apl*, p. 50: f.72/63.
109. See, *e.g.*, *NzḤ19*, p. 1: no. 5/115; *NzḤ20*, p. 7: no. 10/101.
110. *NzḤ18*, p. 182: no. 11/294; *NzḤ20*, p. 115: no. 3/39.
111. See, *e.g.*, *NzH18*, p. 176: no. 3/286; *JfQ5*, p. 49: no. 85-f.89/69.
112. *AI*, vol. 1 (1950), No. 8, p. 7; *AI*, vol. 8 (1962), Nos. 1-2, pp. 38-9.
113. *AI*, vol. 1 (1950), No. 8, p. 7; *Yedī'on*, vol. 1 (1950), No. 8, p. 4.
114. He did not refer to Art. 110 of the *FRL*, which requires the husband to notify the *qāḍī* of the divorce, or to the Marriages and Divorces (Registration) Ordinance, 1919, which prescribes, *inter alia*, the procedure for the registration of divorces.
115. *AI*, vol. 8 (1962), Nos. 1-2, pp. 37-8; *AI*, vol. 9 (1964), Nos. 1-2, pp. 4-6. On registration as a procedural device for the introduction

of reforms in matrimonial matters used in modern legislation of Arab lands see Coulson, *History*, pp. 172 *seq*.

116. *ṬbḤ2*, p. 106: no. 21.
117. The *qāḍī* sometimes stated expressly that the registration of the divorce was inevitable. See, *e.g.*, *JfQ3*, p. 129: no. 204-f.100/64, p. 209: no. 345-f.32/66; *JfQ4*, p. 97: no. 104-f.160/68, p. 107: no. 121-f.80/68.
118. See, *e.g.*, *JfQ1*, p. 99: no. 159-f.35/53, p. 111: no. 179-f.57/53; *ṬbI1*, p. 77: no. 17-f.25/57, p. 108: no. 15-f.31/57; *NzḤ19*, p. 10: no. 3/3, p. 200: no. 8/8.
119. *JfQ4*, p. 17: no. 17-f.67/67. See also *JfQ3*, p. 230: no. 369-f.50/66.
120. See, *e.g.*, *JfQ3*, p. 184: no. 303-f.77/65, p. 206: no. 339-f.339/66; *JfQ4*, p. 5: no. 5-f.98/67, p. 157: no. 191-f.33/69; *ṬbḤ2*, p. 60: no. 25; *ṬbI1*, p. 120: no. 9-f.13/58.
121. See, *e.g.*, *JfQ1*, p. 14: no. 24-f.27/51, p. 70: no. 125-f.103/52, p. 92: no. 147-f.23/53; *ṬbI1*, p. 61: no. 15-f.27/54.
122. *JfQ4*, p. 67: no. 63-f.17/68.
123. See, *e.g.*, *JfQ1*, p. 114: no. 193-f.63/53; *JfQ2*, p. 399: no. 559-f.47/59; *ṬbI1*, p. 33: no. 1-f.10/52, p. 35: no. 4-f.14/52; *NzḤ*19, p. 5: f.3/120; *NzI4*, p. 159: no. 1/6-f.13/54; *AcṬ2*, p. 62.
124. *JfQ3*, p. 148: no. 237-f.140/64; and *JfQ2*, p. 312: no. 484-f.24/58, respectively.
125. *AI*, vol. 8 (1962), Nos. 1-2, p. 39.
126. Criminal File, Tel Aviv 376/59—Attorney-General *vs.* Abd al-Raḥīm Maḥmūd Irāqī. See also Criminal File, Tel Aviv 616/58, *PM*, vol. 22, p. 158. Cf. Goitein and Ben-Shemesh, pp. 132-3; *ha-Tzofeh* of January 7, 1962.
127. *Ha-Yom* and *Lamerhav* of February 15, 1966; *ha-Aretz* of January 3, 1966.
128. *AcṬ2*, p. 48; *AcṬ4*, p. 81: f.19/67; *AcD*8, p. 99: no. 16/70-f.139/68 (the *qāḍī* refused to permit *ṭalāq* because its permissibility "depends according to law on agreement between the spouses").
129. *JfQ2*, p. 327: no. 512-f.65/58, p. 330: no. 518-f.72/58. See also *JfQ1*, p. 114: no. 191-f.58/53; *ṬbI1*, p. 51: no. 12-f.25/53.
130. *ṬbI1*, p. 86: no. 5-f.8/56; *AcṬ3*, p. 84: f.18/58. See also *AcṬ2*, pp. 97, 132; *AcṬ4*, p. 117: f.5/68, p. 142: f.32/68, p. 80-f.18/67; *AcṬ4*, p. 5: f.10/64; *AcQ5*, p. 35: no. 35-f.125/61.
131. See, *e.g.*, *ṬbI1*, p. 61: no. 15-f.27/54; *AcṬ4*, p. 41: f.6/66.
132. See, *e.g.*, *JfQ1*, p. 114: no. 191-f.58/53; *AcṬ2*, pp. 97, 132; *AcṬ4*, p. 77: f.15/67. An essentially similar situation has been found to exist in Iraq. According to modern Iraqi legislation, *ṭalāq* must be performed in court. If the husband insists on exercising his right, he is not debarred from doing so, and he is not required to assign

reasons for the divorce. The legislator intended to allow the husband time to think again as well as to give the *qāḍī* an opportunity to prevent a divorce where, in his opinion, it is unjustified for other than *shar'i* reasons. In other words, the legislator expected to bring about reforms in divorce by judicial means; but the *qāḍīs* did not come up to his expectations: divorce proceedings in court are no more than routine, without the *qāḍīs* trying to influence them. See el-Naqeb, pp. 128-9, 159-64.

133. *ṬbI1*, p. 185: no. 6-f.9/61 (the wife said: "Even though I be strangled or slaughtered [I shall not mind] so long as my husband does not divorce me. I prefer death to divorce").
134. *AI*, vol. 9 (1964), Nos. 1-2, p. 5.
135. Interview with Yūsuf Dasūqī.
136. *AcD8*, p. 99: no. 16/70-f.139/68.
137. See, *e.g.*, *JfQ1*, p. 158: no. 263-f.64/54; *JfQ2*, p. 380: no. 533-f.18/59.
138. See, *e.g.*, *AcṬ3*, p. 243: f.5/63 (the spouses expressed the wish that their marriage be dissolved and "persisted in this wish," and the court granted it), p. 244: f.6/63.
139. See, *e.g.*, *JfQ2*, p. 430: no. 415-f.58/59, p. 436: no. 421-f.18/60.
140. See, *e.g.*, *NzI4*, p. 87: no. 5/46-f.115/50; *JfQ1*, p. 60: no. 95-f.42/51; *Apl*, p. 63: f.13/64.
141. *JfQ3*, p. 145: no. 230-f.108/64, and p. 209: no. 344-f.10/66, respectively.
142. See, *e.g.*, *JfQ1*, p. 275: no. 424-f.29/57; *JfQ2*, p. 527: no. 508-f.62/61; *JfQ3*, p. 329: no. 470-f.30/67; *AcṬ3*, p. 31: f.22[58]; *AcṬ4*, p. 8: f.16/64; *NzH18*, p. 146: f.7/245.
143. Shaykh Tawfīq 'Asaliyya's letter to the author dated December 13, 1974.
144. *ṬbI1*, p. 145: no. 7-f.9/59, *NzI4*, p. 47: no. 2/4-f.6/49.
145. *ṬbI1*, pp. 58, 66: no. 10-f.14/54; *Apl*, p. 12: no. 11, p. 87: f.1/66, p. 20: no. 25.
146. *AcI1*, p. 75: f.43/50; *AcI2*, p. 34: f.26/52; *NzI4*, p. 202: no. 1/8-f.21/59.
147. *AcI2*, p. 36[46]: f.110/52.
148. See, *e.g.*, *NzI4*, p. 222: no. 3/8-f.88/62 and p. 257: no. 9/38-f.42/64.
149. *NzI4*, p. 362: no. 3/26-f.70/68.
150. *Apl*, p. 87: f.1/66.
151. *AcD8*, p. 99: no. 16/70-f.139/68.
152. *Yedi'on*, vol. 1 (1950), No. 7, p. 3.
153. *JfQ1*, p. 43: no. 71-f.38/51, p. 44: no. 72-f.46/51 (the text of the decision of the *qāḍīs'* conference is quoted in these judgments).

154. *AI*, vol. 7 (1959), No. 1, Hebrew Summary, p. 2; *JfQ1*, p. 106: no. 170-f.86/52, p. 111: no. 178-f.41/53, p. 117: no. 199-f.21/52, p. 140: no. 235-f.94/54, p. 145: no. 246-f.6/53; *ṬbI1*, p. 68: no. 5-f.28/54.
155. *Apl*, p. 18: no. 21; *AI*, vol. 7 (1959), no. 1, pp. 29, 31.
156. *ṬbI1*, p. 71: no. 10-f.13/55. See also *Apl*, p. 13: no. 13.
157. *ṬbI1*, p. 98: no. 6-f.10/57.
158. *AI*, vol. 7 (1959), No. 1, p. 29.
159. *Apl*, p. 18: no. 21; *AI*, vol. 7 (1959), No. 1, pp. 29-30.
160. *AcI2*, p. 33: f.83/51, p. 60: f.152/53.
161. *AcI2*, p. 78: no. 10/58-f.60/57 (the judgment was sent to the *Sharī'a* Court of Appeal for confirmation and the wife was meanwhile forbidden to remarry); *AcQ5*, p. 12: f.13/62; *NzI4*, p. 216: no. 1/7-f.64/62.
162. A hint of the *siyāsa* doctrine. See Schacht, p. 54; Coulson, *Succession*, p. 137.
163. *AI*, vol. 7 (1959), No. 1, pp. 29-30; *Apl*, p. 23: no. 30.
164. See, *e.g.*, *JfQ1*, p. 87: no. 137-f.34/52; *JfQ3*, p. 49: no. 79-f.186/63; *JfQ5*, p. 26: no. 26-f.134/62.
165. *JfQ1*, p. 111: no. 178-f.41/53, p. 189: no. 308-f.10/54, p. 48: no. 77-f.37/51.
166. See, *e.g.*, *JfQ1*, p. 43: no. 71-f.38/51, p. 106: no. 170-f.86/52.
167. *JfQ1*, p. 117: no. 199-f.21/52.
168. See, *e.g.*, *JfQ1*, p. 175: no. 289-f.19/55, p. 193: no. 312-f.47/55.
169. See, *e.g.*, *JfQ2*, p. 334: no. 525-f.3/59; *JfQ5*, p. 34: no. 34-f.58/63; *Apl*, p. 18: no. 21.
170. *JfQ1*, p. 189: no. 308-f.10/54[66/55]; *Apl*, p. 19: no. 22.
171. See, *e.g.*, *NzI4*, p. 244: no. 5/15-f.50/64, p. 282: no. 3/3-f.156/65.
172. *NzI4*, p. 344: no. 9/46-f.123/67, p. 351: no. 7/10-f.123/67 and p. 361: no. 1/24-f.36/68.
173. See Anderson, *Dissolution*, pp. 284-5; Coulson, *History*, pp. 186, 188-9; Fyzee, pp. 163-4, 463. See also the Egyptian Personal Status Bill of 1966, published in *al-Ahrām* of August 27, 1966, and reprinted in ai, vol. 10 (1967). Nos. 3-4, pp. 3-4.
174. *JfQ3*, p. 161: no. 197-f.3/69; see also *JfQ5*, p. 52: no. 86-f.161/69.
175. See, *e.g.*, *AcD*6, p. 27: f.60/64; *AcD*8, p. 67: f.17/69.
176. *AI*, vol. 7 (1959), No. 1, pp. 30-2.
177. *Apl*, p. 23: no. 30.
178. See, *e.g.*, *ṬbḤ1*, p. 170: no. 24, p. 182: no. 11; *ṬbI1*, p. 51: no. 12-f.25/53.
179. *ṬbḤ2*, p. 56: no. 21, p. 58: no. 23, p. 129: no. 1, p. 272: no. 63; *ṬbḤ3*, p. 28: no. 37; *JfQ1*, p. 157: no. 261-f.63/54.
180. *NzI4*, p. 179: no. 1/7-f.5/57; *ṬbI1*, p. 249: no. 5-f.8/64; *Apl*, p. 67: f.19/64; *ṬbI1*, p. 284: no. 4-f.8/64.

181. *Apl*, p. 47: no. 69; *ṬbI1*, p. 56: no. 7-f.31/53.
182. *Apl*, p. 63: f.13/64. See also *Apl*, p. 83: f.10/65.
183. *AcD8*, p. 59: f.120/68; and *AI*, vol. 9 (1964), Nos. 3-4, pp. 3-5, respectively.
184. *AcI2*, p. 39: no. 140/52; *NzI4*, p. 214: no. 1/1-f.50/61.
185. *AI*, vol. 9 (1964), Nos. 3-4, pp. 6-7; and *JfQ2*, p. 296: no. 460-f.70/67, respectively.
186. See, *e.g.*, *NzI4*, p. 315: no. 4/5-f.2/67, p. 316: no. 5/6-f.6/67, p. 330: no. 1/27-f.110/67, p. 332: no. 3/29-f.86/67.
187. *Apl*, p. 47: no. 69, p. 54: f.3/64, p. 55: f.4/64, p. 63: f.13/64.
188. See, *e.g.*, *JfQ5*, p. 35: no. 58-f.30/69.
189. *AI*, vol. 9 (1964), Nos. 3-4, pp. 2-5.
190. *Apl*, p. 47: no. 69.
191. See, *e.g.*, *NzI4*, p. 256: no. 8/37-f.151/64, p. 264: no. 4/12-f.7/68, p. 281: no. 2/2-f.151/64, p. 292: no. 2/19-f.30/66, p. 315: no. 4/5-f.2/67, p. 369: no. 6/36-f.72/68; *JfQ5*, p. 35: no. 58-f.30/69. See also *JfQ3*, p. 359: no. 501-f.31/67.
192. *NzI4*, p. 322: no. 3/16-f.15/67, and p. 301: no. 2/28-f.188/65, respectively.
193. *AI*, vol. 9 (1964), Nos. 3-4, pp. 6-7.
194. See, *e.g.*, *JfQ2*, p. 434: no. 421-f.27/59 (the husband denied paternity of the son, and the *qāḍī*, regarding this as a cause of discord between the spouses, appointed arbitrators).
195. See, *e.g.*, *JfQ2*, p. 417: no. 586-f.57/59; *JfQ3*, p. 63: no. 97-f.117/63.
196. See, *e.g.*, *AcQ5*, p. 21: no. 21/63-f.151/62.
197. See, *e.g.*, *Apl*, p. 63: f.13/64, p. 67: f.19/64.
198. *AI*, vol. 1 (1950), No. 7, p. 4; *AI*, vol. 11 (1968), Nos. 1-2, p. 12.
199. S. Nawi told the author that Shaykh Ṭāhir Ḥamād had refused to dissolve the marriages of three minor girls (upto the age of 13) who were brought before him.
200. *JfQ2*, p. 290: no. 451-f.63/57. Shaykh Amīn Qāsim Mudlij, on the other hand, decided that the marriage was irregular and acknowledged the husband's paternity of the children. See *AcD6*, p. 48: no. 49-f.124/64.
201. *AI*, vol. 10 (1967), Nos. 3-4, pp. 5, 8-9, 15, 19, 22; *AI*, vol. 8 (1963), Nos. 3-4, p. 3.
202. See, *e.g.*, *JfQ1*, p. 126: no. 213-f.20/54; *JfQ5*, p. 29: no. 50-f.48/69; *ṬbḤ1*, p. 105: no. 1/73; *NzḤ18*, p. 20: no. 21/84; *NzI4*, p. 231: no. 4/24-f.123/63; *AcṬ2*, p. 143; *AcṬ4*, p. 40[1]-f.40/68.
203. See, *e.g.*, *NzḤ15*, p. 109: no. 5/160; *NzḤ17*, p. 108: no. 17/251; *NzḤ20*, p. 44: no. 1/26.

204. *JfQ4*, p. 57: no. 53-f.150/67, p. 58: no. 54-f.155/67 and p. 67: no. 63-f.17/68.
205. *AcṬ1*, pp. 27-8.
206. See, *e.g.*, *ṬbI1*, p. 77: no. 17-f.25/55; *JfQ1*, p. 266: no. 415-f.13/57; *JfQ5*, p. 49: no. 85-f.89/69; *NzḤ19*, p. 5: no. 3/120; *AcI1*, p. 56: f.3/50; *AcṬ3*, p. 267: f.35/63.
207. *ṬbḤ4*, p. 259: no. 30-f.55/66; *JfQ1*, p. 54: no. 84-f.62/52; *NzI4*, p. 36: no. 52-f.108/47.
208. *JfQ1*, p. 18: no. 30. See also *AcI1*, p. 56.f.3/50. Cf. Granqvist, vol. 2, p. 261.
209. See, *e.g.*, *JfQ1*, p. 148: no. 250-f.9/54; *JfQ3*, p. 161: no. 197-f.3/69; *AcQ5*, p. 34: f.58/63.
210. See Coulson, *Succession*, pp. 19-20.
211. See Shaykh Amīn Qāsim Mudlij, *AI*, vol. 9 (1964), Nos. 1-2, p. 2.
212. *AI*, vol. 9 (1964), Nos. 1-2, pp. 10-11.
213. Remarks taken down at an interview. See also *Ma'ariv* of June 12, 1970.
214. *AI*, vol. 9 (1964), Nos. 1-2, pp. 6-10. The idea of a statutory obligation of the husband to pay compensation to the wife is repeated in Shaykh Ḥusnī's letter to the author of November 22, 1970. See also a suggestion by Advocate Maḥmūd al-Māḍī that "everything should be permitted [by secular legislation] that is not expressly forbidden in the sources of Islamic law." AI, vol. 9 (1964), Nos. 1-2, pp. 7-8.
215. *AI*, vol. 9 (1964), Nos. 1-2, pp. 2-3, 11.
216. See Anderson, *Islamic Law*, pp. 56-7; *idem, Tunis*, pp. 271-2; Coulson, *History*, pp. 209-12; *idem, Conflicts*, pp. 47-8; Schacht, p. 167. These reforms were not mentioned by the *qāḍīs*. See *AI*, vol. 9 (1964), Nos. 1-2, p. 7.
217. Shaykh Ḥusnī al-Zu'bī's letter to the author dated November 22, 1970.
218. Shaykh Ḥasan Amīn al-Ḥabash's letter to the author, no. 2/2/244 of November 19, 1970.
219. *AI*, vol. 10 (1966), Nos. 1-2, p. 83.
220. *JfQ2*, p. 432: no. 418-f.12/60. See also *ṬbI1*, p. 97: no. 5-f.8/57.
221. See, *e.g.*, *NzI4*, p. 90: no. 1/1-f.2/51; *JfQ1*, p. 64: no. 102-f.16/52, p. 116: no. 198-f.62/53.
222. See, *e.g.*, *JfQ3*, p. 63: no. 97-f.177/63 and p. 103: no. 160-f.24/64; *AcI3*, p. 35: fs.29/56, 96/56.
223. See, *e.g.*, *JfQ1*, p. 219: no. 343-f.2/56; *JfQ2*, p. 590: no. 624-f.45/63; *AcṬ2*, p. 86; *AcṬ3*, p. 206: f.10/61; *AcṬ4*, p. 59: f.29/66, p. 133: f.22/68.

224. See, *e.g.*, *ṬbḤ2*, p. 233: no. 8, p. 265: no. 52; *ṬbI1*, p. 192: no. 12-f.20/61; *NzḤ22*, p. 16: no. 5/69-f.97/62, p. 97: no. 1/96-f.149/63, p. 123: no. 4/19-f.36/64.
225. See, *e.g.*, *ṬbḤ3*, p. 58: no. 19.
226. See, *e.g.*, *ṬbḤ2*, p. 3: no. 20; *ṬbI1*, p. 161: no. 2-f.6/60.
227. See, *e.g.*, *ṬbḤ4*, p. 12: no. 45.
228. See, *e.g.*, *ṬbḤ2*, p. 166: no. 49, p. 227: no. 136; *NzḤ23*, p. 162: no. 16/20-f.27/66.
229. *ṬbḤ2*, p. 157: no. 38; *ṬbI1*, p. 100: no. 8-f.28/57. In one divorce under such circumstances, which the author witnessed in court, the husband produced a sum of money previously agreed on with the wife and handed it to her in return for her consent. After the session, Shaykh Ḥasan Amīn al-Ḥabash explained that he did not interfere in the matter of compensation in any way (session of May 26, 1971).
230. See, *e.g.*, *ṬbḤ4*, p. 127: no. 103; *NzḤ23*, p. 43: no. 4/24-f.48/65, p. 183: no. 25/94-f.169/68.
231. See, *e.g.*, *AcṬ3*, p. 91: f.23/58; *ṬbḤ2*, p. 57: no. 22, p. 59: no. 24.
232. See, *e.g.*, *ṬbḤ1*, p. 116: no. 90; *ṬbI1*, p. 73: no. 13-f.9/55.
233. *AcṬ4*, p. 39: f.4/66.
234. Shaykh Ḥusnī al-Zu'bī's letter to the author dated November 22, 1970.

5

Policy Approach to Rural Women's Component Projects: Studies from Least Developed Muslim Countries

Lessons to be learned from a consideration of several projects of this type seem to be the following:

— an informed understand of women's functions and roles should be acquired from the beginning of a project. Flexibility in project management may make it possible to include women where this has not been done from the outset;

— the assumption that women are only interested in the domestic sphere should be questioned and an effort should be made to find out what their traditional activities are and how they will be modified by the project;

— research to find out what women really want, should be conducted with women interviewers due to the restrictions on contacts between men and women in these societies.

(a) Women's Component Project: Western Sahel

The design of (large animal) livestock projects is particularly difficult because of the need to integrate men's herding with women's milk processing, and all livestock production with complementary agriculture. A *project to reconstitute herds after the drought in the Western Sahel* was forced to face a number of problems which became apparent at different stages of implementation. All the women own cattle, sheep, and goats, acquired through gifts, inheritance, and purchases from sales of milk products or grains. From their respective food fields, men are responsible for supplying the household's millet and sorghum requirements, women, for supplying beans, onions, vegetables, and peppers. Women's own grain production is at their disposal and mostly sold. While men's livestock activities in the project were organised through herdsmen's associations, women's were added to the project in a later component centering on an "animation feminine" expert who was also responsible for promoting vegetable cultivation, crafts, basic literacy, and the introduction of appropriate household technology. Due to problems in recruiting this expert, women's livestock activities did not commence until one and a half years after the start of the project. In the meantime an assistant animatrice started that part of the women's component which emphasized their family roles. An initial set of baseline data failed to pick up conflicts between demands on women's time. Included in the recommendation for women's livestock activities was a concentration of births of animals in the rainy season when for age material was most plentiful. This would also provide surplus milk for cheese-making during the rainy season for later consumption and sale. Technically promising from the livestock reproduction and cheese-making viewpoint, this strategy presented problems for women's other activities. Their workload of planting, weeding and harvesting corps in one short rainy season was already heavy. Dealing with a peak of animal births, milking and cheese-making in addition was just not feasible. While the cheese-making in itself might be highly profitable it would have been at the cost of foregoing some other production. Moreover, conçentrating animal births, and therefore milk supply increments, in one season lessened milk availability for consumption and sale at other times of the year when agricultural production was lower. It was only when a second base line study was undertaken that these contradictions were brought to light, and it was realised that the incentives to women to follow the proposed strategy were far from clear. In the meantime men's, quite separate, herding component had gone ahead.

What this case study reveals is the inferior planning of women's production activities when they are not planned at the same time and given the same status as men's. Delaying adequate baseline studies and expecting women's production activities to start only when the "women's component" is ready to absorb them leads to these activities being given a low priority and being badly designed. But compared with another project to reconstitute herds in Mauretania, and a project to improve animal breeds in Benin, for which women were not even mentioned in the project documents, it did make great efforts to integrate women without an established methodology to guide it.

A footnote to rehabilitation after drought and loss of herds might suitably be inserted here. It has already been noted that individually-owned livestock are obtained through inheritance, dowry, or bride wealth. Ownership of cattle is important to women in the event of divorce, and for women's standing in the household. But programmes for the post-drought constitution of Fulani and Tuareg herds gave cattle only to men. Although women should continue to enjoy rights of disposal of the milk and milk products from cows which they care for, their position in the household could be weakened for a generation or two until cattle have been used again for dowry and bride wealth.

Small livestock, such as chickens and goats, are usually exclusively in women's sphere. Eggs and cheese may be sold before the family's nutritional requirements are met because women need a flow of cash income for other household necessities. Projects designed to increase the products of small livestock are frequently aimed primarily at improving the family's nutrition. But they require extra labour and cash inputs. It is not always clear where the cash requirements are to come from, if not from greater sales. Nor can it be easily assumed that women see putting more labour into further self-provisioning output as more important than putting more labour into output for sale. In view of women's often repeated demands to be assisted to earn more money there is something fundamentally a miss in agricultural departments helping men to grow more grains for the market and home economics departments encouraging women to raise output of proteins for family consumption; particularly when women sell foods of high nutritional value in order to buy greater volumes of food of less nutritional value. It may make neither nutritional nor economic sense to allocate scarce resources to greater protein intake if there is a current calorie deficit. Poultry projects have a poor record, with birds dyiny from disease. The explanation is often assumed to be the vulnerability of the new breeds introduced. But it is tempting to believe that an unrecognised problem is that the women themselves are unconvinced of the value of the projects.

(b) Women's Component Projoct: Yemen/Arab Republic

The activities of the various section of a project should be integrated. One of the main goals of this project was to assess the potential for irrigation as well as analysing the need for the supply of drinking water. However, the water management section upto the time of the case study, had not undertaken any activity to educate the village women on water use and hygiene.

(c) Women's Component Project: Ethiopia

In the SIDA project in Ethiopia, the case study reported that the women's component in this project was limited to home economics courses including hygiene, child care, home improvement (light carpentry) and clothing repair. Course content should have been made more pertinent to rural life and the other development aims of the project. However, the need for relevance was not rated highly by the managers of the project. Although the course content was developed to help rural women, the actual role of women as producers and active farmers was not understood.

One of the problems in project design related to the introduction of a women's component in a general project, is the vague definition of the target group as "the farmers", the "rural population", or slightly more specific, "the rural poor". The project management translated these vague terms to mean "mature male farmers", thus limiting the target group by age and sex. In project areas where farming is the main economic activity and where women are actively engaged in agriculture, women should by definition be included in the target group.

According to the study carried out by SIDA, a special women's component in rural development projects would be useful where,

"*(a)* the women are culturally isolated and would be helped and strengthened by a separate programme which addresses their problems, in addition to agricultural extension services;

(b) women are primarily engaged in subsistence activities other than agriculture".

(d) Women's Component Project: Indonesia

In Indonesia, as elsewhere, the traditional roles of rural women are important for the cultivation of certain crops and the production of handicrafts. A special Transmigration Area Development (TAD) sub-project for the development of activities addressed to transmigrant women was financed by the German government. Data was gathered on the socio-economic situation of women in the project area which identified the main problems for women: low literacy rates; high fertility; lack of crop variety resulting in an unbalanced diet and malnutrition: low productivity and incomes; lack of extension services for women; and the lack of women's organisations at the local level.

Close co-operation with TAD experts in agriculture, rural training and extension, aquaculture and health assured the integration of the women's component in the main stream of project objectives. Other reasons for success in the short-term, so far, have been the solicited active participation of the specific target groups in the planning of new project activities; and an approach including a "package of measures" addressed to inter-related problems rather than the proposal of uni-dimensional solutions.

Will Women-specific Projects be of Help?

A key issue throughout this review has been women's access to resources. In many of the general aid projects, access has diminished as a result of the project. This point should be taken into account when reviewing women-specific projects. In other words, the role of projects exclusively for women should be to enhance their access to resources. This should be reflected in the areas of intervention and the potential for integration between these projects and national/regional or community development plans. The general projects were reviewed with a view to examining their impact on women. The review of women-specific projects will keep in mind the hypothesis that such projects isolate women from mainline development activities, and treat them as "consumption items" (*e.g.* maternal and child health services, literacy, training etc. such expenditures are regarded as consumption) on the agenda rather than productive ones. What is their potential for integrating women given our definition?

Before reviewing the women-specific project descriptions made available, some attention will be focused on the objections to women's projects.

(a) Objections to Women-Only Projects

Buvinic and Nieves point out in their study that "The recent experiences in implementing women's projects in developing countries shows that projects fail when participants are expected to perform too many complex tasks and when welfare-oriented organisations attempt to develop production-oriented projects." "Women's programmes in developing countries have repeatedly and systematically translated production objectives into sewing, handicrafts and other "traditionally" female activities during implementation, and failed—in part because the tasks have been excessive, difficult and non-familiar to the women, and in part because they have little economic potential."

In a review of six such projects in rural Senegal, Savane points out that none of them meets the criteria of projects acceptable for funding by the ILO, *i.e.* projects which generate regular income for the participants. However, other activities carried out by women which generate irregular income were identified. With help in improving production methods and marketing, profits would increase and ensure women modest but regular incomes.

In Savane's evaluation the objectionable aspects of such projects were reported to be the following:

— the main purpose of most of these projects was not income generation but home economics;

— with one exception, these projects could not be made profitable in any durable or substantial manner for a number of reasons, such as: the type of activity, the poor environment, absence of employment possibilities, high cost of production, etc.;

— the projects were set up as an extra activity that women should be involved in, in addition to their already heavy workloads and were of little or no benefit to them, which explains the progressive decline in participation;

— the activities were constantly interrupted, due to rapid turnover in project staff; the women had not been taught to take over for themselves;

— these projects are characterised as "social" and the staff assigned to them by the Division of Human Resources, is not competent or interested in the technical and managerial tasks necessary to make these projects viable. They could in no way provide guidance with regard to agricultural work or handicraft production from the raw materials available.

— and finally, no study of the communities involved was made to give the project management and in-depth, informed understanding of the problems of the people there, consequently inappropriate activities were proposed. For example, the need for technologies to alleviate women's work is urgent, but those measures proposed were unsuitable.

In Loufti's opinion, "the overall objective which provides the context for a discussion of strategies for women's advancement and rural development, is growth with equity and participation." She advocates "strategic separatism" a term used by Boulding. This is essentially the same idea put forward by the SIDA project cited for women's component projects: "...separation is sometimes necessary under patriarchal structures, for women to gain experience and confidence, enabling them to integrate with men on more equal terms".

(b) Design and Appraisal of Women-Specific Projects

The Voluntary Fund for the Decade for Women (VFDW) made available 23 descriptions of women-specific projects. These projects had been approved for funding by the consultative committee of the VFDW in 1982. It is too early for evaluation. However, the design and appraisal elements and the areas of intervention can be reviewed for their potential impact in the light of the pitfalls mentioned above. Although these projects may be considered a biased sample of women-specific projects, the appraisal and objectives will be examined. It is difficult to judge whether these projects will actually up-grade the women beneficiaries, without base-line knowledge of what existed before. Nevertheless, the areas of intervention and the definition of the target groups will provide some clues as to whether they are on the right track according to our criteria.

Most of the projects in this category had mixed target groups and objectives. The areas of intervention range from training in "integrated" health and agriculture (Five projects), one of these overlapped with access to credit and a revolving fund, income-generation in various branches such as increasing food supplies, training of staff to identify areas of income-generation, and textiles (11 projects), training for employment (two non-rural projects and one rural), energy conservation and training in the use of woodburning stoves (two projects covering six countries), one workshop in development planning with participants from five Asian countries with training in project design. (This workshop was part of more comprehensive development programmes in the countries represented.) Finally, there was one action research project with on-the-job training for female social researchers.

Many of the descriptions mentioned community participation and self reliance as components of the projects. The most striking aspect of these projects was an *awareness of the multi-dimensional roles and functions of women,* something we found missing in the general aid and women's component projects. Only time will tell, whether the income-generation project develop into viable enterprises as outlined above. However, these projects definitely show more potential for ultimately leading to integration because they address women's multiple problems with their participation in the solution.

(c) Problems Identified with Women-Specific Projects

A special problem for women-specific projects is the institutional framework in which they are undertaken and the implications for co-ordination between different ministries in the host country for projects with several objectives: for example, water, health, and income-generation. The key questions here are how the institutional mechanisms and human resources, (technical and managerial competence and outreach capabilities) work in the implementation phase given the power structure between ministries. For example, it is difficult for a junior ministry such as the Ministry of Social Affairs to co-ordinate activities which depend on a more powerful ministry.

Institutional Framework of Women-Specific Projects

Buvinic in her penetrating analysis of why women's projects misbehave traces the problem to the institutional framework of women-specific projects. The period immediately following Second World War, saw the development of two parallel worlds of development and relief agencies in the 1950s and 1960s. The World Bank and its affiliates represented the world of economic growth and a host of international and national private voluntary agencies, the other branch of development assistance.

By and large, women's projects are implemented by "women-based institutions...are organisationally capable of executing welfare, but not production-oriented projects". It is generally found that these institutions invariably, translate production objectives into welfare actions.

As in the cases cited by Savane above, the personnel of these institutions do not have the technical capacity to implement income-generating projects for women.

Other institutional difficulties are illustrated by the following example from Asia, which is one of the ten projects reviewed by Carloni in a study carried out for FAO. The women-specific project in question, combined a strong poultry component with vegetable growing and home economics/nutrition advice and was located in the Ministry of Social welfare. "As long as the follow-up project was primarily an agricultural production project it had government funding priority. As soon as it become a women's project, with social welfare objectives, it lost its priority for Funding. If it can be demonstrated that is a common occurrence, it will strengthen the case for integration of women in large agricultural projects as opposed to women's projects".

This example coupled with Buvinic's observations outlined above would make Blumberg's suggestions for overcoming the difficulties inherent in the institutional framework very pertinent. "...more people with demonstrated expertise in women in development (should be hired) both within Third World government ministries and within the various donor agencies". Such hiring practice are necessary at the mission and bureau levels. According to Blumberg, the present practice of adding women's concerns to programme officers "whose main job assignment lies in other areas" is less effective than that suggested above.

If such personnel are hired by aid agencies they should build on the awareness of the multi-dimensional roles and functions mentioned above which seem to be the most positive and the most effective aspect of women-specific projects. Palmer suggests that the "reason why women-only projects look more carefully at multifunctions of women is obvious; they specialise on women, and team members are not diverted to other things. How can we get the best of this into evaluation procedures at all stages for a general project? The only solution is to get in at the very earliest identification stage. If necessary send a woman on her own for three weeks to scout around and establish questions for the first proper team to answer"

Along with the institutional framework in the host country, the question of *donor co-ordination* on certain co-financed projects should be examined. If there is a common ideology behind projects, there may be room for complementarity to avoid overlapping, for example reporting on projects could be integrated.

The Multiplicity of Women's Roles

A number of comments received in response to an earlier drafts of this paper indicated the need to reconsider the so-called welfare component or outcome of women-specific projects. Elmendorf, Van Wijk-Sijbesma, Srinivasan, Timpson, Thomas, Blumberg and Date-Bah among others, point out that the "welfare" aspect can be interpreted more positively. These authors' research deals, respectively, with: women, water and sanitation projects, education projects, supports for mothers and health. All working emphasise the necessity of considering the "whole" women in her reproductive and productive roles and caution against a one-sided emphasis on income-generation projects. The essential points is that there is a need for flexibility in the approach to women and the design of projects, *i.e.* we should start where the women are. The way to reach women who "are on the edge of physical survival" is not with a literacy project but one which will provide support services (day-care, etc.) and alleviate physically burdensome tasks such as fetching water by bringing potable water systems closer to their communities.

Blumberg suggests that health projects are under-rated with respect to their impact on women. She points to three positive aspects of those projects: they are often labour-intensive employers of village-level women; the women who participate gain greatly in self-esteem and autonomy, as well as gaining respect from others in their communities and finally they "may act as role models whose accomplishment inspire increased educational attainment for girls".

Timpson who is working on the Water Decade at UNDP brings to our attention the importance of avoiding an "over-emphasis on economic productivity, which can obscure other personal development and self-fulfilment goals which are part of women's rights and which may be non-economic or not achievable through income—generating activities...".

Elmendorf demonstrates how women's water and sanitation roles can be the key to health and integrated development "a missing element in much other sector planning". In one case the necessity may be for an income-generating project to precede a social one in order for the latter to function properly. An example of where this happened comes from the experience of Dr. Pairat Decharin of the Thai Community Development Department who explained that their emphasis in the 1960s was on training programmes in nutrition and home economics for women, including personal hygiene and sanitation. Due to a slow start and a lack of response from women they realised that income-generating projects were necessary before they could make progress in other areas. Elmendorf has found that "this concept is confirmed by other women in development research and agency experience".

Elmendorf found further evidence of this idea in Sri Lanka where it was observed that income-generating activities where a necessary entry point so that efforts to improve sanitation and health could be more successful.

Similar experiences are reported by Acharya and Bennett for Nepal. "For most women, participation in traditional programmes in health and family planning, education, nutrition and child care, etc. is a *luxury* they cannot afford. Unless the time women spend away from household and agricultural chores can bring in some visible contribution on family income, neither they "nor their households will feel that the time is *justified.* Time is in fact a crucial issue for women...". The authors added that women's workloads, as well as the seasonal and daily variation in their activities should be taken into account and lead to the development of labour-saving technologies in villages to lighten these burdens.

In fact Elmendorf points out that: "When income-generating activities are made available in combination with the introduction of labour-saving village technologies, time and energy can be channelled into more productive activities. Acharya and Bennett also point out that women's increased *visible* contribution to the household especially if it is in the form of cash, usually brings them greater decision-making power in domestic allocations of funds which means that women potentially can influence spending of money for operation and maintenance of water supply and sanitation system".

Thus the chain of events may be from economic towards economic/social. Elmendorf's paper is especially interesting because it gives specific case of the nature of the relationship between economic and social projects and how they can be interdependent and how they can progress from one to the other and back again. The order needed for the projects is not fixed.

A good example of an understanding of women's multiple roles and the issue of social and/or economic is provided by Elmendorf and Isely who used a theoretical framework developed by Chen to show the chain of events set in motion by the improvement of water supplies. "...water supplies (can) affect nutrition and/or energy availability through various mechanisms. Increased household food can become available through home gardens, animal husbandry, or by cash income. With more accessible water sources, women can use their time saved for more efficient household management or storage, processing, distribution of food and more attention to child feeding. Energy expended by women and children in water drawing and carrying would be reduced by more accessible water sources. Last, but not least, the reduction of chronic and acute infectious diseases and infestations could reduce the wastage of nutrients..." which result in lower physical energy.

The combination of social and economic concerns in projects is also illustrated by Srinivasan in regard to literacy interventions which "package" literacy with basic services, "many women's programmes have begun by combining literacy with nutrition and health activities focused on the child and the range of basic services in the 'mix' is being increasingly broadened."

The "package" or mix approach has several distinct advantages over traditional single-purpose literacy interventions. The emphasis here is on facilitating women's access to technical knowledge, skills and services which make improvements, in their daily lives possible. Harmon (112) points to an added advantage, as long as educational programmes convey information regarded by participants as relevant and functional the likelihood of sustained attendance increases.

As Srinivasan points out, "In many instances, however, the developmental 'mix' may not be a mix at all. Separate services coexist without the benefit of a unifying concept or a co-ordinated plan of action. Learning from experience of the need for both integration and relevance, the trend now is to include a strong component of income-generating activities which seem to appeal to women and which serve as a binding factor." Srinivasan also mentions the Bolivian project included in those financed by VEWD presented previously where the range of activities includes: weaving, tailoring, cooking, crafts, basic accounting, hygiene, latrine construction, vegetable growing, home management, family relations, women's role in society and co-operatives. The crux of the matter in regard to 'welfare' criticism of women's programmes shared by so many observers is not so much in the provision of services but in *how* they are organised. The criticism is aimed at the passive role attributed to the beneficiaries by the projects' organisers who do not consult the communities about the services to be provided.

Furthermore, the inclusion of different components "cafeteria" style in a project is no guarantee of integration "...in testing for integration perhaps it may be less important to ask 'Does the project include multisectoral components? than 'what is the underlying philosophy which unifies the different elements of the project? To what extent does the order of introducing these different elements represent an evolutionary process rather than chance or expediency".

Dixon proposes the following list of conditions for the creation of women-specific projects which are similar to those we proposed in relation to "women component" projects discussed earlier. These projects can provide respect for *cultural values* which are opposed to the association in public of unrelated males and females:

— the recognition of the needs for girls and women to

"catch up" with men, *e.g.* in training for skills and professions previously closed to them;

- consideration of the specific problems of women-headed households when they represent a high proportion of the households in the community;
- consideration of the prevailing sexual division of labour, and women's specialisation in certain tasks, such as food production, small animal raising or vegetable marketing, which may need assistance to increase their productivity and then returns of their labour;
- provision of safeguards against the likelihood that men would receive the returns of women's labour, for example, by selling the goods that women produce or by becoming, as household heads, the formal members of co-operatives based on women's work;
- flexibility in planning for women who want their own activities, such as revolving credit clubs or marketing associations, in order to achieve a measure of self-reliance or to avoid conflict or competition with men.

MAJOR ISSUES IN IMPLEMENTATION, MONITORING, ACCOUNTABILITY

A quick overview of available data is sufficient to observe the level of resources devoted to general aid projects as compared with women-specific projects. The cost of the former usually amounts to millions of dollars while the latter never surpasses thousands of dollars. This is one good reason for focusing our discussion of the major issues in implementation, monitoring, accountability and flexibility on general aid projects. Other units which is a small sub-sample of the projects listed in the data was composed in an effort to select agro-food projects, a key area to test our underlying assumptions about project success and the common assumption made by project planners that the household is a homogeneous unit. Thirteen projects of the three types are included in the main, eight general aid projects, three component and two women-specific projects. The table includes a number of variables which are crucial to our analysis:

the executing agency in the host country: the number in the target population, the percentage of women included, the focus of the project (economic or social) productive or welfare-oriented; benefits from the project for women; and positive or negative consequences of the project for women. Although the potential for reaching a larger target group is greater for general aid and component projects, these projects do not realise this potential. It seems in general that increased agricultural productivity has meant more work for women and no more control over resources or access to these resources. In Peru, however, the general provision of water for the families in one area had only positive effects. By saving women three hours a day in water collection, more time was left for income earning and cash saving activities. These two tables demonstrate that a critical review of accountability at various levels to adapt these projects to the needs of the *whole* population is essential.

The integration of women should be part of the professional responsibility of all those involved in project management. This in fact is the thrust of the work on this subject at the World Bank which has been a pioneer in conducting training workshops for Bank staff involved in the design and implementation of project. These workshops aim at sensitising technicians with analytical tools to detect the effects on women in project areas. USAID held similar workshops for AID personnel in the Fall of 1983. The Population Council has developed and continues to develop materials to be utilised in the training of planners. The French Cooperation has begun research on a methodology to set up similar procedures. And last but not least, the DAC High-Level Meeting adopted unanimously (29 November 1983) "Guiding Principles to Aid Agencies for Supporting the Role of Women in Development". Adoption of the Guiding Principles was an expression of recognition of the importance of the role of women in development, an issue which requires consideration by policy makers in aid agencies.

(a) Appraisal and Impact Analysis

How difficult, time-consuming and costly is appraisal or impact analysis? The initial efforts of the Population Council were "appraisals" which combined the use of secondary data bases and short field trips of two to three weeks carried out by experienced consultants. The purpose of the first two case studies of the impact of large scale development projects on women (A Series for Planners) was to draw attention to how the inclusion or exclusion of a consideration of women's roles may affect projects. The first study in this series, the NEMOW case was a composite of two actual development projects for which data was available which illustrated the 'interdependence of women's roles and development".

The second study focused on sex role differences in the farm household and provided a planning methodology for development projects to incorporate the gender dimension. However, subsequent work by the same agency has revised the time estimate upwards for appraisal and impact analysis with the addition of computerisation of the results.

Impact analysis, *i.e.* ex-post evaluation of the project's impact on women is reported to be a more difficult and costly endeavour. According to Singh, an evaluation analyst in CIDA, collecting baseline information and conducting impact analysis is a time consuming and expensive proposition. Depending on the quantity of information and the depth of analysis required, anywhere from four to six months and 50000 to 70000 US dollars, may be required, for a modest effort. In the AID evaluation report of Honduras five to six months was also considered necessary for the collection of data and subsequent impact analysis.

Given these costs and time consideration, perhaps the suggestion of Guerrero at the Inter-American Development Bank, represents a useful strategy: If development projects have negative effects on women it is imperative that during project development these be specified quantitatively to the extent possible in order to obtain a more accurate estimate of overall project feasibility. It is suggested therefore, that there be a discussion of the way in which the issue of women can be incorporated in the methodologies required for assessing project feasibility.

In the previous section, the project cycle of three general aid projects was presented to illustrate how attention to crucial variables in relation to the projects' objectives can indicate what we should be looking for "If we are concerned about eliminating huge areas of indifference and ignorance" and how to avoid major blunders. As Palmer points out, what we need are reliable approximations and reliable qualitative information on socio-cultural structures, relations of economic exchange within the households, the sexual division of labour in different tasks and on different crops, and the way different sources of cash income are earmarked (and by whom) for different household consumption requirements. The studies by Palmer and Burfisher and Hornstein are brilliant examples of what can be done to forestall major blunders by utilising secondary sources. The original assumptions of the project can be revised for example in the light of calculations on heavier workloads for women (especially higher seasonal peaks). Palmer further maintains that three to four weeks is sufficient to obtain and report on a relevant data base. Longer periods indicate a lack of understanding of what to look for in relation to planners' needs. Ideally, a competent woman ought to be in on an identification, monitoring and evaluation team. A woman's brief should be held at the earliest stage onwards and be closely integrated with what the other investigators are doing. Any delay means *ad hoc* supplements for women dissociated from the rest of the project.

Review of these initiatives must include another dimension: the developing country side. Where are the obstacles to the implementation of projects which would in effect integrate women into development according to the criteria set out earlier? Where do we have to start in making integration a standard operational requirement of all projects as part of the professional responsibility of project management? Could one of the problems be that the appraisal evaluation has to concentrate on the factors that the project management can influence?

Other colleagues working in related fields at OECD were consulted. It is interesting to note that the DAC Expert Group on Evaluation has found that the lessons identified have long been recognised. The question therefore arises as to why these problems and deficiencies continue to occur. There are two kinds of constraints to project implementation and it is important to distinguish those based in developing countries and those linked with donor countries. For our purposes, these two sides of the picture in evaluation should be examined with a specific focus on issues related to women. As mentioned earlier, it is important to understand the nature of the constraints: ideological, structural or administrative.

Evaluators in the Expert Group were given a limited mandate to focus on the evaluation of the appraisal and implementation of individual projects. However, they suggest that project identification be more closely linked with country programming in planning aid. Socio-economic, sectoral and institutional analysis should replace an excessively project-specific orientation.

The salient points from both OECD sources are: the need for donor co-ordination, flexibility and more grass-roots participation in all phases of the project.

(b) Donor Co-ordination

The DAC Expert Group on Evaluation suggested that greater co-ordination among donors in country programming is needed with special emphasis on co-ordinating the policy dialogue when non-project aid is involved. There needs to be more co-ordination in the collection of base-line data including better briefing before leaving home with data which meets the criteria for "valid decision-making and responsible management". If outside technical assistance is needed for the preparation of project requests, it should be financed as part of the donor's overhead costs and not as part of the projects. The quality of studies done in the preparatory stage of projects should be improved and the time allocated for project formulation increased. Donors working in the same countries, on co-financed or similar projects could pool their information and thus save time and financial resources. This is particularly important for the integration of women in development project since the integration requires more attention in getting the appropriate information on local conditions.

(c) Flexibility

Flexibility is of particular importance to women's concern for the following reasons:

— there may be a need to lay down certain pre-conditioning structures or resources for women to take advantage of general project interventions;
— there may be inadequacies of base-line data concering women, or design faults which need to be addressed after the basic design and during implementation. In other words with a new subject we cannot expect to get predicted effects right. Therefore, there is a need for flexibility in design options, so that courses can be changed midstream;
— there may be need for an investment component (*e.g.* domestic water supplies) which has a long gestation period and which particularly affects women, if certain project inputs are delayed this delay may cause chaos in some other aspect of the project's implementation.

The importance of flexibility in project design and implementation are associated with monitoring, timing of interventions, synchronisation and experimentation. The latter would include the implementation of smaller less ambitious projects with a pilot phase to allow feedback. However, the difficulty of synchronisation should not be underestimated.

Flexibility in implementation can be estimated by observing whether the project design includes: a process evaluation component, feedback mechanisms and a reserve fund item in the budget. An analysis of the period of time allowed between fund disbursements will also provide information on the amount of flexibility.

One member of the AID evaluation team (132) for the rural roads projects in Kenya felt that AID needed to "study further the extent to which the sequencing of development needs to be an administrative or aid priority". In this view, the lead investment in roads, without follow-up will have been untimely. The author of this annex to the report stated that, "integrated time-phased development undertaken on a regional basis, *i.e.* purposefully planned and co-ordinated development activities which are implemented over a period of time," are preferable to single sector investment, such as roads, or simultaneous integrated development undertaken on a localised basis as in integrated rural development projects.

(d) Participation

A plea was made for more grass-roots participation in the OECD sources and at ILO in all phases of the project including design. This is especially important for integration. Now that participation of the beneficiaries is seen as desirable it is important to establish at the outset that beneficiaries are individuals as well as households. Otherwise the quest for participation will stop at male heads of household who may see things differently from women. Participatory research is difficult but not impossible. If projects are to offer rural women equipment, facilities and service they must be relevant to their needs and priorities. "...the best way to discover those needs is to ask. Poor women whose primary economic activity is cattle raising and dairying, *e.g.*, are unlikely to request an embroidery project..." (135). Built-in mechanism of accountability can be developed with grass-roots participation.

And finally, the effort must involve male allies as well as women ... men and who are already or potentially supportive of women's advancement can be identified within key structures...", as well as male support within the family and community. The latter is an important point in relation to socio-cultural practices and more information is needed.

The first level to look for allies is in the woman's family and household. However, as Date-Bah and Stevens point out in an article on rural women in Africa and technological change, the literature on rural women poses a major sociological problem for the researcher in terms of identifying male allies. The first problem is that women are often treated as isolated individuals in the introduction of new techniques and equipment. It has been reported that by and large, men to the exclusion of women are thought how to use new technology even if women were doing the work for which the new techniques are being introduced.

However, the main sociological problem according to Date-Bah and Stevens is the male image project by the literature: men and women living the same households and villages seem to be leading parallel lives, this is especially true of the portrait for Africa. Husbands are portrayed as callous individuals who have no feeling for their wives, the mothers of their children. This image is certainly generated by the resettlement project in Burkrina Faso presented earlier in this paper, where it was reported that some husbands refused to provide the necessary funds for grinding sorghum for family meals, although their income had increased considerably. "This picture tends to reflect a type of human society where the sexes lead separate lives without interacting and sharing ideas. It would appear that it is on this premise that a number of projects aimed at improving the lot of women in the rural areas have been planned. These projects have thus tended to focus only on women and therefore have committed the same mistake they set out to rectify."

However, rural women do not live in isolation and if we want to find male allies we have to try to enhance the complementarity of men's and women's roles rather than plan for them isolation to counteract past discrimination. Date-Bah and Stevens suggest that the introduction of new technology is one opportunity to change the present state of affairs. "Thus technological change for rural women should be planned and implemented in such a way that it leads to an improvement in the relationship between the rural couple and generally between members of the rural family and between males and females in the village." Co-operatives would also provide a way of enhancing collaboration rather than separation.

Shaheed, a researcher from Pakistan indicates that projects having a specific female target, need to elicit male support from within the community, if for no other reason than to alley fears and minimise or counter probable opposition from the more powerful male half of the community. The essential point is that to be allies, men have to have a stake in what happens to women, and perceive them as part of the solution to development problems. As Carloni states they have to be convinced that the successful outcome of projects depends on including women.

Other ways of cultivating male allies are to meet the men where they are, *i.e.* to address women's issues through development plans as suggested by Miralao at the Asian and Pacific Development Centre in Malaysia. This entry point has an advantage over specific women's programmes which may operate in isolation of more basic economic and social processes. At this level as well, areas for complementarity and co-ordination between government policies and aid projects could be made more explicit.

Another suggestion along the same lines comes from Sarthi Acharya at Tata Institute of Social Sciences in Bombay. Her proposal aims at strengthening national economic planning and developing a continuum between the grass-roots level and the the national planning bodies. The aid agencies in this regard can work in close co-operation and make suggestions as a necessary condition before any aid is granted. In addition, she suggests that governments will have to place a higher priority on rural development than they have in the past. "...the rural base itself has to be strengthened for evolving an alternative path of economic transformation." Thus projects with positive results for women can only be implemented if rural development is taken seriously as a strategy for development at large.

De Arellano, Regional Director for the Organisation of American States' Inter American Commission on Women, indicates from her experience, a strategy which can be successful at the grass-roots and at the same time "touch" the different levels necessary to create a systematic impact on women's lives. "...One must employ elements from both the 'component' and 'specific' projects. This, of course, implies a certain amount of flexibility and willingess on the part of the financing agency." Furthermore, according to De Arellano, the relative success of the Inter American Commission on Women technology project in Bolivia and Ecuador and its applicability to ten additional Latin American countries, can be attributed to having combined the phases which "We now know work". Her impression is that the women in Development process has to come this in a number of countries: a women-specific project which has its national *locus* in an ongoing development effort that has partial responsibility for monitoring, while respecting its "speciality". "This means *including sympathetic and interested males in all phases* (and levels) of planning, implementation, and evaluation (technicians, community men, grassroots promoters)."

As Ingrid Palmer points out confrontation is an open invitation to chauvinism, it provides "more heat than light". The traditional relations between men and women can be expanded, not perverted, by realistic incentives and opportunities for both men and women.

TENTATIVE CONCLUSIONS AND FUTURE RESEARCH

Women-Specific Projects

This review has shown that all three types of projects, *i.e.* general women's component and women-specific can be useful if properly designed and co-ordinated. However, the lessons learned from the implementation of some women-specific and component projects is that they are too welfare-oriented. Future projects should avoid the home economics approach and focus on income generating activities which are relevant and useful to the women participating. However, the main point in regard to these projects is that it is not their welfare aspect *per se* which is objectionable. There is nothing wrong with the "right" kind of welfare and the provision of basic needs such as potable water. Women-specific water and health projects can have positive synergistic effects on women's income generating activities. It is also important to remember that there is no fixed entry point to reach women. As pointed out throughout this discussion in order to reach women are on the brink of survival their needs must be met as they perceive them. It is also essential to remember that these projects to successfully integrate women must have an underlying philosophy of cohesive evolution which leads to development and not charity. Help them to help themselves.

The institutional framework and personnel of women-specific projects seem to be major obstacles to integrations because evidence presented in this paper shows that too often the agencies responsible for women-specific projects are not capable of implementating income-generating projects, their personnel does not have the necessary training or management skills. Another problem is that as soon as women are relegated to "welfare" concerns they become marginal in the perception of those in control of budget allocations such as the Ministry of Planning or Agriculture: they lose their priority for funding and their projects flounder as a result.

General Aid and Component Projects

As mentioned earlier, given the vast resources devoted to general aid and most component projects and the negative impact that the majority of them have had in terms of women's access to resources, a way of changing this state of affairs must be found. The project cycle approach used in the presentation of three general aid projects in the text and questions asked in regard to two other projects of this type illustrate how the lessons we have learned from the shortcoming of such projects can improve the design and implementation of future projects of this type. Three of the four components projects presented also show the need for starting early in the consideration of the major areas which are known to affect women, instead of tacking on activities for women which are not relevant to their occupations and concerns. Furthermore, it can be argued that unless this is done, enormous waste and deprivation will be the result of too many development projects.

Appraisal and prediction analysis implies action on a number of levels, stating and revealing areas of negative impact is not enough. In addition to the project cycle approach, one way to more positive results for these projects is to distinguish and identify those mechanisms which are based in developing country institutional structures and those which arise in donor agencies. However, the part played by the former and the latter may not be entirely separate. The responsibility, for example, for the allocation of land to the male head of household may be the result of developing country-donor interaction in the past when different systems of production were envisaged.

One major obstacle to equitable distribution of benefits in the implementation of projects seems to be donor agency and developing country ideology in regard to the capabilities and functions of women. How can change be brought about? Preaching may just alienate project management, who should be the major target for training in impact analysis such as that provided by the Bank and USAID. Unless this training is perceived by project manager as a means of improving their professional performance rating its "impact" will not be enough to enhance their ability to implement project objectives in all their ramifications.

One way to see if such training has been effective would be a review by the Bank and other agencies who have run training workshops, to study and analyse the characteristics of the participants in relation to the type of projects they have subsequently implemented, their level of responsibility, the nature of the critical points of resistance concerning the training message, *i.e.* ideological, structural or administrative.

General aid projects will not reach women and improve their lot, unless armed with an informed understanding of their roles and functions. This means that the "training" mentioned above has to be addressed to those involved all along the programming and project cycle. Conviction of the importance of this issue by top management will help other staff to integrate these ideas in their performance.

Where are the areas for donor co-ordination and flexibility in existing projects? Innovation in the design of new projects which takes into account the lesson learned above is essential to increase food production and improve family nutrition. Technology which aims at reducing the non-paid workload of women, to free them for income-generating activities is needed. But how can we ensure that women will retain control over the income they have generated?

This paper is one step among many in the development of the analytical tools for the inclusion of women in large-scale development projects. As stated elsewhere, this kind of analysis is in its infancy. More materials on urban projects are needed, however, what is most urgent is not another "overview" of impact of urban project but in-depth case studies using the analytical tools outlined in this paper on specific projects and the problems all along the project cycle.

The essential thrust of this approach to project analysis is to differentiate between "empirical (data) knowledge and cognitive (understanding) knowledge, and the appropriate balance between the two. We cannot demand hung empirical investigations for each proposed project." What is important is our own cognition of the general impact of economic change on women. If we understand, then we have the capacity to recognise the essential points *i.e.,* we know what to look for in any field investigation of a new project. "General cognition mean the ability to set up questions or hypotheses, as well as the awareness of what fact are needed to test the hypotheses. Transmitting our understanding to male planners will come from the drip-drip of our educational efforts". In the meantime they may need a little convincing with the aid of some empirical data from different setting such as that provided in the review of projects.

Future Research

Further research is envisaged beyond the UN Conference to Review and Appraise the UN Decade for Women in July 1985. The comments and materials received in response to an earlier draft of this paper have substantially altered plans for future research. Our research should address the most essential or crucial areas for women. The result of concentration and reflection with specific project materials at hand, points to the need for attention to links between the micro and the macro levels in the food chain.

We have seen that women are frequently invisible in development plans and project documents. The research proposed would try to demonstrate how this invisibility is linked to the common problems of women as food producers and providers in different seating. Such research must combine a conceptual and sample framework in systematic information "gathering at the micro and macro levels. This approach is needed to provide a typology of situations and results. The identification of certain kinds of information can improve "visibility". Knowledge of regional agricultural and socio-cultural patterns can point us in the right direction and indicate what we need to know about project or selected areas for study.

Issues

Decisions taken by producers as to what, how and for whom to produce vary according to preferences which are not only related to food provisioning. By focusing on key socio-cultural groups in specific countries the motivations and rationale of these groups for the production of given crops would become apparent.

One issue relates to the question of *how* production is increased. This is an issue raised by Mellor and Johnston who emphasise the importance of increasing *productivity* as part of the growth of output. For our purposes, it is even more important to ask *by whom* will production be increased, men or women? This raises the possibility that men and women producers may have goals conflicting with each other and with those of governments in regard to the cultivation of given crops. For example, governments may want a surplus in given staples such as wheat, maïze or rice to be produced for urban consumers who are politically more articulate and powerful than the rural producers. However, women are often not engaged in the production of the crops the government has earmarked for food self-sufficiency or may not give priority to the latter for various reasons. It become important, therefore, to consider in concrete cases the implications of the fact that women are not usually cultivating "self-sufficiency" crops or that they are often unremunerated for their work on these crops.

Another issue is the need for more research focused on the household and farm division of labour and how all family members are affected by the type of production unit in which they live, there is still little understanding of how the household level and the women in them are related in practice to national strategies for food self-sufficiency. Furthermore what is known about farming systems must be articulated to include women in the analysis as we shall illustrate below.

A balanced appraisal of a food policy for self-reliance would include expertise from several disciplines: economics, agronomy, nutrition, sociology, anthropology and ecology. A food systems approach is essential to an understanding of how food problems are linked to economic structure and varying internal and external forces.

Variables

The key variables for examination of women's participation in agriculture are:

(i) the extent of smallholder agriculture,
(ii) the extent to which the agricultural product is sold on local markets,
(iii) the flow of and cumulated male outmigration,
(iv) the types of crop(s) cultivated.

An examination of data in regard to the crops designated for self-sufficiency by governments as compared to the crops cultivated by women is essential; they are most often not the same. In other words, if production targets for self-sufficiency are not related to the crops women cultivate, then their contribution to food strategies is masked (or undermined) or taken for granted and yet may not be forthcoming, or taken into consideration in planning for self-sufficiency. There is evidence that the food crops produced by women provide a kind of "safety net" for the farm family significantly influencing the amount of risk male farmers are willing to incur in the production of other crops.

The multiplicity of women's roles and competing demands made on their time marks studies of women's time allocation including the seasonality aspect an essential component in any food equation.

For instance, since cassava can grow also in depleted soils, it is often planted at the end of the rotation cycle in Africa. Cassava has also replaced yams in some areas of West Africa where male outmigration is heavy since its cultivation need less land preparation. These considerations indicate that the characteristics of the crop have to be investigated. Another characteristic of this crop is its perishability after harvesting, (it keeps well in the ground) Food strategies concern not only production, but also processing, storage and distribution. Therefore, processing technology would have to be developed to cope with any increased output in this crop. Storage becomes problematic otherwise.

Since food strategies are also concerned with the balance of payments and agricultural exports, the fact that some roots, tubers and other crops produced by women are not competitive on international markets and indeed are not exportable, is of relevance. However, for Africa at least, they are important components of national diets in many countries, which will continue to be so for number of decades. Furthermore, the resilience and "root retention" of African populations for their traditional foods may conflict with the government's objectives for a "self-sufficiency crop" as in the case of Nigeria. The planting of wheat was delayed by farmers in the Kano River of Nigeria. The planting of wheat was delayed by farmers in the Kano River scheme because their food (sorghum) comes first. This could also be said for the cultivation of yams in regard to certain ethnic groups such as the Baoule in the Ivory Coast.

Peasant producers may not only decide that their foods come first but that producing a surplus is not worthwhile in terms of prices, lack of production supports and indebtedness. This is clearly a frequently occurring phenomenon, was in indicated in reports from Mexico.

Elements of a Conceptual and Sample Framework for Comparative Research

A first step in constructing a sample of countries or regions within them would be to identify areas where the cluster or constellation of the key sufficiency. The analysis in research of this kind should identify the characteristics of the actors in relation to the crops they are producing and how they relate to national food policies. For example, Thailand which is self-sufficiency in rice could be compared to Mexico whose, stated goals are self-sufficiency in maize and beans in central and southern Mexico or a Sahelian country such as Burkina Faso which has not achieved its objectives of self-sufficiency. For specific regions in these countries, a preliminary examination would "plot" the key variables on a chart or axis. Since, for instance, in Mexico the crisis in food production is on rainfed land in the centre and south where smallholders cultivating maize and beans predominate, research should focus on the distribution and size of agricultural holdings, the intra-household sexual division of labour, migration patterns etc. to find out how women fit into food strategies for self-sufficiency.

Based on this "objective data" (ecological area, crops cultivated, migration patterns, type of holding, intra-household division of labour, etc.) a series of hypotheses could be developed with these specific populations in mind.

Perhaps the best way to start would be to examine specific food and agricultural projects while they are being designed or just before implementation or at other stages with the understanding that all executed stages of any given project would be analysed on the basis of:

- available information at those past stgaes, with indication of information missing;
- examination of assumptions made of how recipients would respond to the project;
- examination of the interaction of recipient ministry(ies) and donor agencies;
- examination of resources available, and the prioritisation of their expenditure and their relevance;
- examination of flexibility of options paying particular attention to the closing off of options at each past stage;
- and identification of ideological, information, or administrative convenience, misjudgements of women's concerns.

After such an examination of projects, we would know if the type of data mentioned above is available. Work at the project level would fill the gap in our knowledge in regard to a number of questions: crops cultivated by women with what complementarity with men?: women's time allocation and seasonal patterns, what are their needs: financial, technological, and access to income etc. and how are these needs being met currently. These initial forays would provide clues and information as to how this micro picture might add upon a larger scale and what the implications are for planners.

Policy Implications and These Variables

There is repeated reference in the literature to the importance of smallholders (one of our key variables in regard to women) for agricultural production. In fact, Mellor and Johnston advocate an emphasis on a "unimodal" pattern of agricultural development on smallholdings rather than a dualistic pattern of cultivation. This is advised because agriculture is the most important potential source of income and employment in low-income countries. Increases in productivity must be envisaged which employ the abundant labour in most low-income countries. Therefore, emphasis must be placed on gradually increasing the productivity of small farmers. The technological and other innovations to bring this about should be adapted to these labour abundant populations rather than emphasising capital which is usually scarce.

The food systems approach suggested are beginning of this section, is also a way of linking nutritional need with access to resources to satisfy that need. This focus is more helpful than the welfare-oriented approach too often associated with women.

In other words, it is no longer enough to state that women have pivotal roles in any food strategy, we have to find out what these are in the larger perspective. With an examination of data and an analysis of how the key variables interact we can acquire an informed understanding of how women can in the food equation. It is only with knowledge of this kind that a consistent set of measures can be designed whose implementation will enhance the role of women in food systems in a number of settings.

Research of this kind can spell out the implications for governments in terms of the economic costs unsuccessful food strategies for food self-sufficiency. Without further research women may continue to remain "invisible" for planners with the accompanying negative consequences for the outcome of food strategies.

Advocacy certainly has a role to play, but it must not stop at pure rhetoric and continued neglect, we must begin to examine the available data. Countries do operate under constraints, they do next foreign exchange from agricultural exports, but the pitfalls of taking food production by women for granted must be made evident with careful examination and analysis of concrete situations.

ANNEXURE

UNDP PROGRAMMES FOR WOMEN: A SUMMARY

The Action-Oriented Assessment of Rural Women's Participation in Development forms part of UNDP's evaluation programme, undertaken jointly with Participating and Executing Agencies. It is also the latest in a series of continuing activities aimed at promoting and increasing women's participation in development projects and programmes supported by UNDP. Thus, in 1975 educational and informational activities were initiated,[1] followed by detailed *Guidelines on the Integration of Women in Development.*[2] An attempt has also been made during the past five years to monitor the progress achieved in involving women in projects.[3] In the process of time it has become clear that while there has evolved a greater acceptance and fuller understanding of the role of women in development, difficulties are encountered in actually programming for women's participation in development. The chief aim of the current UNDP Assessment is therefore to improve the United Nations system's capability to offer programming advice to governments at the project level concerning these matters.[4]

A further purpose of the study is to make a special contribution to the World Conference of the United Nations

Decade for Women (WCUNDW), to be held in Copenhagen in July 1980. The Conference will review and assess, at the mid-point of the United Nations Decade for Women, the progress and obstacles encountered in attaining the objectives of the Decade and prepare a programme of action for its second half (1980-1985), designed to implement the World Conference of the International Women's Year (WCIWY) in 1975.[5] Within this framework and UNDP's mandate of providing technical co-operation, the Action-Oriented Assessment was conceived as a joint Agency/UNDP undertaking.

In view of the magnitude and complexity of women's role in development, the need for selectivity in approaching the problem was obvious. As many international resolutions and recommendations have emphasized the need to pay special attention to rural women,[6] who also constitute a large majority in the developing world, it was decided to limit the Assessment to this particular section of society. The Food and Agriculture Organization (FAO) was invited to be the lead agency among other agencies with substantial mandates in rural development, *i.e.,* the International Labour Organisation (ILO); the United Nations; United Nations Educational, Scientific and Cultural Organization (UNESCO); United Nations Industrial Development Organization (UNIDO) and World Health Organization (WHO). In addition, the Regional Commissions have been involved to varying degrees and three funding organizations—United Nations Fund for Population Activities (UNFPA); United Nations Children's Fund (UNICEF) and World Food Programme (WFP) have collaborated where possible on the study. UNDP has co-ordinated the exercise and prepared the final report in consultation with the agencies.

Interagency meetings were held in the fall of 1978 to establish a methodology for the exercise. It was agreed that the best way of handling the conflicting demands of broad geographic coverage and the need for intensive examination of specific problems at the country and project levels would be to divide the Assessment into two parts:

(i) desk reviews, which would attempt to give a brief outline of the situation of women in each of the four developing

regions, including relevant technical co-operation projects; and

(ii) country missions.

Against the backdrop of the four regional reviews, four country case studies, one for each of the main developing regions, constitute a major part of the Assessment. These studies include two main parts: a profile of the situation of rural women in each of the four mission countries, *i.e.,* Rwanda, the Syrian Arab Republic, Indonesia and Haiti,[7] followed by proposals for technical co-operation that were formulated by each mission in close consultation with respective governments.

The selection of mission countries was based on two main considerations: first, that the government be interested in receiving such a mission, and second, that UNDP resources for technical co-operation be available to permit programming of activities of special interest to rural women. As resources for the current programming cycle, covering the years 1977-1981, were in many instances fully committed, the number of countries that could be considered for missions was quite limited.

Concerning the substantive content of the study, it was agreed to concentrate on the sub-theme of the World Conference, namely, rural women's employment, health and education, with the important proviso that all aspects of women's work were to be included under employment. In addition, rural women's role in development planning and implementation is discussed, but briefly, since data on this topic are scarce.

Apart from these general regional reviews and specific country case studies, the exercise contains a short summary of a few global and interregional projects of special interest to women. Findings and recommendations for action are presented in a concluding chapter.

Introduction

The concern of the present action-oriented study is limited to the problems faced by rural women in developing countries. However, to fully appreciate these problems, it is helpful to see them in the wider perspective of women's situation as it appears to have evolved and to exist in all cultures. While class or social ranking is a general and basic factor in women's as well as men's fate in life, the special problem faced by women is that there are two systems of stratification in operation.

The second system concerns women's position *vis-a-vis* men in public and private life. It is in this sense that women are facing problems of discrimination peculiar to them and it is this universal problem that lies behind the designation of the International Women's Year in 1975, followed by the current United Nations Decade for Women. Since the origins of present systems of social organization go back to prehistoric times, it is not possible to be definite about the history of the present situation. However, it seems quite clear that the discriminatory feature is something that has emerged as part of the process of cultural and technological evolution, a basic feature of which is population increase, accompanied by an intensified competition for resources. In the beginning we may have had no more than a functional, not necessarily rigid division of labour, similar to what is still found, or was until recently found, among peoples living at the subsistence level. As societies become increasingly stratified, discrimination against women appears to emerge as an inevitable feature. As such it typically varies significantly with class at the same time as it cuts across class stratification.

The intensity of discrimination is highly variable, ranging from a show of public deference to men of no or minor practical significance to a state of severs subjugation.[8] A common denominator is that under conditions of rapid change and increasing competition for scarce resources, as at present in the majority of developing countries, discrimination tends to become more pronounced (unless mitigated through the intervention of political organizations and authorities[9]). In the following brief outline an attempt will be made to indicate some principal features of the current situation.

Rural Development and the Changing Division of Labour Between Men and Women

(a) General Overview

The current tendency in developing countries is generally, as just noted, towards a rather rigid, but not static, division of labour between men and women. Although new options may exist for the privileged few, for the large majority of women, particularly in rural areas, development has not brought change for the better but rather the opposite. An important reason for this situation is that men tend to appropriate the more lucrative employment opportunities that become available as part of the introduction of modern technology. As a result, a modified division of labour may emerge but it is as rigid as the old pattern, except that women are shifted to less rather than more attractive task.[9a] Very briefly, the process may be explained as follows.

The original basis of ˛all sexual division of labour is undoubtedly men's and women's different role in human reproduction. In societies at the subsistence level, of which there are very few left, women where generally responsible for such tasks as the gathering, production and processing of food for the family; the care, education and socialization of small children; the fetching of fuel and water; and local trade or exchange of surplus products. A common feature of these tasks is that they could usually be performed near the home. Men, on the other hand, went hunting and fishing, often far from the home; assisted in clearing the ground under burn and slash agriculture; conducted long-distance trade and were responsible for the security of the community. Children of both sexes assisted their parents and were thus trained to assume their adult roles in due course.[10] By way of generalization, one may conclude that men's and women's tasks were related to their differential roles in securing the survival of the family. Even so, many activities were not directly, if all, related to physical differences but were assigned as need and interests indicated. Additionally, in small communities or relatively self-contained households, it was often not possible to be unduly strict in the matter and men and women occasionally assisted with each other's tasks.

As societies have become more complex and stratified, division of labour has becomes more rigid, within as well as between the sexes, and ultimate authority and power have, practically without exception, become vested in a male elite.[11]

These matters, a strictly enforced sexual division of labour, often imbued with the absolute command of religious beliefs, and the maleness of public authority, appear essential to any understanding of why development seems as a rule to have had an adverse effect on the role and status of women.

First of all, a basic feature of development is to introduce new and modified technologies, inevitably accompanied by changes in economic and social organization, with a view to increasing the total output of society's productive resources, human and non-human. Additionally, as part and parcel of the development process, population has been growing at a very high rate, thereby greatly intensifying the competition for often precariously scarce resources. A general consequence of these and related factors is that development has as a rule been accompanied by complex and painful societal disruptions. As urban areas have generally been favoured over rural areas in the allocation of resources, the rural population has been particularly hard hit by these negative effects of development, which may be summarized as having led to the by now well-known polarization of society into rich and poor. A closely associated but until recently overlooked phenomenon is the intensified dichotomization of the relationship between men and women, leaving women relatively worse off than men even though both sexes obviously are very hard hit by the effects of the impoverization of large sectors of the rural population (many of whom migrate to urban areas in search of a better life).

In this context it is also highly relevant to consider the changing relationship between the private family and society at large. The increasingly specialized methods of production that constitute the core of the development process, require, *inter alia,* ever-larger units of economic and social organization. As a result, the family progressively loses its role as a relatively independent economic and social unit. Gradually, a large number of both decision-making and other functions are transferred to society at large. In the course of this transformation, men's and women's functions in the private and public spheres of life tend to become more and more lopsided, with men losing touch with family life and problems and women understanding less and less of the workings of the public machinery. In many ways this is a well-recognized phenomenon but its political and administrative implications for men's and women's joint responsibility for societal well-being remain largely unexplored and would seem to deserve special attention, not least, not least by women.[12]

Given the world as it is, with men overwhelmingly in charge of the public sphere and women often left to handle the private sphere as best they can, it is not surprising that women are forgotten in development planning and implementation and find themselves shortchanged in the process. When they protest and want to change the situation, they are faced with grave handicaps *because* of their inferior position.

(b) Manifestations of Women's Problems

Women's special problems manifest themselves across the board but can in large measure be traced to three main areas: the data base for development planning; education and training, including extension services; the technological change, not least its social implications.

In the book-keeping system of development, *i.e.,* the statistics used for the preparation of development plans, women (and girls) have generally been seen as consumers, not as producers. It is in varying degrees recognized that they are in need of public services, such as health care and education. The contribution of such services to the productivity of labour is, however, not well understood and is usually ignored. Moreover, women's work, in particular rural women's work, is often not counted statistically. This alleged lack of contribution to the productive effort, in combination with a general shortage of funds, tends to give women a low priority as recipients of public support.

A primary reason for not including women's work in the computation of the Gross National Product (GNP) is that so much of it is performed in the family setting. Additionally, it is often of a subsistence nature. On both counts such work, when performed by women, tends to be excluded from official statistics.[13] According to generally accepted standards, it should be recorded as "unpaid family labour" if it concerns production that may, at least in part, be sold on the market. In many countries such work is recorded, in many others it is not fully recorded or omitted entirely. The reason for non-recording is usually that the societal ideal is that women should not perform such work, in particular not field work. It should be done by men or, in parts of India, *e.g.,* by hired lower-caste women.

Another reason for non-recording of women's work is that it is to a large extent labelled domestic work and this is conventionally excluded from statistically recognized work. The exclusion is particularly misleading as concerns rural women's work in developing countries where it often includes all post-harvest processing of grains and the fetching of water and fuel, in addition to child care, cooking and preservation of food and other house-keeping duties.[14]

Still another reason for non-recording appears to be what has been called "occupational multiplicity", *i.e.,* the necessity individuals or households to combine several economic activities—often in the course of the same day—in order to subsist.[15] In principle this phenomenon is not limited to women; it also applies to men and children.[16] Often it appears, however, as if more occupational options are available or explored by women.[17] The lack of reporting of such activities appears mainly to reflect the limitations of commonly used concepts and methods of gathering employment information. Typically, simple retrospective questions are asked concerning the amount and kind of work performed the previous week, say. The questionnaires leave no room, and the interviewers have no time or instructions for how to handle the complex stories that are covered by the term "occupational multiplicity" (assuming that those questioned would recall all of their different occupations).

For all of these three sets of reasons, official statistics on rural women's labour force participation are generally of very limited use. Often all they indicate is that women's work is understated, often grossly so. So far, the only remedy is intensive time-use studies, of which an increasing number have become available in recent years. A general finding of these is that women work at least as much, often considerably more, than men. In some instances it has also been found that the prevalent ideas of rural underemployment, of men or women, are very misleading. Overemployment with pitifully low returns is a more accurate description. Such data also seem to confirm that conventional questionnaires concerning economic activities, even when great care is taken to include unpaid family labour, *e.g.*, may nevertheless result in considerable under-reporting.[18] The main drawback of time-use studies is their high cost and limited coverage, usually a village.

Because of its wide ramifications, the discrimination against women in matters of education and training is probably the most damaging of all. It is a well-documented phenomenon that will be discussed in all subsequent regional reviews and country case studies. It is of course also closely related to technological change and it is more than coincidental that the educational gap between men and women, boys and girls, is widest in technical fields. Not infrequently, most lines of technical education and training, including agricultural education, are closed to girls, even though such education would help them substantially in carrying out their traditional tasks. The obstacles to change are, however, not limited to formal admittance but are also firmly entrenched in traditional attitudes of both men and women, making it difficult for girls to avail themselves of many forms of technical education even where the legal barriers have been removed. In the few areas where women as a rule admitted—often because they are less indispensable—they are generally employed in relatively subordinate positions, such as nursing and the teaching of girls and young boys. Needless to say, these matters vary a great deal from country to country and exceptions exist. Additionally, changes in practice and attitude seem to be spreading. Nevertheless, as a generalization of some of the key problems responsible for the inferior position of adult rural women in developing countries, the above comments seem valid.

Nothing illustrates more clearly than women's lack of access to modern technology, closely linked to the pervasive bias against women in technical education and training, that women's problems in becoming part of the development process, as participants and beneficiaries, are not limited to the obstacles raised by class and scarcity (which are equally men's problems and, in a men's world, affect men more directly than women) but involve admittance to the male hierarchy of power and status. At any rate, it is difficult to find any other explanation for the bias encountered in matters of technological change, where the general rule is that whenever the change leads to improved income-earning opportunities, men tend to avail themselves of these, even if the work affected was formerly in the domain of women's duties. Examples of the latter case will be found in the Indonesian case study.[19] Here it seems that the replacement of female by male workers may in one instance—harvesting—be justified by changes in the nature of the work, as the new methods require more physical strength than the old methods. However while displacement of significant numbers of male workers is usually viewed as calling for remedial action of some sort, this is very rarely the case with female workers.

Other common examples along the same lines concern the offering of agricultural training and extension services to men while the work is being done by women.[20] The net effect of such programmes is mainly a drain on scarce resources. In part this bias in favour of men goes back to colonial times when female farming was seen as inferior by the European administrators,[21] but it also fits the pattern of a more general bias in favour of men.

In short, there is a consistent tendency to allocate resources to the advantage of men, leaving women behind in all aspects of development. Rural women must in the vast majority of cases continue to do their work without the assistance of education, training, and improved technology, the only significant change being that, with more surviving children, the workload becomes heavier and output tends to fall as competition for land and other scarce resources intensifies. With a growing recognition that this state of affairs acts as a deterrent to development and is harmful not only to women but to society at large, the next question concerns the strategy for change: how and by what means can women become active participants in rural development? Interestingly enough, the tentative answer to this question has in large measure been provided, or implied, by the continuing re-evaluation of development strategies that constitutes an important element of development itself.

Rural Women's Participation in Development—Indicated Strategies

The re-evaluation of development strategies reflects of course the growing experience and manifestations of development, not least changes in the political structures that have occurred since development became an issue of global concern during the second half of the 1940's. As a result, development priorities have gradually become much more varied. Earlier there was, with a few notable exceptions, a very strong emphasis on concentrated capital-intensive development in those sectors of the economy deemed to have the greatest prospects for integration (or further integration) into the international market system. The dominant measure of development was the rate of growth of the GNP. More broad-based development, the stated goal of all development plans, was supposed to follow gradually through more or less automatic multiplier or spread effects.

In due course it became increasingly clear that the spread effect of this strategy was very weak. Rather, this general approach to development was found to be the prime mover towards increasing economic and social stratification, the rich getting richer and the poor getting poorer, which soon emerged as a prominent feature of development, internationally and nationally.

From the continuous debate of these matters, it has since the late 1960's become increasingly clear that development must, without neglect of the growth issue, concern itself with the need for structural and institutional change to ensure that the benefits become more equitably distributed. No less important than the equity issue, is the realization that the prospects for development improve with wider participation.

From the point of view of rural women's role in development, these matters are of primary importance since they have been a major factor in at long last gaining women some recognition as active contributors to development. In what follows a number of current issues of special interest to rural women will be identified and suggestions made on possible policies or strategies of special interest to them.[22]

At this point it should also be noted that we are in the present study primarily concerned with rural women's problems as they present themselves within the developing countries, as this is where the majority of opportunities for technical co-operation present themselves. This should, however, in no way make us lose sight of the importance for women—and men—of the severely disadvantaged position of developing countries *vis-a-vis* industrial countries in their efforts to attain full sovereignty and a higher level of living for their peoples. The establishment of the New International Economic Order[23] is therefore of primary concern to the women in the developing countries, in particular those in the poorest countries. In the international as well as the national arena, women have special problems related to such matters as conditions of work and transfer of technology, etc.[24] In either case, the initiatives for remedial action will mainly have to be generated within countries, and key efforts need to be aimed at the adoption of policies that will "promote the participation and advancement of women in all fields of work, provide them with equal educational opportunities, and such services as would facilitate housework."[25]

Because so much of the development effort has been deficient in its attempts to reach the common people, there is now widespread agreement that the revised development strategies need to be more broad-based and people-oriented. For such strategies to succeed, they must combine two basic principles. On the one hand they must provide for a wide distribution of benefits and services like health care, education and training, productive employment, credit, marketing, fuel, water, sanitation and protection against environmental degradation, in particular the loss of cultivable land through erosion. On the other hand, to make such policies a realistic alternative, a greater mobilization of people as productive agents must be achieved. Their labour, capability, motivation and enterprise in bettering their own conditions must be stimulated. In both respects, women's role in development, not least in rural areas, deserves special attention.[26]

For rural women, new initiatives are particularly urgent in matters of agricultural production, cottage and small-scale industry, credit, marketing, energy, technology, potable water supply, sanitation, primary health care, education and training.

Special attention to women's role in agricultural production, including animal husbandry, is justified on several counts, First, the continuing re-evaluation of development strategies has, *inter alia* involved an assessment of the relative importance of rural *versus* industrial/urban development. As a result, the consensus now is that rural development had been grossly neglected. Major factors behind this conclusion were the realization that absolute poverty was a common phenomenon of frightening proportions and that many countries were beginning to lose the ability to feed their rapidly growing populations.

Second, as part of the increased interest in rural development, and often quite coincidentally, women's crucial role in agricultural production, as well as other aspects of rural life, has emerged or, willy-nilly, been "discovered" (a dairy project could, *e.g.*, not be launched without the participation of women, since they were entirely responsible for the milking and care of the cows). Most important is probably the recognition of the crucial role women play in food production. If they have any access to land at all, they grow at least part, often all or most of the food the family consumes, and they often participate in the production of marketable food supplies and other agricultural crops as well. Additionally, they are everywhere traditionally responsible for the processing, preparation and preservation of food. Other common tasks include the care of animals, and, of course, the care of children, house-keeping and the fetching of fuel and water.

Rural women are also traditionally occupied in cottage industries of various kinds and in the local trade of the output of such industries and other products, in particular surplus food. As the shortage of cultivable land intensifies, non-agricultural occupations have assumed greater and greater importance as the main source of income. Under all too common conditions of extreme poverty, the opportunities for reasonably productive and remunerative work are scarce indeed. Additionally, rural women have difficulties in engaging in income-generating activities because of their general lack of modern education and training and their hard and time-consuming responsibilities in the above-mentioned tasks of food processing (*e.g.* pounding and other processing of grain) and the fetching of fuel and water, often requiring many hours of work a day. Finally, given these conditions, both the women themselves and their families, in particular the children, are prone to suffer from further impediments in the form of illness and general weakness and debilitation. To assist them in their work, rural women are primarily obliged to rely on their daughters, who consequently are drawn into the same conditions of life and all too often fail to obtain the same educational opportunities as the boys.

Even from this very brief account of rural women's responsibilities, it will readily be seen that women carry a very substantial responsibility for the maintenance of rural life. However, since all or much of this work is of a subsistence nature, performed at home, rural women have, as noted earlier, generally been ignored by the planners.[27] As a result they continue to perform their work, which is increasing on account of larger family size and increasing pressure on land and other resources, without any assistance in the form of education, training and improved technology. If the commonly advocated, more broad-based rural development effort is to succeed, an inescapable conclusion would seem to be that rural women must be given increased support, designed to enable them to perform their traditional as well as new tasks in a more productive and rewarding way.

In respect of agricultural production, women's work must be treated as the important part of the farm family's work that it is and extension and other services should be designed to meet women's as well as men's needs. At present there are often, hardly any agricultural extension services for women. Furthermore, if the women is, in fact, the head of the household, as increasingly and frequently happens, she should be treated as such.

In plans for the development of non-conventional energy sources, such as woodlots, bio-gas, and small-scale generation of electricity, women's energy needs for cooking as well as for other purposes, in particular small scale industry, should be considered.

Similarly, women have a pressing need for improved tools and implements and other appropriate technology to assist them in their hard and time-consuming work in farming, food-processing, fuel and water portage and other household activities. They also need assistance aimed at employment creation, *inter alia,* through the development of arts and crafts production into more efficient small-scale industrial undertakings, based on traditional as well as non-traditional, locally available raw materials. Of special importance is technical education and training in such projects as accounting, co-operative organization and marketing, and increased facilities for credit.

Finally, there is the large area of social and physical infrastructure, covering such services as education, health care, water and sanitation. As concerns education, there is above all a need to make educational facilities available to girls on an equal basis with boys. There is also a general need for curriculum reform, aimed at making education more relevant to the needs and opportunities of society.

In matters of certain services that have until now generally been provided through face-to-face contact with a professionally trained public employee, the consensus seems to be that the delivery system must undergo radical change because it is only reaching a tiny fraction of the rural population. The change must be towards community based delivery systems, in which members of the village population are selected, at least in part through popular participation, to serve as lay agents in their own villages. In addition to taking care of special cases, referred to them by the local agents, professional staff should in large measure devote their time to the training and supervision of the community-based system. This approach, practised in the People's Republic of China and on a smaller scale in many other countries, would in appropriate forms seem to be particularly relevant in the development of more effective preventive and curative health care systems and extension services.[28]

The majority of rural women in developing countries is also in great, sometimes desperate, need of improved water supply and sanitation facilities. Apart from the provision of the physical facilities, successful programmes in these areas require extensive training and education in matters of both maintenance and use. Other serious environmental problems concern very poor housing and soil erosion, leading to large-scale loss of cultivable soil.

More could be said about rural women's needs, but, even as is, the list may seem prohibitive and unrealistic. Nevertheless, it is not possible to shorten the list. Instead, the emphasis must be put on the potential but under-utilized productive contribution of rural women and their families. Given an opportunity to improve their conditions of life, there is every reason to believe that the productive effort and capability would be commensurate with the task of more broad-based development. In getting the process started, the most crucial factors are in most instances not necessarily lack of physical resources but the capacity for organization and the rather fortuitous factor of leadership. In these in other matters, the role of women is only rarely taken into account.

To conclude, if the poor are to be given a fair opportunity to participate in the development effort, there is every reason to consider the participation by women as full and equal partners as a major factor in this effort. In this words, as there are two systems of social stratification, there are two problems of integration, that of the poor and, especially within but also beyond this problem, that of women. Without the active participation in rural development of women, no strategy is going to succeed within the foreseeable future.

Notes and References

1. See UNDP, Governing Council, Nineteenth Session 15-31 January 1975, "Action by UNDP in response to General Assembly Resolution 3202 (S-VI) on the Programme of Action on the Establishment of a New International Economic Order. The Integration of Women in Development." Note by the Administrator. 7 November 1974. (DP, 83); Ester Boserup and Christina Liljencrantz, *Integration of Women in Development—Why, When, How,* UNDP, New York, 1975; Irene Tinker and Michele Bo Bramsen (eds.), *Women and World Development,* Overseas Development Council, Washington, D.C., 1976; UNDP, *Women in Development—Courses for Action* (audiovisual aids and discussion guides).
2. UNDP, Programme Policy and Evaluation Division, *Guidelines on the Integration of Women in Development,* 25 February 1977. (G3100-1).
3. See UNDP, Governing Council, Twentieth Session 11-27 June 1975, "General Review of Programmes and Policies of UNDP—The Integration of Women in Development." Report by the Administrator. 5 May, 1975. (DP/127); UNDP Governing Council, Twenty-fifth Session 12-30 June 1978, "Role and Activities of UNDP. Report by the Administrator. Addendum "Integration of Women in Development." 12 May, 1978. (DP/319/Add.3).
4. Independent of the present exercise, UNDP has approved the financing of three sub-regional programme officers under the guidance of a co-ordinator, attached to the Asian and Pacific Centre for Women and Development and one women's affairs officer to each of the four multinational programming and operational centres (MULPOCs) that have been established in Africa. This assistance is part of the regional programmes for Asia and the Pacific and Africa, respectively.
5. Preparatory Committee for the World Conference of the United Nations Decade for Women: Equality, Development and Peace, "Report of the Preparatory Committee on its Second Session, "United Nations Headquarters, 27 August-8 September 1979. (A/CONF, 94/PC/12).
6. See, for example, United Nations. General Assembly resolutions 3505(XXX). Integration of women in the development process; 3520(XXX), World Conference of the International Women's Year; 3523(XXX), Women in rural areas (*G.A. Official Records, 30th Session. Supplement No. 34* (A/10034); 31/175, Effective mobilization of women in development (*G.A. Official Records, 31st Session. Supplement No. 39* (A/31/39); 33/200, Effective mobilization and integration of women in development (*G.A. Official Records, 33rd*

Session. Supplement No. 45 (A/33/45); as well as World Conference of the International Women's Year, *Declaration of Mexico—Plans of Action,* United Nations, 1975; World Employment Conference, *Declaration of Principles and Programme of Action,* WEC/CW/E. 1, ILO, 1976; WHO, *Report of the International Conference on Primary Health Care,* Geneva, 1978; World Conference on Agrarian Reform and Rural Development, *Report,* FAO, 1979.

7. The amount of information available varies from country to country.
8. See, for example, Mead Cain, Syed Rokeya Khanam, Shamsum Nahar, "Class, Patriarchy and Women's Work in Bangladesh." *Population and Development Review,* Vol. 5, No. 3, 1979, pp. 405-438, Shirley Lindenbaum, "Ideology and Control: Women's World Position in Traditional Societies." In Jean 0, Barr(ed)., *Third Women: Factors in Their Changing Status.* Duke University, Centre for International Studies, Durham, N.C. 1976, pp. 51-64. Because of the great importance of class differences, it is sometimes claimed that women's inferior position is mainly a matter of class. See, for example, Gelia Castillo, "The Changing Role of Women in Rural Societies: A Summary of Trends and Issues." Agricultural Development Council, *Seminar Report.* New York, 1977, pp. 5-6; Ann Stolert "Class Structure and Female Autonomy in Rural Java." *Signs,* Vol. 3, No. 1, 1977, pp. 74-89. While class may indeed be and usually is a major determinant of women's options, this does not rule a male/female dichotomy operating within and across class boundaries. At the current juncture of history, the matter seems to be the prevailing situation.
9. See, for example, Elizabeth Croll, *Women in Rural Development The People's Republic of China,* ILO, Geneva, 1979.

9a. Additionally, under the most extreme conditions of Poverty both men and women may find themselves outside the system of societal norms of behaviour, forced to accept any type of work that may or may not come their way.

10. Roy G.D. Andráde, "Sex Difference and Cultural Institutions." In Liam Hudson (ed.), *The Ecology of Human Intelligence.* Penguin Books, London, pp. 15-49; Lindenbaum, *op. cit.,* p. 53.
11. D' Andrade, *op. cit.,* p. 23; Lindenbaum, *op. cit.,* p. 55.
12. This observation is included as an important principle in the Declaration of Mexico. See World Conference of the International Women's Year, *op. cit.,* para. 20. It has also been discussed by Ulla 01 in "A Case for Women as Co-Managers: The Family as a General Model of Human Social Organization." In Irene Tinker and Michele Bo Bramsen (eds.) *op. cit.,* pp. 105-128.
13. By contrast, all able-bodied men are generally enumerated as economically active (not infrequently their work input is less than that of women).

14. In this context it is of interest to note that while the attitude towards women's in work in developing countries is in part attributed to the practices followed in industrial countries, census reports of Great Britain during the last century indicate a more sympathetic view of the matter. Thus, in the 1881 report is, *e.g.*, stated (following it a comparison of the extent of male *versus* female economic activities): "It must be remembered, however, that a very large number of wives and daughters assist their husbands and fathers in business, and also that the most important of all female occupations, and that which occupies the largest number, is altogether omitted from reckoning, namely the rearing of children and the management of domestic life. To make the comparison at all a fair one, we should take into account the existence of the 4, 437, 962 wives and, were we do so, the proportion, of occupied women would be much the same as that of occupied men." British Parliamentary Papers, *1881 and 1891 Censuses, England and Wales.* 1881 General Report, 1891 Preliminary and General Rpeorts. Irish University Press, Shannon, Ireland, 1970, p. 43; See also *ibid.*, p. 347 and *The Census of Great Britain in 1851.* The numbers and Distribution of the People, their Ages, Conjugal Condition, Occupations and Birth Place. Longmen, Brown, Green and Longmans, London, 1854, p. 64.
15. Lambros Comitas, "Occupational Multiplicity in Rural Jamaica." In L. Comitas and D. Lowenthal (eds.), *Work and Family Life: West Indian Perspectives.* Doubleday-Anchor, New York, 1973, pp. 156-173.
16. See paras, 399-402 for a discussion of this type of employment in Indonesia.
17. See, for example, Stoler, *op. cit.*, p. 89.
18. For an illustrative discussion of all these problems, see in particular Chapter III.3(2) (iii) below.
19. See paras, 414, 421 below.
20. Irene Tinker, "The Adverse Impact of Development on Women." In Tinker and Bo Bramsen, *op. cit.*, pp. 22-24.
21. Ester Boserup, *Woman's Role in Economic Development.* St. Martin's Press, New York, 1970, p. 53 ff.
22. A fuller discussion of current development issues may be found in various reports that address themselves to the formulation of a strategy for the Third United Nations Decade for Development, 1980-1989. See, *e.g.*, United Nations, *Official Records of the Economic and Social Council, 1979, Supplement No. 7* (E/1979/37) and *ibid., 1980, Supplement No.* 2 (E/1980/3), which also contain references to other reports.
23. United Nations, General Assembly Resolution 3201 (S-VI).

24. See, *e.g.*, United Nations Economic Commission for Africa, *The New International Economic Order—What Roles Women?* E/CN. 14/ ATRCW/77/WD3, 31 August, 1977; United Nations General Assembly, *Development and International Economic Co-operation: Effective Mobilization of Women in Development.* A/33/238/Corr. 1, pp. 5-6.
25. World Conference of the International Women's Year, *op. cit.* para. 20.
26. For references, see footnote 22 above.
27. Because of the common negative attitude towards women's work outside the home, urban women suffer to a considerable extent from similar neglect.
28. For a detailed discussion of mainly health care based on these principles, see V. Djukanovic and E.P. Mach, *Alternative Approaches to Meeting Basic Health Needs in Developing Countries.* A joint UNICEF/WHO Study. WHO, Geneva, 1975; Kenneth W. Newell (ed.), *Health by the People.* WHO, Geneva, 1975; UNICEF, "Basic Services for Children in Developing Countries." E/SCEF/L. 1342, 12 March, 1976.

6

Islamic Rights of Motherhood—I Custody of Children

Legal Background

Islamic law distinguishes between guardianship (*wilāya*) and the custody of minor children (*ḥaḥāna*). Having regard to the interest of the minor, who needs the proximity of a woman, it lays down that the mother has the best title to *ḥaḍāna,* provided that she meets the conditions of eligibility to this task, *viz.,* that she is adult, of sound mind, honest, responsible and capable of seeing to the minor's education and well-being and is not an apostate (*murtadda*). The mother's right is independent of the legal relationship between the parents; it does not lapse on her divorce. But if after her divorce she marries a stranger, *i.e.,* a man not a *maḥram* (a kinsman of the child within the forbidden degrees), she is denied the right to *ḥaḍāna* so long as the marriage exists. Where there is not a mother or where the mother is denied the right to *ḥaḍāna* for any reason, that right passes to the maternal grandmother and to other female cognative relatives in the order of degrees of kinship and then to female agnative relatives in the same order: only in the absence of eligible women does the right pass to the father and then to male agnatic relatives (*'aṣabāt*) entitled to succession, again in the order of degrees of kinship. The period of *ḥaḍāna* ends when the child is seven in the case of a son or nine in the case of a daughter, whereupon the child passes into the charge of the father. The custody of the children in no way affects the father's natural guardianship over their persons. He owes them maintenance during the *ḥaḍāna* period.[1]

The Women's Equal Rights Law, which grants the mother the status of a natural guardian of the children, does not refer expressly to custody,[2] but although Section I provides that "a man and a woman shall have equal status with regard to any legal act," the mother's precedence over the father in the matter of custody remains unimpaired owing to Section 6, which provides that "this law shall not derogate from any provision of law protecting women as women."[3] The Capacity and Guardianship Law, 5722-1962 expressly includes the right to the custody of the children in the guardianship of the parents (Section 15); but again, equality in this sphere between father and mother does not do away with the mother's precedence as to custody, although it introduces certain deviations from *shar'i* law. The law provides that where the parents of a minor live separately for any reason they may, with the approval of the court, agree between themselves which of them is to have custody of the minor, and in the absence of such an agreement or if the agreement is not carried out, the court may determine matters of custody at its discretion, having regard to the interest of the minor, "provided that children up to the age of six shall be with their mother unless there are special reasons for directing otherwise" (Section 25). In other words, the *ḥaḍāna* period has been shortened and like treatment has been prescribed for sons and daughters.

The Exercise of the Right to Custody by the Mother

As a rule, a mother enjoyed her right to custody of her minor children. She did not need confirmation of this right from the court unless someone challenged it. The *sijills* thus reflect only those cases in which the mother wished to exercise this right or someone wished to deny it to her. The questions of custody naturally arose where the parents did not live together. It especially did so where they were divorced and sometimes where the mother was widowed, but it might also concern a married woman who for some reason had left her husband's house or whose husband had deserted her. There is ample evidence of women of different marital status demanding that the court confirm their right to custody of their children, reject attempts from various quarters to deprive them of this right, or direct that children who were taken from them against their, the women's will be returned to them.[4] A woman sometimes stressed that her right to custody of her children was based on both religious and secular law,[5] and she might enlist the help of the execution office or the welfare officer to realize it.[6]

In dozens of cases of divorce by agreement it was expressly indicated that the children were to remain in the custody of the mother and that the father was to pay maintenance for them or custody money to the mother.[7] In one case, the father undertook to transfer some land and a house to the children.[8] If the divorce agreement does not indicate that the wife renounced her right to custody—and most divorce agreements do not—it means that she continued to have custody. Moreover, a mother sometimes had custody of her children even after the expiration of the *ḥaḍāna* period. This appears from cases in which a relative demanded to take charge of them on the *shar'i* ground that the period had expired. Several years sometimes passed under these circumstances before application was made to the court for relief against a woman who seemed to be unwilling to give up her children.[9] It may be assumed that retention of the children beyond the *ḥaḍāna* period was more frequent than would appear from the *sijills*. It was especially likely to occur in cases where the mother brought them up and provided for all their needs by her own efforts or at any rate did not claim maintenance from the father.[10]

In many dozens of cases, the wife at the time of the divorce renounced the custody money or maintenance for the children, provided that they remained in her custody, and she might undertake to keep them at her own expense even after the expiration of the *ḥaḍāna* period; sometimes it was stipulated that if she went back on this undertaking she would have to pay monetary compensation to the husband,[11] and occasionally she renounced everything due to her by virtue of a *shar'ia* right, *i.e.*, maintenance for the children, accumulated maintenance for herself, dower and maintenance for the waiting-period, provided the children remained with her. Renunciation as aforesaid was particularly frequent where the wife's right to custody had lapsed for any reason.[12]

In many cases, the mother concluded an agreement with the father as to the custody of the child. Most of these agreements were made incidentally to divorce. The agreement might relate to the realization of the wife's *shar'i* right. Thus, for instance, a wife might reserve to herself the choice between keeping the child until he no longer needed her or until the expiration of the *ḥaḍāna* period.[13] The agreement might provide that the wife should keep the child even after that period; usually it imposed certain conditions, such as a limitation of the period of custody,[14] the provision of education during the period of custody,[15] permission for the father to see the children from time to time,[16] careful protection of the children and abstention of the mother from remarrying,[17] and prohibition of the mother (and the child) from living outside the father's place of residence without his consent.[18] A frequent arrangement between the parents was the division (*tawzī* or *taqsīm*) of the children between them: the girls might be handed over to the mother and the boys to the father,[19] but the opposite might also occur.[20] The mode of division seems to have depended on the circumstances of the case; anyhow, there was a tendency to give young children to the mother.[21] Sometimes the child, on reaching puberty, was allowed to choose the parent with whom he would live.[22] A woman might on divorce undertake to assume custody of her husband's children by another wife in addition to her own children and even to pay compensation if she infringed the undertaking. These conditions were probably forced on the woman, who strove to her utmost to attain her release, in return for the husband's consent to divorce her.[23]

The proportion of endogamous wives enjoying the right to *ḥaḍāna* was particularly high in rural society, but it is doubtful whether there was a causal connection between endogamy and the exercise of this right. In fact, if endogamy indeed had any effect here it should have been in the opposite direction, for blood-relationship between the spouses restricts the wife's freedom of action as compared with the position in exogamous marriages. The main factor here was the woman's economic and social position, which was especially significant in the case of divorced and widowed women. A certain measure of economic independence, freedom of movement and social contact is essential to a woman's ability to bring up her children. In traditional society, the structural solution of such problems is the divorced or widowed woman's return to her father's or brother's house, where she stays until—as soon as possible—she marries again (although she loses her right to *ḥaḍāna* if she marries a stranger): this solution is to be understood in terms of kinship and property relations.[24] But in recent years, widows and divorced women have shown an increasing tendency not to return to their fathers' or brothers' houses. Rosenfeld discerned this tendency in the Galilean villages he studied. He notes that widows of all ages were then permitted to keep their children without remarrying. He attributes this to the rapid transition from the extended to the nuclear family.[25] The economic and social position of women varied according to their type of settlement: in the towns, especially the mixed towns, they enjoyed greater economic independence and freedom of social contact than in other types of settlement, a fact which is reflected in the *sijills*.

Deprivation of Women's Right to Custody

Besides the cases where women enjoyed their right to *ḥaḍāna* and even retained their children beyond the *shar'i* period, there were many cases in which they were deprived of this right for *shar'ia* and other reasons. The most frequent reasons were termination of the *ḥaḍāna* period[26] and marriage to someone not of a forbidden degree of kinship to the children; such a marriage was regarded as an orthodox *shar'i* ground for deprivation of *ḥaḍāna*, and its validity was usually not disputed even by the mother.[27] Moreover, the mother might on her own initiative deliver the children into the custody of relatives in the order of their entitlement to *ḥaḍāna,* either because she was unable to support them or because she could not devote herself to them owing to her duties toward her new husband and her children by him or because the new husband objected to the presence of children not his own.[28] Occasionally the spouses agreed at the time of the divorce that the children should remain in their mother's custody until she remarried, when they were to pass into the charge of their father.[29] As stated, the dissolution of the mother's marriage to a stranger removes the ground for the denial of her right to *ḥaḍāna,* and there were in fact cases in which she wished to reassert it under these circumstances.[30]

The qualifications for *ḥaḍāna* were framed in accordance with the norms of a traditional society in which the inferiority of women is a basic feature. On the other hand, Muslim women in Israel—in the towns, and also in the large, developed villages—enjoyed a greater measure of economic independence and social contact than they ever had before. Their behaviour and habits did not conform to orthodox concepts and gave rise to demands that *ḥaḍāna* be denied to them on various grounds: moral flaws in their conduct and the pursuit of disreputable occupations[31]; frequent absence from home for various purposes,[32] especially work, causing the children to run wild[33]; exploitation of the child for heavy work in the employ of strangers or non-Muslims[34] disobedience and being declared rebellious (*nāshiza*),[35] etc.

A woman might not accept the removal of her children from her custody and might try to frustrate it in various ways. To an attempt to disqualify her from *ḥaḍāna* on the ground that she would leave the house and thereby neglect her children, one woman reacted by declaring through her lawyer that such an argument was "untenable and invalid from a *shar'i,* a secular-legal and a modern social point of view," since it was intolerable that a woman should be imprisoned in her house and not be allowed to go out on housekeeping errands.[36] In another case, the wife admitted that her *shar'i* right to *ḥaḍāna* had lapsed and passed to the paternal grandmother, but her devotion to her little daughter deeply touched the grandmother, and with the latter's consent it was decided that the little girl should divide her time between the two women.[37] A woman might try to disqualify others from *ḥaḍāna* in order to assure it to herself. Thus, in one case, a divorced woman contended that her former husband had their children live together with his second wife and that they were "like orphans" at his house.[38] In another case, a woman asked that her daughter's father be disqualified from *ḥaḍāna* because she had brought up the girl by her own efforts, without assistance from him; he had abandoned them at their gravest hour (during the evacuation of Jaffa in 1948); he had no house where he might bring up the girl properly, in fact, no fixed abode at all; he wished to smuggle the daughter out to an Arab country and give her into the custody of his sister; and in addition, "she will lose her legal right to be a national of this country and to be heir to her mother"; a previous smuggling attempt had ended with the killing of a person; the man was a drunkard and had broken a promise he had made in court during the Mandate to give up drinking; he was "sinful (*fāsiq*), unreliable and could not be entrusted with an educational task, with the protection of honour and its preservation from decay . . . he had already violated the honour of a virgin."[39]

In dozens of cases, a woman renounced her right to *ḥaḍāna*. It seems that only in a few cases did she do so of her own free will—because she wished to join her new husband abroad, because she had married a stranger or for other reasons.[40] It may be assumed that a woman was generally not inclined to give up that right. In most cases, the renunciation was made on divorce, or more exactly, was the condition or one of the conditions for the husband's consent to divorce his wife. In some cases, the judgment states expressly that the wife waived her right to *ḥaḍāna* on condition that the husband divorce her or "in return for" (*muqābil*) a divorce,[41] *i.e.*, as a last resort to obtain her freedom. In one case, the wife opposed a divorce for fear that she might have to give up her two-year-old son.[42] In some cases, a woman was divorced during pregnancy and compelled to renounce her unborn child.[43] Lest the wife were to withdraw her renunciation, the husband frequently stipulated that she would have to forgo future claims in respect of her children and that if she changed her mind and wished to exercise her *shar'i* right she would have to maintain the children at her own expense or even pay compensation to him as a fine (*gharāma*) for infringing the agreement.[44]

A woman might set a series of conditions to allay as far as possible the bitterness of her renunciation of the right to *ḥaḍāna*. In the case of a very young or unborn child she might stipulate that before he was handed over to his father he should be in her custody for one or several years[45]; that she be enabled to see the child from time to time and to buy him presents and clothes; that the child, if a girl, be allowed to stay the night at her house[46]; and lastly, that if any of these conditions was infringed or the father neglected or caused injury (*ḍarar*) to the child, she should be entitled to claim her right to *ḥaḍāna* and the child should return to her.[47] But these conditions were not routine; as a rule, the wife renounced her right to *ḥaḍāna* on divorce without any conditions. In fact, the divorce agreement sometimes states expressly that the renunciation was made "unconditionally and unreservedly" in return for her freedom.[48]

Only in a few cases—all involving women from urban types of settlement—did the *ḥaḍāna,* when the mother was debarred from exercising it, pass to the maternal grandmother.[49] Usually under these circumstances it passed to the paternal grandmother[50] or to another of the agnatic relatives (*'asabāt*), especially to an uncle,[51] the grandfather,[52] or a brother.[53] The custody of the children is a very important matter. Where questions of succession were involved, in addition to kinship relations, considerations relating to the estate would also occur.[54] In traditional society, not only do men take precedence over women, but also agnatic relatives over cognatives ones, and this finds its expression in the sphere of the custody of children.

The *Qāḍīs* and Custody

The *qāḍīs* were not inclined to apply the provisions of the *sharī'a* where an agreement existed between the parties concerning custody of the children, even if this agreement was in flagrant contradiction of the religious-legal norm. Thus, for instance Shaykh Ḥasan Amīn al-Ḥabash and Shaykh Mūsā al-Ṭabarī confirmed agreements leaving the children in the mother's *ḥaḍāna* although she was married to a stranger.[55] The *qāḍīs* almost blindly confirmed divorce agreements in which the wife renounced the custody of her young children.[56] The will of the parties, as manifested in an agreement, was thus stronger than religious-legal provisions, and it might happen that a *qāḍī* would not permit the parties to exercise their *shar'i* rights once the agreement was in force. In one case, the parents agreed that their son should be in the mother's *ḥaḍāna* until he was 19; a few years later, the father changed his mind, but Shaykh Ṭāhir al-Ṭabarī decided that the question of the implementation of the agreement was not within his competence and referred the parties to a civil court.[57] The contents of the agreement were determined in accordance with local custom, and the *qāḍī* did not interfere as to its details. In fact, he sometimes used arbitration to solve disputes in matters of *ḥaḍāna* without resort to *shar'i* sanctions. Thus, in one case, a woman claimed that her husband—both belonged to the al-Huzayyil tribe—had taken her daughters from her by force. Shaykh Ṭāhir Ḥamād succeeded in ending the dispute "thanks to Allāh" on certain conditions, including restoration of the daughters to the mother, and appointed a famous Shaykh and chief of the al-Huzayyil tribe, who had probably taken part in the arbitration, to serve as a supervisor (*murāqib*) whose decision was to be binding in the event of any difference of opinion between the spouses. In another case, the same *qāḍī* adjourned the hearing in the hope that the couple would reach a settlement, and in doing so suggested solving the dispute in one of the following ways: the daughter should be in the custody of her father, who would provide for her upkeep, but should spend her nights at her mother's house, or she should be sent to a boarding-school.[58]

In the absence of agreement between the parties, the *qāḍīs* had no choice but to apply the religious law. If there was not a clear *shar'i* ground disqualifying the mother from *ḥaḍāna,* they all took care that she was not deprived of this right: that her children were under her control and that the agnatic relatives paid the children's maintenance and the *ḥaḍāna* money. All the *qāḍīs* stressed, with some differences in wording and style, that *ḥaḍāna* was the mother's right and that she took precedence in this regard over the father and every member of her or his family.[59] Moreover, some *qāḍīs* held that a mother's right to *ḥaḍāna* never lapsed and that if she had renounced it she might cancel her renunciation.[60]

The same degree of strictness was shown by the *qāḍīs* in upholding the right to *ḥaḍāna* of women other than the mother, in the order prescribed by Islamic law. Thus, for instance, Shaykh Ḥasan Amīn al-Ḥabash and Shaykh Mūsā al-Ṭabarī repeatedly decided that the maternal grandmother's right was prior to that of the paternal grandmother.[61] Where relatives were unwilling to exercise *ḥaḍāna,* the *qāḍīs* compelled them to do so, again in strict adherence to the prescribed legal order.[62] The *qāḍīs* required the relatives to pay maintenance to the minors in accordance with their share in the latters' inheritance.[63]

Although this attitude of the *qāḍīs* was very advantageous to the mother, it seems that its motive was not, as a rule, her best interest or that of the child, but the wish to apply the provisions of the *sharī'a* unswervingly. This is suggested by their frequent references to Qadrī's collection of laws of personal status, and to Ibn Ābidīn's interpretations.[64] The same motive underlay Shaykh Ṭāhir Ḥamād's opposition to giving a Muslim baby girl of unknown paternity into the custody of a Christian family. He decided that handing the girl over to a non-Muslim for guardianship or adoption was forbidden because it was "contrary to the Muslim *sharī'a.*" On another occasion, he opposed a Jewish family's having the custody of a 15-year-old Muslim girl because "Jewish tutelage is contrary to the *sharī'a.*"[65]

The most significant test of a *qāḍī*'s attitude regarding a woman's rights to *ḥaḍāna* occurred where a bid was made to disqualify her on one of the *shar'i* grounds. These grounds, are, as stated, based on the norms of traditional society, and a difficulty arose when it was to be determined whether the habits and behaviour of a woman in contemporary society were consistent with the conditions of eligibility to *ḥaḍāna* or whether she was disqualified.[66] None of the *qāḍīs* called into question the fact that a woman's right to custody of her children lapses on the termination of the *ḥaḍāna* period. Shaykh Ḥusnī al-Zu'bī in one case dismissed the plea of a woman that her child was still of tender age and in need of maternal care and female attendance. In another case, he decided that a girl should be returned to her father because after the *ḥaḍāna* period he was entitled more than anyone else to have custody of her."[67] The same attitude was usually taken where a woman was legally disqualified by reason of her marriage to a man not of one of the forbidden degrees of relationship to the children.[68] In one case, a man asked that his former wife be declared disqualified because she had married a stranger. While the case was pending, the woman was divorced by her second husband, and Shaykh Ṭāhir Ḥamād thereupon declared her again eligible for *ḥaḍāna* because "she was now free to attend to her children."[69]

The position is different with regard to the appraisal of a woman's personal qualifications, which are vaguely defined by the *sharī'a* and whose interpretation is by the nature of things subjective, dependent on each *qāḍī's* philosophy. Two diametrically opposed attitudes may here be distinguished, an orthodox-conservative one and a liberal one.

Shaykh Ṭāhir Ḥamād was the most typical representative of the orthodox school. He measured a woman's eligibility for *ḥaḍāna* in terms of traditional society, in which women are confined to their homes, debarred from social contacts and outside employment. It therefore did not appear difficult to convince him that a woman who regularly left the house, especially for work, and had close contacts with strangers and non-Muslims, was not fit to have custody of her children.[70]

On the other hand, there were *qāḍīs* whose attitude to a woman's eligibility for *ḥaḍāna* was liberal in that they did not regard her social liberation and freedom of movement as grounds for disqualification. This attitude found its main expression in the judgments of Shaykh Ḥasan Amīn al-Ḥabash. Thus, in one case, this *qāḍī* dismissed a man's action to disqualify his divorced wife from *ḥaḍṭna* on the ground that she frequently left the house, abandoning her little girls in the street. He accepted the wife's argument that this demand was unfounded in religious-legal, secular-legal and social respects and that it was intolerable that in this modern age a woman should be confined to her home and not allowed to go out on housekeeping errands. The ex-husband appealed to the *Sharī'a* Court of Appeal, which set aside the judgment, declaring that the court below had dismissed the action without entering on the substance of the case and that it should have enabled the man to prove that the girls were neglected as a result of their mother's leaving the house. Shaykh Ḥasan Amīn al-Ḥabash appealed against the setting aside of his judgment, but his appeal was dismissed.[71] The difference in attitude between the two levels of jurisdiction was not confined to the procedural aspect, but expressed different social philosophies.

Shaykh Ḥasan Amīn al-Ḥabash and Shaykh Ḥusnī al-Zu'bī did not regard a wife's disobedience or having been declared rebellious a sufficient ground to disqualify her from *ḥaḍāna*.[72] They did not regard it as unlawful if a woman who fled from her husband's house to her premarital abode took her children with her. Shaykh Ḥasan decided in one case that *ḥaḍāna* was "bound up with the *ḥāḍina* herself and not with her place of residence," but that the latter could not, in any event, be a ground for disqualification if it was her own parents' house.[73] This attitude, which is not contrary to the *sharī'a,* corresponds to the liberal social outlook of the two *qāḍīs*.

There were definite deviations from the religious-legal norm under the influence of Israeli legislation. Signs of this influence were the application of the principle of the best interest of the child, which is alien to Islamic law,[74] and resort to the welfare officer. Thus, in one case, Shaykh Amīn Qāsim Mudlij rejected an attempt to disqualify a mother from *ḥaḍāna* because she had married a stranger on the ground that under the Women's Equal Rights Law both parents are the natural guardians of their children and that Section 25 of the Capacity and Guardianship Law enables the court to deal with the question of custody in accordance with the best interest of the children: since in that case this interest required that they be with their mother, the *qāḍī* refused to take them from her.[75] Shaykh Ṭāhir Ḥamād in one case disqualified a woman from *ḥaḍāna* because of unchaste behaviour and decided that the best interest of the child required that he be handed over to his father, and in another case he decided that it was best for the daughter if she was left in the *ḥaḍāna* of the mother.[76] He and Shaykh Ḥasan Amīn al-Ḥabash, sitting as a Court of Appeal, decided, in reliance on the Women's Equal Rights Law, that a daughter's best interest required, in the circumstances of the case, that she remain with her mother or with both her parents so long as they remained husband and wife.[77]

A welfare officer's task is to examine the circumstances of each case involving a minor and to recommend to the court the most desirable solution. He is guided by the principle of the child's best interest. His status and mode of operation are regulated by the Welfare (Procedure in Matters of Minors, Mentally Sick Persons and Absent Persons) Law, 5715-1955.[78] The *qāḍīs* availed themselves a great deal of the services of this official, who attended the hearings of the court and prepared a memorandum (*taqrīr*) recommending a suitable candidate for *ḥaḍāna*. Shaykh Ḥusnī al-Zu'bī noted that the *qāḍīs* regularly relied on this memorandum in deciding which of the parents was eligible for *ḥaḍāna*[79]; he, at any rate, frequently had recourse to the welfare officer and always accepted his recommendations. Thus, in one case, it had been contended that a woman's work as a teacher led to neglect of her daughter and that she should therefore be disqualified from *ḥaḍāna*. The welfare officer declared that the daughter should be left with the mother and the *qāḍī* decided accordingly. In another case, the welfare officer declared that although the children loved their mother, who was very devoted to them and did not want to join their father, who had neglected them until then, their interest required that they be handed over to the father because they needed education and a trade, which only he was able and willing to provide. The *qāḍī* decided in accordance with the welfare officer's recommendation. He had asked his opinion although he, the *qāḍī,* had already found that the mother's marriage to a stranger disqualified her from *ḥaḍāna* according to *shar'ia* law.[80] This case shows that the welfare officer's intervention was not necessarily in favour of the woman if he determined the best interest of the child in accordance with traditional concepts. A similar attitude toward the welfare officer has been taken by other *qāḍīs* in recent years.[81]

An ambivalent attitude is discernible where the *qāḍī* applied substantive elements of the two systems, the secular and the religious, at one and the same time. This was particularly so in the case of Shaykh Ḥusnī al-Zu'bī. In one instance, he decided that the best interest of the children required that they should be with their grandfather and not with their mother, who had remarried and had a small child to look after, and then he went on to declare that the grandfather was their *shar'i* guardian. In another case, he said that "the court must exercise its discretion, having regard to the best interest of the minor, in accordance with the power vested in it by the Women's Equal Rights Law of 1951 and the Capacity and Guardianship Law of 1962," and added that the mother was the child's natural guardian according to the [secular] law and the holder of the right to *ḥaḍāna* according to the *sharī'a*.[82] In yet another case, he declared that the spouses had not yet reached agreement as to *ḥaḍāna* in accordance with Section 24 of the Capacity and Guardianship Law, that the mother had the strongest title to the office under Article 380 of Qadrī's collection and the strongest claim to custody of the children upto the age of six under Section 25 of the Capacity and Guardianship Law, that the court had considered the matter with reference to the best interest of the minors, that no-one had sought to disqualify the mother from *ḥaḍāna* and that she was therefore eligible under Article 382 of Qadrī; and "in reliance on the *shar'i* provisions and the Capacity and Guardianship Law" he decided that the minors should be given to the mother. He also referred to Goitein and Ben-Shemesh and to al-Abayānī.[83] A similarly ambivalent attitude was adopted by Shaykh Amīn Qāsim Mudlij and Shaykh Tawfīq 'Asaliyya.[84] Such an attitude was also reflected in the stand taken by the *qāḍīs* concerning the Egyptian Personal

Status Bill of 1966, which, *inter alia,* proposed raising the age of *ḥaḍāna* to 11 years for boys and 13 years for girls.[85]

Notes and References

1. Qadrī, secs. 380-94, 420. See also Fyzee, pp. 189-92; Schacht, p. 167; Levy, pp. 140-3; Abu Zahra, pp. 154-6.
2. The Legal Adviser to the Ministry of Social Welfare, interviewee M. Horvitz, was of the opinion that the custody of children is included in guardianship.
3. See Schereschewsky, pp. 203-5; Silberg, pp. 420-1.
4. See, *e.g.*, *JfQ2*, p. 528: no. 579-f.108/62 (a divorced woman asked that her children, whom their imprisoned father had entrusted to a stranger, be handed over to her); *JfQ3*, p. 144: no. 229-f.123/64 (the wife alleged that the husband had taken her two daughters from her by force), p. 272: no. 411-f.93/66; *ṬbI1*, p. 29: no. 14-f.34/51, p. 65: no. 2-f.1/55, p. 99: no. 7-f.23/57 (a widow asked that the court order her husband's children by another woman to return her daughter to her), p. 215: no. 10-f.6/63; *AcQ4*, p. 91: f.106/60; *NzI4*, p. 251: no. 5/29-f.133/64, p. 279: no. 3/38-f.159/65.
5. See, *e.g.*, *JfQ2*, p. 502: no. 462-f.90/61; *ṬbI1*, p. 237: no. 25-f.21/63; *AcQ5*, p. 54: f.88/63 (the wife said that custody was "her natural right according to religious and secular law").
6. See, *e.g.*, *NzI4*, p. 311: no. 6/40-f.149/66, p. 298: no. 1/25-f.29/66, p. 309: no. 4/39-f.115/66, p. 362: no. 2/25-f.115/66, p. 376: no. 8/45-f.68/68.
7. See, *e.g.*, *JfQ5*, p. 29: no. 50-f.198/69, p. 67: no. 115-f.227/69; *ṬbI1*, p. 35: no. 4-f.14/52; *NzḤ23*, p. 37: no. 4/18-f.39/65; *AcṬ3*, p. 42: f.32/57; *AcṬ4*, p. 110: f.48/67.
8. *NzḤ24*, p. 257: no. 7/81-f.155/69.
9. See, *e.g.*, *JfQ1*, p. 41: no. 70-f.39/51 (daughter, aged 12 at the time of the hearing), p. 108: no. 173-f.49/53 (son, over ten years of age); *ṬbI1*, p. 20: no. 2/3-f.7/50, p. 90: no. 11-f.36/56.
10. See, *e.g.*, *ṬbI1*, p. 141: no. 4-f.4/59 and p. 143: no. 6-f.7/59, p. 90: no. 11-f.36/56; *NzI4*, p. 130: no. 3/29-f.115/52, p. 259: no. 2/2-f.111/64.
11. See, *e.g.*, *JfQ1*, p. 229: no. 254-f.18/56; *JfQ3*, p. 157: no. 254-f.130/64; *JfQ5*, p. 60: no. 102-f.211/69 (the wife undertook to support her daughter "voluntarily, for the sake of Heaven" and renounced the daughter's maintenance on condition that she was left in her charge so long as she was in need of protection, "even if she [the mother] should remarry"); *NzḤ17*, p. 272: no. 19/49; *NzḤ18*, p. 212: no. 9/34; *NzḤ22*, p. 48: no. 13/38-f.58/63; *AcṬ2*,

p. 3: f.?/50, p. 74 (the wife, who was pregnant at the time of the divorce, undertook that if she gave birth to a live child she would suckle him, bring him up and support him with her own money for seven years), p. 159 (if she went back on her undertaking to support her son gratuitously she would pay his father IL 500); *AcṬ4*, p. 8: f.16/64 (the wife undertook to bring up the children at her expense "for life"). The practice has also been observed in Iraq. See el-Naqeb, pp. 161-2.

12. See, *e.g.*, *AcI2*, p. 7: f.6/51 (the woman had married a stranger); *AcṬ4*, p. 23: f.8/65.
13. *AcṬ3*, p. 76: f.11/58. See also *AcṬ3*, p. 14: f.8/57. The father also sometimes reserved such a choice to himself. See, *e.g.*, *AcṬ2*, p. 44; *NzI4*, p. 173: no. 3/8-f.28/65.
14. See, *e.g.*, *NzI4*, p. 145: no. 1/12-f.25/53 (the parents had made an agreement that the mother should have custody of the son until he was 19 and that if the father infringed the agreement by claiming the son he should pay a fine of IL 500), p. 378: no. 1/46-f.128/68.
15. *NzI4*, p. 362: no. 2/25-f.115/66.
16. See, *e.g.*, *AcI3*, p. 31: no. 22-f.62/56, p. 34: no. 27-f.81/56.
17. *AcD8*, p. 110: no. 27-f.90/70. See also *AcD7*, p. 66: f.26/67.
18. *AcṬ3*, p. 44: f.34/57.
19. See, *e.g.*, *JfQ3*, p. 329: no. 470-f.30/67; *AcṬ3*, p. 148: f.43/59, p. 195: f.38/60.
20. See, *e.g.*, *AcṬ4*, p. 82: f.21/67, p. 85: f.24/67.
21. See, *e.g.*, *AcṬ4*, p. 139: f.29/68.
22. *JfQ3*, p. 329: no. 470-f.30/67.
23. *AcṬ2*, pp. 25, 78.
24. See, Rosenfeld, *Peasants*, pp. 40, 132, 152; Baer, p. 59.
25. Rosenfeld, *Peasants*, pp. 41-2. See also *ibid.*, pp. 152-3.
26. See, *e.g.*, *JfQ2*, p. 315: no. 491-f.38/58; *JfQ3*, p. 30: no. 50-f.144/63, p. 133: no. 208-f.95/64; *ṬbI1*, p. 20: no. 2/3-f.7/50; *NzḤ18*, p. 154: no. 17/255; *NzI4*, p. 130: no. 3/29-f.115/52, p. 259: no. 2/2-f.111/64.
27. See, *e.g.*, *JfQ1*, p. 3: no. 5-f.5/51, p. 95: no. 151-f.22/53; *NzI4*, p. 178: no. 1/6-f.21/57; *AcI2*, p. 48: f.57/53; *ṬbI1*, p. 95: no. 11-f.36/56 (the woman contended that she had married an agnatic (*'aṣabī*) relative of her daughters and that her right to custody had therefore not lapsed).
28. See, *e.g.*, *ṬbI1*, p. 19: no. 6-f.14/51, p. 163: no. 4-f.10/60; *JfQ5*, p. 84: no. 144-f.264/69. See also *NzI4*, p. 302: no. 1/29-f.97/66.
29. See, *e.g.*, *JfQ5*, p. 58: no. 99-f.204/69; *JfQ4*, p. 128: no. 149-f.122/68; *AcṬ4*, p. 53: f.21/66 and p. 54: f.22/66, p. 91: f.29/67, p. 110: f.48/67.
30. See, *e.g.*, *JfQ1*, p. 262: no. 409-f.3/57.

31. See, *e.g.*, *JfQ1*, p. 196: no. 317-f.61/55 (the wife had fled from the husband's house, lived with a strange man "and joined a nest of corruption"); *JfQ2*, p. 383: no. 537-f.58/58 (the magistrates' court had convicted the wife of a civil offense); *Ṭbl1*, p. 29: no. 14-f.34/51 (the wife had subsisted by begging).
32. See, *e.g.*, *JfQ1*, p. 157: no. 262-f.49/54; *Ṭbl1*, p. 237: no. 25-f.21/63 (the wife went out on household errands).
33. See, *e.g.*, *JfQ1*, p. 196: no. 317-f.61/55; (the wife frequently left the house for the purpose of supporting the husband); *JfQ2*, p. 502: nos. 462/3-f.90/61; *JfQ3*, p. 9: no. 15-f.74/63 (it was contended that the wife took employment with Jews), p. 327: no. 468-f.16/67 (the husband contended that the wife worked "from morning to four o'clock in the afternoon and that he did not know where she was at midday"); *Ṭbl1*, p. 215: no. 10-f.6/63; *NzI4*, p. 298: no. 1/25-f.29/66 (the husband alleged that because of her teaching job the wife neglected their daughter and deprived her of "natural suckling").
34. See, *e.g.*, *JfQ2*, p. 467: no. 488-f.13/61; *Ṭbl1*, p. 20: no. 2/3-f.7/50.
35. *NzI4*, p. 349: no. 3/6-f.162/67; *Ṭbl1*, p. 215: no. 10-f.6/63, p. 228: no. 19-f.20/63.
36. *Ṭbl1*, p. 237: no. 25-f.21/63.
37. *AcI1*, p. 67: f.34/50.
38. *JfQ1*, p. 262: no. 409-f.3/57. See also *NzI4*, p. 145: no. 1/12-f.25/53.
39. *JfQ1*, p. 41: no. 70-f.39/51. See also *JfQ1*, p. 108: no. 173-f.49/53.
40. *NzḤ19*, p. 15: no. 1/9; and *NzḤ*18, p. 154: no. 17/255, respectively. See also *NzḤ20*, p. 158: no. 1/100; *JfQ3*, p. 238: no. 276-f.66/66; *AcQ5*, p. 7: no. 7/63-f.153/62.
41. See, *e.g.*, *JfQ3*, p. 252: no. 391-f.77/66; *AcṬ3*, p. 236: f.13/62, p. 261: f.22/63. For the same practice in Iraq see el-Naqeb, p. 161.
42. *Ṭbl1*, p. 108: no. 15-f.31/57 and p. 109: no. 16-f.24/57.
43. See, *e.g.*, *NzḤ*20, p. 113: no. 10/36; *NzḤ21*, p. 29: no. 3/53.
44. See, *e.g.*, *NzḤ*20, p. 63: no. 3/52; *NzḤ24*, p. 149: no. 7/47-f.84/68, p. 187: no. 6/100-f.184/68; *JfQ3*, p. 124: no. 194-f.16/64; *AcṬ2*, pp. 88, 91.
45. See, *e.g.*, *AcṬ2*, pp. 111, 174; *AcṬ3*, p. 39: f.29/57; *AcṬ4*, p. 123: f.11/68; *JfQ2*, p. 557: no. 560-f.104/62; *JfQ3*, p. 295: no. 435-f.132/66.
46. See, *e.g.*, *AcṬ2*, p. 91, *AcṬ4*, p. 23: f.9/65, p. 58: f.28/66, p. 121: f.9/68 (the wife might visit her children but not at their father's house, and the children might visit her at her house once a week

"from sunrise to sunset"), p. 123: f.11/68; *JfQ4*, p. 178: no. 226-f.68/69; *JfQ5*, p. 38: no. 63-f.159/69.

47. See, *e.g.*, *AcT3*, p. 37: f.27/?, p. 80: f.15/58; *AcṬ4*, p. 47: f.14/66, p. 121: f.9/68.
48. See, *e.g.*, *AcṬ3*, p. 80: f.15/58.
49. See, *e.g.*, *JfQ5*, p. 115: no. 194-f.289/69); *NzI4*, p. 76: no. 2/28-f.72/50. See also *NzI4*, p. 265: no. 3/15-f.41/65 (the mother entrusted the daughter to her brother for temporary custody during her rebelliousness and absence from her husband's house, and the brother kept her for six years and eventually handed her over to the girl's cousins; the father feared that the 45-years-old girl's chastity would be impaired; the cousins were willing to return her to her father on condition that he first reimburse them for her maintenance and the expenses incurred by them in bringing her up).
50. See, *e.g.*, *ṬbḤ2*, p. 133: no. 8, p. 253: no. 35; *NzI4*, p. 162:no. 1/11-f.46/54, p. 254: no. 4/33-f.147/64; *AcṬ4*, p. 136: f.25/68.
51. See, *e.g.*, *JfQ3*, p. 147: no. 234-f.128/69; *ṬbI1*, p. 90: no. 11-f.36/56; *ṬbH4*, p. 121: no. 98.
52. See, *e.g.*, *NzI4*, p. 302: no. 1/29-f.97/66; *AcD6*, p. 52: f.135/64.
53. See, *e.g.*, *ṬbI1*, p. 20: no. 2/3-f.7/50; *NzI4*, p. 314: no. 2/3-f.14/67.
54. See chapter "Guardianship," pp. 265-6.
55. *ṬbI1*, p. 90: no. 11-f.36/56; and *AcI2*, p. 7: f.7/51, respectively.
56. See, *e.g.*, *AcD6*, p. 13: f.22/64; *NzI4*, p. 254: no. 4/33-f.147/64; *JfQ4*, p. 178: no. 226-f.68/69.
57. *NzI4*, p. 145: no. 1/12-f.25/53. See also *NzI4*, p. 378: no. 1/46-f.68/68.
58. *JfQ3*, p. 144: no. 229-f.123/64; and *JfQ2*, p. 467: no. 488-f.13/61, respectively. See also *AcQ4*, p. 54: f.199/59.
59. See, *e.g.*, *JfQ2*, p. 411: no. 578-f.71/59; *JfQ3*, p. 9: no. 15-f.74/63; *ṬbI1*, p. 115: no. 4-f.39/57; *AcI3*, p. 37: no. 33-f.115/56, p. 72: no. 48-f.112/57; *NzI4*, p. 197: no. 4/8-f.17/59, p. 295: no. 6/23-f.24/66, p. 312: no. 1/1-f.163/66.
60. See, *e.g.*, *JfQ2*, p. 536: no. 534-f.56/62; *ṬbI1*, p. 40: no. 10-f.26/52.
61. See, *e.g.*, *NzI4*, p. 76: no. 2/28-f.72/50; and *AcQ4*, p. 93: f.105/60, respectively.
62. See, *e.g.*, *JfQ3*, p. 243: no. 381-f.62/66; *ṬbI1*, p. 19: no. 6-f.14/51.
63. See, *e.g.*, *JfQ1*, p. 62: no. 100-f.59/51.
64. See, *e.g.*, *JfQ3*, p. 158: no. 255-f.124/64; *ṬbI1*, p. 40: no. 10-f.26/52, p. 99: no. 7-f.123/57; *AcQ5*, p. 60: f.143/63.
65. *JfQ1*, p. 15: no. 26, and p. 16: no. 27/8-f.33/51, respectively.
66. Cf. Fyzee, p. 190.
67. *NzI4*, p. 259: no. 2/2-f.11/64, and p. 265: no. 13/15-f.41/65,

respectively. A similar attitude is reflected in decisions of Shaykh Mūsā al-Ṭabarī and Shaykh Amīn Qāsim Mudlij. See, *e.g.*, *AcI2*, p. 48: f.57/53; *AcQ5*, p. 15: f.59/61; *AcD6*, p. 63: f.175/64.

68. See, *e.g.*, *JfQ1*, p. 1: no. 5; *JfQ3*, p. 30: no. 50-f.144/63 (Shaykh Ṭāhir Ḥamād); *ṬbI1*, p. 163: no. 4-f.10/60 (Shaykh Ḥasan Amīn al-Ḥabash): *NzI4*, p. 309: no. 4/39-f.115/66, p. 314: no. 2/3-f.14/67, p. 314: no. 2/3-f.14/67 (Shaykh Ḥusnī al-Zu'bī).

69. *JfQ1*, p. 262: no. 409-f.3/57.

70. See, *e.g.*, *JfQ1*, p. 196: no. 317-f.61/55; *JfQ2*, p. 467: no. 488-f.13/61, p. 502: no. 462-f.90/61, p. 502: no. 463-f.91/61.

71. *ṬbI1*, p. 237: no. 25-f.21/63; *Apl*, p. 56: f.6/64, p. 59: f.9/64. See also *Apl*, p. 5: no. 4, p. 29: no. 37. A *sharī'a* court in Iraq once disqualified a mother from custody, on the application of her husband, on the ground that she was a Communist: the court of appeal disqualified also the maternal grandmother on the ground that she lent support to her daughter. See el-Naqeb, pp. 192-3.

72. *ṬbI1*, p. 215: no. 10-f.6/63; *NzI4*, p. 349: no. 3/6-f.162/67.

73. *ṬbI1*, p. 228: no. 19-f.20/63. See also *NzI4*, p. 376: no. 8/45-f.68/68.

74. See Anderson, *Patriarchal Family*, p. 232.

75. *JfQ3*, p. 157: no. 254-f.130/64.

76. *JfQ1*, p. 196: no. 317-f.61/55. See also *JfQ1*, p. 261: no. 408-f.11/57.

77. *Apl*, p. 31: no. 41. See also *AcQ5*, p. 30: f.116/61 and p. 8: f.21/63. Modern Iraqi legislation likewise adopted the principle of "the best interest of the child" in matters of custody, but to no effect because the *qāḍīs* did not apply it; they continued to adhere to Ḥanafī principles as regards the Sunnites and to Ja'farī principles as regards the Shi'ites. See el-Naqeb, p. 200.

78. The welfare officer within the meaning of this law has no standing in the *sharī'a* court unless summoned by the *qāḍī* (sec. 2); the *qāḍī* may summon him, but is not required to do so. The Attorney-General, on the other hand, may intervene in proceedings of the *sharī'a* court whenever he wishes to do so by virtue of his powers under the said Welfare Law or under the Capacity and Guardianship Law (Sec. 8). The Attorney-General has delegated his powers under these two laws to the District Welfare Officer of the Ministry of Social Welfare (as intimated by the Legal Adviser of that Ministry, M. Horvitz). See Schereschewsky, p. 380. For simplicity's sake, the various functionaries of the Ministry of Social Welfare are hereinafter described by the term "welfare officer."

79. *AI*, vol. 10 (1967), Nos. 3-4, p. 9.

80. *NzI4*, p. 298: no. 1/25-f.29/66, and p. 309: no. 4/39-f.115/66,

respectively. See also *NzI4*, p. 280: no. 1/1-f.111/64, p. 311: no. 6/40-f.149/66, p. 353: no. 3/13-f.145/67, p. 362: no. 2/25-f.115/66, p. 376: no. 8/45-f.68/68. Advocate Darwish told the author of a case in which he persuaded the *Sharī'a* Court of Nazareth to leave a child with his mother, having regard to his best interest, although he was past the age of *ḥaḍāna;* the *qāḍī* decided accordingly in the light of an opinion of the welfare officer.

81. See, *e.g.*, *AcṬ4*, p. 136: f.25/68; *JfQ3*, p. 244: no. 382-f.50/66.
82. *NzI4*, p. 302: no. 1/29, and p. 335: no. 8/34-f.93/67, respectively.
83. *NzI4*, p. 376: no. 8/45-f.68/68 (al-Abayānī, pt. 2, p. 85).
84. See, *e.g.*, *AcD7*, p. 26: f.92/66; *JfQ5*, p. 84: no. 144-f.264/69.
85. *AI*, vol. 10 (1967), Nos. 3-4, pp. 5, 15, 9-10, and 19, respectively.

7

Islamic Rights of Motherhood—II Guardianship of Children

Legal Background

Islamic law distinguishes between guardianship over the person (*wilāya al-nafs*) and guardianship over property (*wilāya al-māl*). *Guardianship over property concerns especially* administration of the inheritances of minor heirs (*wiṣāya*). The inequality between men and women is apparent in this sphere as well. The father alone is the natural guardian of his children, and this status corresponds to the patriarchal concept, which regards him as the head of the family. Although a woman is not disqualified from guardianship, she does not serve in this capacity by virtue of blood-relationship, the power is vested in her by appointment only, either by the legal guardian, in which case she is an "elected guardian" (*waṣī mukhtār*), or by the *sharī'a* court. Article 974 of the *Mejelle* prescribes a combined series of legal guardians and appointed guardians. The status of legal guardian is given only to the father and the agnatic ancestors in ascending order (grandfather, great-grandfather, and so forth). A woman is also discriminated against as to the power to deal with property under her guardianship. Guardianship terminates when the minor reaches puberty. According to the *Mejelle* (Section 986), pubescence begins at the age of 12 in the case of a boy and nine in the case of a girl, and is completed in both cases by the age of 15.[1]

The Women's Equal Rights Law, 5711-1951, enabled a woman to be a natural guardian of her children and abolished the discrimination against her embodied in Article 974 of the *Mejelle* and in other provisions of religious law. Section 3(a) of the Women's Equal Rights Law provides: "Both parents are the natural guardians of their children; where one parent dies, the survivor shall be the natural guardian." At the same time, the court is competent to deal with matters of guardianship, both over the person and the property,[2] "with the interest of the children as the sole consideration" (Section 3(b)).[3] Section 1 of the law, which prescribes equal status for a man and a woman with regard to any legal act, abolished the restrictions imposed by religious law on a woman's capacity to deal with the property of minors under her guardianship. Apart from the new rules expressly laid down in the law, matters of guardianship are still to be dealt with in accordance with religious precepts.[4] The religious court is to follow the new rules unless all the parties are 18 years of age or over and have agreed before the court, of their own free will, to litigate in accordance with the law of their community (Section 7).

The Capacity and Guardianship Law, 5722-1962, supplements and develops the principles established by the Women's Equal Rights Law. It distinguishes between natural guardians and guardians appointed by the religious court. Natural guardianship is based on complete equality of the parents as to their duties and rights with regard to their children: they are the natural guardians of the children (Section 14); they are to act in agreement and co-operation (Section 8); on the death of one of them, the guardianship of the minor is vested in the other (Section 28). The principle of equality finds expression also in the status of the children: the same age (18 years) is fixed for daughters and sons for the termination of guardianship (Section 3). The law does not distinguish between the person and the property of the minor; both come within the scope of the duties of parents toward their children (Section 15), which implies the mother's equal entitlement with the father to deal with the property of the minor children.[5] Under certain circumstances, the court may appoint a guardian for the minor alongside one or both of the parents (Sections 17-29 and 33). There is nothing to prevent the appointment of a woman as guardian of a child not her own. The court acts at its discretion in this matter, with the interest of the ward as its sole consideration (Section 35); it is not tied to the rigid order of agnates or their testamentary appointees,[6] and even if the appointment of a testamentary guardian is confirmed, this does not affect the natural guardianship of the surviving parent (Section 64).

The Capacity and Guardianship Law gives civil authorities standing in matters of minors. The Attorney-General and the welfare officer are authorized to intervene in certain ways (including the institution of legal proceedings) if, in their opinion, it is appropriate to do so in order to protect the minor (Sections 68-70).[7] There is some doubt as to the applicability of this law in *sharī'a* courts. Some think that the provisions relating to guardianship are intended also for religious courts and supercede the religious law. Others say that since this law does not contain an express provision in the matter, as is customary in some other laws, the religious law continues to apply.[8]

Women as Guardians of Their Children

Women were guardians in about half the approximately 500 cases in which guardianship orders were issued by *sharī'a* courts. In most instances, they were guardians of their own children. Usually the woman was the sole guardian, but in several dozen cases a *nāzir* or additional guardian, was appointed, who was either the father, or an agnatic relative of the minor, or a stranger. The *nāzir's* task is to supervise the guardian's activities, lest the children or their property suffer damage.[9] In some cases, a divorced woman became the guardian of her children after some time; in others the spouses agreed to this at the time of the divorce.[10] In dozens of cases, women were appointed guardians over children not their own; such women were either blood-relations of various degrees or strangers. A woman is not disqualified from guardianship under these circumstances even according to the *sharīʻa,* and Israeli legislation is of no significance in this context. In most cases, the woman was an agnatic relative: a germane sister (*shaqīqa*),[11] a paternal aunt (*ʻamma*)[12] and especially the paternal grandmother,[13] but in some instances the maternal grandmother was appointed[14] or even a non-blood-relation, as when a woman became guardian of her husband's children by another wife or of a girl of unknown parentage.[15] The common feature of most of these latter appointments is that the mother and the agnatic relatives had died or were found ineligible for one reason or another.

The majority of guardianship orders deal with the property accrued to minors by way of inheritance.[16] The principle motive for seeking appointment as guardian was thus the property aspect. In many dozens of cases, the woman, very soon after the issue of the guardianship oder, applied to the *qāḍī* for permission (*idhn*) to carry out various transactions in respect of property of the minor: to sell it, to exchange it for other property, to consolidate rights scattered over several properties in a single property, to receive compensation for expropriation, and so on.[17] In dozens of cases, a woman applied for a succession order for the estate of her late husband on the very day she was appointed guardian over the property of her children.[18] A woman's appointment as guardian is thus the clearest possible indication of her capacity to hold and dispose of property.

As a matter of fact, such an appointment was nothing new. A sample from the *sijills* of Jaffa and Nazareth of the Ottoman era reveals that women, of different degrees of relationship to the minor, were appointed in about one-quarter of the cases in which guardianship orders were issued by the courts. Evidence of such appointments is found also in the *sijills* of Jaffa and Nazareth of the Mandate era,[19] but it seems that they were less frequent then than in Israel.

The *sijills* contain evidence that Israeli Muslim women were alive to their status as natural guardians of their children and claimed their rights as such, sometimes with express reference to the relevant legislation.[20] In some cases, a distinction (unknown in secular law) was made between guardianship over the person of the minor, in respect of which the woman sought confirmation (*tathbīt*) of her status, and guardianship over the property of the minor, in respect of which she sought appointment (*naṣb*).[21] In one case, a woman asked that the uncle of a minor girl be removed from the office of guardian and that she be appointed in his stead, being her mother and the natural guardian of her person and property, as the general law required; in another case, a woman contended that the Knesset had empowered her to handle the affairs of her minor children and that there was no need for the appointment of a guardian by the court; and in yet another case, a woman applied to the High Court of Justice when it seemed to her that the *sharī'a* court was about to deprive her of her status as a natural guardian of her children.[22] In several cases, both parents were appointed guardians of their children, sometimes with express reference to secular legislation or with the remark that "the parents are the natural guardians,"[23] in open contradiction of the *shar'ī* concept.

It may thus safely be affirmed that Israeli legislation has materially affected the position of women as guardians. But it seems that it is not the only or principle factor, for in most of the cases in which a woman was appointed guardian of her children the appointment was made not by virtue of her legal status but either because there was no natural guardian (in the *shar'ī* sense) or person elected by such a guardian,[24] or because the natural guardian was disqualified by old age, illness or the like,[25] or the office had fallen vacant owing to dismissal, resignation or death of the agnatic guardian.[26] The *maḍbaṭa* (petition) frequently notes the mother was worthy of the office because of her outstanding qualities, "that there is no-one in the land worthier of the *wiṣāya* than the mother,"[27] that her appointment was in the best interest (*maṣlaḥa*) of the minor, or the like.[28] But in all these cases, the mother's appointment was made *ex gratia* and not as of right, or as a provisional measure pending the availability of a natural guardian. Thus, in a case in which the mother had taken the place of the paternal grandfather owing to his inability to serve, the *maḍbaṭa* stated that the grandfather had permitted (*ajāza*) the mother to be a legal guardian (*waṣī shar'ī*) of the minors, and in another case, in which the mother replaced the absent father for seven years, the *maḍbaṭa* stated that "a guardian was required for the duration of the father's absence."[29] Where a woman was appointed guardian of her children on her own initiative, she was frequently careful to point out that there was no natural or elected guardian and that she was capable of carrying out the task.[30] The appointment was usually initiated by the signatories to the *maḍbaṭa*, who were close to the family and could be relied on to know the situation, while the woman agreed to serve, sometimes without material reward.[31] In some cases, the father of the minor appointed the mother, his wife, to be *waṣī mukhtār* on his behalf after his death, and she accepted the appointment.[32]

Urban women provided twice as many guardians as corresponded to the proportion of urban Muslims among the total Muslim population. They enjoyed a better economic and social position than their sisters in other types of settlement, which was also reflected in their ability to handle property matters connected with the office of guardian.[33] Isolated instances of women being appointed guardians occurred in Beduin society, mostly among the Galilean Beduin, who were at a more advanced stage of sedenterization than those of the Negev.

On the other hand, there seems to have been no causal connection between female guardianship and the type of marriage (endogamy or exogamy). The orders are almost equally divided between the two types. It may thus be concluded that blood-relationship between the spouses was not a serious obstacle to the wife's seeking to exercise her right.

Nor did education, at any rate at that time, affect the position of women as guardians. The *Sharī'a* Courts of Ṭayyiba and of Nazareth had the guardian sign the order of appointment. The *sijills* of these courts record only a few cases in which a woman actually signed the order with her name (as distinct from her fingermark (*baṣma*) in other cases).[34] There can be no doubt that education will leave its imprint when the generation of girls who grew up in Israel reaches the stage at which the question of guardianship becomes relevant to it.

Deprivation of Women's Right to Guardianship

In half the cases of orders issued by the courts, women were not appointed guardians of their children. One must of course take into account the fact that some of these orders were issued when the mother was no longer alive or before the enactment of the Women's Equal Rights Law. At the same time, it may be assumed that in other cases the question of guardianship did not arise while the father was alive because as a natural guardian under religious law he did not require appointment or recognition of his status.[35] It thus appears that in a large proportion of cases women did not serve as guardians of their own children. It might happen that they refused the office from the outset or resigned from it on various grounds.[36] In many dozens of cases, they renounced their right to guardianship and consented, ostensibly of their own free will, to the appointment of various agnatic relatives. In some cases, the renunciation was in favour of other women, especially the maternal grandmother and other cognative relatives.[37] Women might make their renunciation dependent on certain conditions, such as a specific mode of distribution of the estate among the heirs,[38] or withdraw their renunciation on various grounds.[39]

There appear to be various causes of a woman's renunciation of her right to guardianship of her children or of her deprivation of that right. It seems that the woman who renounced was usually not aware of her legal right and accepted the right *shar'i* order of agnatic guardians and their appointees (Article 974 of the *Mejelle*). Thus: in one case, a woman said: "I cannot perform the functions of a *waṣī* and have no *shar'i* right to this guardianship unless the court so wishes . . ." and later she added (apparently after her legal right had been explained to her): "It is all the same to me whether I am a legal or an illegal *waṣī*—I renounce my right to this guardianship and shall content myself with being the *ḥāḍina* of my children . . . and let the court select whom it sees fit to be *shar'i* guardian. . . ."[40] In many cases, a woman agreed to or acquiesced in the appointment of the paternal grandfather as the guardian of her children or even resigned the office in his favour in the belief that he preceded her in the order of priority.[41] Also significant in this context is the fact that there was not a single case of a woman being appointed sole guardian while the children's paternal grandfather was alive, unless he had renounced his *shar'i* right for some reason, such as old age or inability to perform the task.[42]

A woman might be disqualified from guardianship (frequently even in her own view) because she was unfit by *shar'i* and traditional standards or incapable of fulfilling the task properly. Justifications for this were marriage—after being widowed or divorced—to a stranger, *i.e.*, a man not within the forbidden degrees of kinship to the minor[43] (this was the principal ground); neglect of the children[44]; immoral conduct[45]; inexperience and inability in matters of property, especially as regards dealing with the authorities[46]; illness[47], and various other circumstances.[48]

Pressure within the family over questions of property might force renunciation. Where the renunciation was in favour of the paternal grandfather or uncle, it is very doubtful that it was voluntary. Both had strong reasons for wishing to prevent the fragmentation of the family property after the death of the children's father, and this was comparatively easy to achieve as guardian of their property. In fact, as regards the grandfather, this is the institutionalized method which has received *shar'i* sanction by his recognition as a natural guardian. In one case in which the mother wished to oust the grandfather from the guardianship on the ground that he was incapable of looking after the children's property owing to weakness of mind, he said that he was a *shar'i* guardian by the grace of God: "It is God, praise be to him, who appointed me over him [the minor] and no-one but He is authorized to dismiss me from this *wilāya*."[49] The institutionalized method by which the paternal uncle (*'amm*) prevents fragmentation of the family property is to marry his sons to the minor girls or to gain control over the property through guardianship. Thus, in one case in which a woman renounced her guardianship over her daughter in favour of the daughter's uncle, the daughter was the wife of that uncle's son.[50] In another case, the uncle and guardian "was always trying to marry his sons to his brother's minor daughters in spite of the latter's minority and against their will. He also tried to gain control of the property of the minors . . . and in fact gained such control."[51] The Jaffa *sijill* describes a long drawn out, complicated dispute between the brother and the uncle of some minor girls over the management of the girl's share in the estate of their grandfather, who had been a wealthy Jaffa resident. They were alternately appointed guardians of the property of the girls and dismissed for dereliction of duty, and the girls were not free of them until they reached puberty.[52]

Paradoxically, the welfare officer, a creation of the Knesset, contributed to the curtailment of women's rights as guardians of their children. As stated, he is guided in his considerations by the child's best interest which does not always coincide with the best interest of the mother. The welfare officer translated this principle into terms accepted in traditional Muslim society, in which a woman's ability to provide for the subsistence and education of children is inferior to a man's and in which the kinship factor is still of importance. As a matter of fact, he did not propose candidates for guardianship but weighed up the candidates proposed in the *maḍbaṭa,* and these were generally selected on traditional considerations. He relied chiefly on the opinions of local welfare workers, who were familiar with social realities and supplied him with the relevant facts. He might recommend in principle the appointment of a guardian in addition to the one proposed in the *maḍbaṭa* but leave the choice of the person to the *sharīʿa* court or to the local council on the assumption that they would know how to find a candidate suitable from the point of view of the child's best interest.[53] There was not a single instance of the welfare officer disqualifying someone proposed for the office. In almost none of the cases in which the mother was appointed was it on his initiative.[54]

The appointment of a guardian alongside the mother, which in several cases was requested by her because she found it difficult to manage the affairs of the minor,[55] was not an innovation but had undoubtedly been given considerable encouragement in Israel by the intervention of the welfare officer. The Legal Adviser to the Ministry of Social Welfare explained that his ministry encouraged the appointment of two or more guardians with a view to preventing collusion and embezzlement of the property of the minor.[56] The addition of a guardian beside the mother ostensibly confirmed her right to the natural guardianship of her children without prejudice to the best interest of the child by traditional standards. The appointment of an agnatic relative, especially the paternal grandfather, who is a natural guardian under religious law, alongside the mother is a compromise between the norm of secular law and the social custom supported by the *sharī'a*. In several cases, the mother and the grandfather demanded to be guardians—by virtue of secular and religious law respectively—and both were appointed.[57] The appointment of the husband's brother or son beside his widow maintained some equilibrium between the interests of the wife and those of the husband's family.[58] In one case, the welfare officer suggested appointing a guardian from the wife's family in addition to the guardian from the husband's family proposed by the *maḍbaṭa*.[59]

In other cases, the welfare officer's intervention to the detriment of the mother was more explicit. Thus, on one occasion, he deprived her of her right to guardianship on the traditional ground that she had married a stranger, and joined the signatories of the *maḍbaṭa* in proposing that the minor's sister be appointed in her stead.[60] In another case, he supported a proposal to appoint an agnatic relative as guardian in addition to the mother, who had married a stranger, and in this connection remarked that the mother's natural guardianship was confined to the persons of the children whereas the agnatic relative was fully entitled to control the management of the entire property, although the distinction between guardianship over the person and over the property does not exist in Israeli legislation.[61] In other cases, the officer accepted the mother's renunciation of the guardianship and agreed to the appointment of an uncle or other agnatic relative even though it was not certain that the renunciation had been of her own free will.[62] In this way, the welfare officer, perhaps unwittingly, sanctioned the restriction of women's rights to guardianship by the court, and even their total deprivation of that right, since his intervention was based on the principle of the best interest of the child, by virtue of which the court may deviate from the provisions of Section 3(a) of the Women's Equal Rights Law. This sanction shields the *qāḍī* from a plea of *ultra vires* on a question of material law.[63]

The *Qāḍīs* and Guardianship

Most *qāḍīs* were alive to the status of women as natural guardians of their children, although some discovered it rather late.[64] They sometimes noted expressly in the order that the appointment of the mother or of both parents was made in reliance on Israeli legislation.[65] They might even point out to the woman or indicate in the order that as the mother she had the status of a natural guardian.[66] In several cases in which a guardian other than the mother was appointed, such as the paternal granfather, who, as stated, is a natural guardian according to the *sharī'a,* this was only done after the mother had renounced her right or agreed to the appointment.[67] Such a renunciation or agreement is not required by religious law, and the author has not encountered it prior to the enactment of the Women's Equal Rights Law.

As stated, the Knesset gave wide discretion to the court to appoint someone other than the natural guardian "with the interest of the children as the sole consideration." In several cases, this principle was consciously applied by Shaykh Ṭāhir Ḥamād and Shaykh Ḥusnī al-Zu'bī when appointing someone other than the mother.[68] Shaykh Tawfīq 'Asaliyya also sometimes applied it, though not with reference to Israeli legislation.[69] He and Shaykh Ḥasan Amīn al-Ḥabash made a point of inviting the welfare officer to the hearings of the court, asking his opinion as to the appointment of a guardian and acting in accordance with it, and if the welfare officer was absent from the hearing, he was reserved the right to oppose the appointment.[70] The alertness of the *qāḍīs* to the status of women as natural guardians should probably be attributed in no small measure to the presence of the welfare officer in court.[71]

At the same time, in all cases in which the mother served as guardian, including also cases in which the *qāḍīs* treated her as a natural guardian, she was *appointed* by the court, as had been usual before the enactment of the Women's Equal Rights Law and as in the case of a woman's guardianship of children not her own.[72] This is, of course, a distorted interpretation of the law since a natural guardian does not require appointment.[73] The distinction between natural guardianship and guardianship by court appointment exists also in Islamic law and was thus not strange to the *qāḍīs*: Shaykh Ṭāhir Ḥamād mentioned it in one case in connection with Israeli legislation.[74] Shaykh Ḥasan Amīn al-Ḥabash explained to the author that the court did not really appoint a natural guardian, because he was appointed by Allāh, but only supplied him with a formal certification of his guardianship for the purposes of his contacts with the authorities.[75] In fact, in some cases, Shaykh Ṭāhir al-Ṭabarī gave a certificate of guardianship (*tathbīt wilāya*) to natural guardians within the meaning of the religious law, and Shaykh Ḥusnī al-Zu'bī, on several occasions, issued such documents to women as natural guardians within the meaning of the general law, although he restricted their powers to the persons of the children and officially *appointed* other guardians for their property. Similarly, other *qāḍīs* issued certificates to natural guardians—within the meaning of the religious law—of the persons of minors and at the same time *appointed* them guardians of the property.[76] It thus seems that some *qāḍīs* tended to limit the mother's natural guardianship to the person of the minor; an express indication of such a tendency is contained in a decision of Shaykh Ḥasan Amīn al-Ḥabash. Shaykh Ṭāhir Ḥamād declared in one case that the guardianship of the persons of the children was indeed vested in both parents by law but that, since the mother had not asked to share the guardianship of the property with the father, he assigned this function to the father alone.[77]

On the other hand, there were cases in which the *qāḍīs* applied religious law to matters of guardianship and adhered to the order of guardians prescribed by Article 974 of the *Mejelle* as if nothing had happened. Shaykh Mūsā al-Ṭabarī and Shaykh Amīn Qāsim Mudlij regarded the father (but not the mother) and the paternal grandfather as natural guardians.[78] Most *qāḍīs* were in the habit of confirming an elected guardian (*waṣi mukhtār*) appointed by a *shar'i* natural guardian.[79] Shaykh Mūsā al-Ṭabarī himself appointed his wife to be *waṣī mukhtār* of his children after his death,[80] and in another case a woman contended in the High Court of Justice that this *qāḍī* had meant to deprive her of the guardianship through the children's aunt, who had been elected to the office by their father.[81] In most of the cases in which the mother was appointed it was after it had been found that "there is no real grandfather and no elected guardian on his behalf" or after the *shar'i* natural guardian had renounced his position for some reason not relevant to the status of women as natural guardians[82]: under such circumstances, the *qāḍīs* did not, when the mother was alive, necessarily appoint her.[83] They continued, in accodance with the *shar'i* norm, to disqualify a woman from the guardianship of her children on the ground that, after being widowed or divorced, she had married a stranger.[84] Since the father's remarriage did not disqualify him under religious law from the natural guardianship of his children, this practice of the *qāḍīs* constituted discrimination against women and was thus quite out of keeping with Section 1 of the Women's Equal Rights Law.[85] Shaykh Ṭāhir Ḥamād in one case appointed a 16-year-old girl guardian of her brother on the ground that she was physically mature, adding that her maturity was not conditional on her having reached the age of 18, the appointment thus being made in conscious disregard of the general law.[86]

The *qāḍīs* sometimes sought support for the appointment of a guardian, at one and the same time, in substantive elements of both legal systems, the religious and secular, though based on utterly different philosophies. Thus, Shaykh Mūsā al-Ṭabarī in some cases gave as reasons for the appointment of the mother as guardian of the children that she was a natural guardian within the meaning of Israeli law and that the father had left neither a legal guardian nor an elected guardian behind him.[87] Shaykh Amīn Qāsim Mudlij in one case appointed the mother in reliance on her consent, on Section 1 of the Women's Equal Rights Law and on the *sharī'a*[88]; and Shaykh Tawfīq 'Asaliyya on one occasion based the appointment of the father on his being "the one among the guardians and agnatic relatives (*aṣaba*) who is nearest to the children, and on Section 14 of the Capacity and Guardianship Law."[89]

The only way to circumvent the provisions of the Women's Equal Rights Law relating to gurdianship (and its other substantive provisions) is, as has been noted, by the parties agreeing to litigate in accordance with the law of their community. But in none of the orders appointing someone other than the mother guardian of her children, sometimes in express contradiction to her wishes, did the author find that the mother had in fact been asked or had agreed to apply religious law to matters of guardianship. It does not seem that the *qāḍīs* were alive to this question; at any rate, the author found no evidence to this effect in the *sijills*.

Notes and References

1. See Qadrī, arts. 420 *seq.*, 435 *seq.*; Fyzee, pp. 188, 193-4, 198; Abu Zahra, pp. 156-7; Levy, pp. 143-4; Silberg, pp. 407-8, 410; Schereschewsky, pp. 375-6; Vitta, p. 183; Zadok, pp. 66-7, 70; Eisenman, pp. 365-6. *KP*, Vol. 9, p. 2004 col. 1, p. 2005 col. 2 (remarks by the Minister of Justice in the Knesset).
2. In the opinion of the Ministry of Justice, the two kinds of guardianship were mentioned "not in order to differentiate between them but to combine them." See *IFB,* Explanatory Note, p. 149.
3. See Silberg, pp. 414 *seq.*; Women's Equal Rights Bill, 5711-1951, p. 19.
4. *E.g.*, the distinction between sons and daughters as to the expiration of the period of guardianship remains in force. See Silberg, pp. 412-3.
5. On the other hand, parental control over the person and property of the child is curtailed with a view to equating parents as far as possible to appointed guardians, but there is no discrimination between the parents in this respect (see Sec. 22).

6. The enactments repealed by this law include, *inter alia,* arts. 941-7, 957-97 of the *Mejelle* (Sec. 82).
7. See *IFB,* Explanatory Note, pp. 133-4, 148-61, 172-89; Explanatory Note to Capacity and Guardianship Bill; *KP,* Vol. 32, p. 45 col. 2, p. 47 col. 2, p. 49 col. 2 (remarks by the Minister of Justice on the first reading of the bill), p. 3077 col. 1-p. 3080 col. 1 (remarks by the Chairman of the Constitution, Legislation and Juridical Committee concerning this bill).
8. See Shaki, p. 266; *KP,* Vol. 34, p. 3095. At any rate, Sec. 3 of the Women's Equal Rights Law, which deals with matters of guardianship, was not repealed by the law under reference.
9. See, *e.g.*, *JfQ2*, p. 379: no. 532-f.17/59 (the guardian required the supervisor (*nāzir*) to consent to any act of transfer in respect of the property); *AcD*6, p. 43: f.106/65.
10. See, *e.g.*, *JfQ1*, p. 144: no. 244-f.51/54; *JfQ4*, p. 101: no. 112-f.66/68, *AcD*8, p. 74: f.91/69.
11. See, *e.g.*, *JfQ3*, p. 245: no. 383-f.16/66; *AcQ5*, p. 36: f.71/63.
12. *NzḤ24,* p. 267: no. 6/9-f.17/70.
13. See, *e.g.*, *JfQ3*, p. 206: no. 340-f.46/65; *ṬbḤ2,* p. 133: no. 8; *NzḤ*24, p. 22: no. 4/68-f.11/66.
14. See, *e.g.*, *JfQ1*, p. 242: no. 375-f.30/56; *NzḤ14,* p. 116: no. 8/76.
15. *JfQ1*, p. 90: no. 144-f.3/53, and p. 15: no. 26, respectively. See also *NzḤ24,* p. 57: no. 11/22-f.41/67 (appointment of paternal uncle's wife), p. 192: no. 3/106-f.191/68 (step-mother, who was also a blood-relation of the children).
16. Only in two cases was guardianship over the persons and not over the property of the minors referred to. In both, Negev Beduin sought to use the mechanism of execution to recover a minor girl who had been abducted or fled from their house; their suit was allowed. See *JfQ2*, p. 553: no. 554-f.97/62, p. 582: no. 606-f.32/63.
17. See, *e.g.*, *AcQ4*, p. 7: no. 7/59-f.49/59; *JfQ3*, p. 216; no. 353-f.36/66, p. 348: no. 490-f.58/67; *ṬbḤ2*, p.54: no. 20; *NzḤ23*, p. 153: no. 8/12-f.7/66.
18. See, *e.g.*, *JfQ4*, p. 70: no. 66-f.4/68 and p. 71: no. 67-f.19/68; *ṬbḤ2*, p. 222: no. 130 and p. 223: no. 131; *NzḤ23*, p. 84: no. 5/63-f.107/65 and p. 85: no. 6/46-f.108/65; *AcIr3*, p. 146: no. 41-f.65/52 and p. 147: no. 42-f.106/52.
19. See, *e.g.*, *JfḤ19*, p. 47: no. 310, p. 104: no. 416; *NzḤ14*, p. 16: no. 68, p. 20: no. 72.
20. *JfQ2*, p. 388: no. 543-f.30/59; *JfQ3*, p. 25: no. 40-f.128/63; *ṬbḤ2*, p. 246: no. 26; *ṬbḤ3*, p. 31: no. 42; *AcD*6, p. 26: f.59/64; *AcD*7, p. 15: f.65/66; *NzḤ24,* p. 144: no. 2/42-f.75/68.

21. See, *e.g.*, *NzḤ24*, p. 86: no. 2/56-f.120/67, p. 224: no. 1/37-f.85/69. This matter is discussed above, pp. 272-3.
22. *NzI4*, p. 329: no. 5/29-f.100/67; *JfQ3*, p. 224: no. 364-f.58/65; High Court of Justice 187/54—Ḥalīma Sulaymān Barriyya *vs. Qāḍī* of the *Shar^a* Court of Acre *PD*, vol. 9, p. 1193. Parts of the judgment are quoted by Goitein and Ben-Shemesh, pp. 242-5.
23. See, *e.g.*, *JfQ2*, p. 553: no. 554-f.97/62; *ṬbḤ3*, p. 36: no. 48.
24. The *maḍbaṭa* usually notes that "there is not a paternal grandfather or *waṣī mukhtār.*" See, *e.g.*, *JfQ3*, p. 304: no. 444-f.138/66; *NzḤ19*, p. 14: no. 8/8; *AcI2*, p. 55: f.124/53; *AcQ4*, p. 28: f.119/59.
25. See, *e.g.*, *NzḤ21*, p. 176: no. 5/47-f.70/62.
26. See, *e.g.*, *NzḤ20*, p. 3: no. 5/96; *AcQ4*, p. 7: no. 7/59-f.49/59; *AcD6*, p. 66: f.192/64; *AcD8*, p. 52: f.141/68.
27. *JfQ1*, p. 146: no. 247-f.56/54. See also *NzḤ22*, p. 57: no. 9/47-f.73/63.
28. See, *e.g.*, *JfQ3*, p. 309: no. 448-f.143/66; *NzḤ23*, p. 171: no. 3/30-f.42/66.
29. *NzḤ20*, p. 40: no. 3/20, and p. 13: no. 9/110, respectively.
30. See, *e.g.*, *AcI2*, p. 55: f.124/53.
31. See, *e.g.*, *JfQ4*, p. 71: no. 67-f.19/68; *ṬbḤ2*, p. 25: no. 64; *NzḤ21*, p. 5: no. 8/23; *AcD6*, p. 64: f.157/65.
32. *JfQ1*, p. 168: no. 277-f.14/55; *ṬbḤ2*, p. 72: no. 39; *NzḤ19*, p. 76: no. 3/76; *AcI2*, p. 62: f.16/54; *AcIr3*, p. 67: no. 64/56-f.87/56.
33. In several cases, it was noted that a transwoman managed her husband's property even during his lifetime. See, *e.g.*, *JfQ1*, p. 90: no. 144-f.3/53, p. 168: no. 277-f.14/55.
34. See, *e.g.*, *ṬbḤ2*, p. 232: no. 6; *NzḤ24*, p. 213: no. 8/25-f.58/69.
35. See, *e.g.*, *NzḤ24*, p. 121: no. 1/12-f.21/68.
36. See, *e.g.*, *NzḤ19*, p. 182: no. 7/74; *NzḤ21*, p. 132: no. 4/60-f.95/61; *AcIr2*, p. 145: no. 40-f.129/52; *AcD8*, p. 68: f.49/69.
37. See, *e.g.*, *JfQ3*, p. 326: no. 467-f.25/67; *AcD6*, p. 37: f.75/65; *NzḤ17*, p. 201: no. 28/278; *ṬbḤ2*, p. 235: no. 12.
38. See, *e.g.*, *JfQ2*, p. 379: no. 532-f.17/59; *JfQ3*, p. 165: no. 267-f.6/65.
39. *JfQ2*, p. 534: no. 520-f.54/62 (the woman at first consented to the appointment of the children's uncle as *waṣī* for their property; later she contended that her renunciation had been made while she was very ill with grief at her husband's death and that now she had recovered she had reassumed control of the children; the uncle resigned and the mother was appointed in his stead).
40. *NzḤ17*, p. 172: no. 21/337.
41. See, *e.g.*, *NzḤ21*, p. 133: no. 5/61-f.96/61; *NzḤ23*, p. 14: no. 5/91-f.156/64.

42. See, *e.g.*, *NzḤ23*, p. 14: no. 5/91-f.156/64 (when the grandfather recovered from sickness, the mother was dismissed and the grandfather reappointed).
43. See, *e.g.*, *JfQ3*, p. 30: no. 51-f.147/63; *TbḤ2*, p. 133: no. 8; *NzḤ24*, p. 192: no. 3/106-f.191/68; *AcD*6, p. 37: f.75/65.
44. See, *e.g.*, *JfQ3*, p. 245: no. 383-f.16/66; *NzḤ21*, p. 156: no. 2/21-f.27/62.
45. See, *e.g.*, *NzḤ23*, p. 141: no. 18/122-f.185/65; *AcIr3*, p. 118: no. 38/57-f.152/57.
46. See, *e.g.*, *JfQ3*, p. 270: no. 409-f.100/66, p. 328: no. 469-f.27/67; *NzḤ17*, p. 201: no. 28/278; *NzḤ19*, p. 36: no. 3/33; *ṬbḤ1*, p. 122-f.6/10.
47. See, *e.g.*, *NzḤ24*, p. 78: no. 4/46-f.101/67; *JfQ3*, p. 279: no. 418-f.102/66.
48. See, *e.g.*, *NzḤ21*, p. 43: no. 1/8-f.11/60.
49. *NzI4*, p. 52: no. 3/15-f.26/49.
50. *NzḤ19*, p. 178: no. 3/70. See also *AcIr3*, p. 164: no. 3-f.29/58 (a man was appointed guardian of his female cousin).
51. *NzḤ20*, p. 3: no. 5/96. Cf. Rosenfeld, *Peasants*, p. 145.
52. See *JfQ2*, p. 318: no. 497-f.42/58, p. 337: no. 529-f.13/59, p. 442: no. 434-f.9/60, p. 476: no. 500-f.52/61 (another guardian was appointed for the girls), p. 483: no. 516-f.61/61 (here, too, the guardian was dismissed by reason of embezzlement of property of the wards), p. 551: no. 550-f.95/62.
53. See, *e.g.*, *ṬbḤ3*, p. 79: no. 48; *ṬbḤ4*, p. 121: no. 98.
54. See, *e.g.*, *ṬbḤ3*, p. 88: no. 61: *ṬbḤ4*, p. 57: no. 16. See also *ṬbḤ3*, p. 36: no. 48; *ṬbḤ4*, p. 93: no. 65.
55. See, *e.g.*, *JfQ3*, p. 249: no. 388-f.75/65; *NzḤ*24, p. 144: no. 2/42-f.75/68.
56. Interview with M. Horvitz.
57. *NzḤ24*, p. 213: no. 8/25-f.58/69, p. 252: no. 1/75-f.145/69. See also *AcD*8, p. 57: f.126/68; *ṬbḤ3*, p. 49: no. 10.
58. See, *e.g.*, *ṬbḤ1*, p. 18: no. 9/35; *ṬbḤ3*, p. 92: no. 66; *JfQ3*, p. 323: no. 463-f.19/67; *AcD*7, p. 48: f.30/67; *NzḤ19*, p. 66: no. 9/68.
59. *ṬbḤ3*, p. 107: no. 16.
60. *JfQ3*, p. 245: no. 385: f.16/66.
61. *ṬbḤ4*, p. 300: no. 6-f.13/68.
62. See, *e.g.*, *AcI3*, p. 105: no. 135-f.158/58; *NzḤ24*, p. 111: no. 6/83-f.175/67.
63. See High Court of Justice 187/54. Quoted by Goitein and Ben-Shemesh, p. 244.

64. See *ṬbḤ2*, p. 244: no. 22: *ṬbḤ4*, p. 279: no. 10-f.15/67; *JfQ2*, p. 587: no. 542-f.29/59: *AcD6*, p. 26: f.59/64.
65. See, *e.g.*, *JfQ2*, p. 553: no. 554-f.97/62; *JfQ3*, p. 348: no. 490-f.58/67, p. 364: no. 508-f.82/67; *AcD6*, p. 26: f.59/64.
66. See, *e.g.*, *JfQ2*, p. 534: no. 520-f.54/62; *JfQ3*, p. 216: no. 353-f.36/66; *ṬbḤ2*, p. 244: no. 23; *AcD6*, p. 16: f.55/65.
67. See, *e.g.*, *JfQ1*, p. 141: no. 237-f.31/54; *JfQ4*, p. 131: no. 155-f.137/68; *AcIr3*, p. 17: no. 15/55-f.42/55; *AcD6*, p. 39: f.36/64; *ṬbḤ4*, p. 121: no. 98.
68. See, *e.g.*, *JfQ2*, p. 318: no. 497; *NzḤ24*, p. 33: no. 82/2-f.142/66.
69. See, *e.g.*, *JfQ4*, p. 38: no. 37-f.140/67. See also *NzḤ*24, p. 96 no. 12/66-f.140/67.
70. *ṬbḤ2*, p. 15: no. 19, p. 244: no. 23; *JfQ3*, p. 244: no. 382-f.50/66.
71. See, *e.g.*, *ṬbḤ3*, p. 5: no. 6. This was also the opinion of interviewee Horvitz of the Ministry of Social Welfare.
72. See, *e.g.*, *ṬbḤ1*, p. 31: no. 10/56; *NzḤ14*, p. 71: no. 3/12; *JfQ1*, p. 15: no. 26, p. 90: no. 144-f.3/53.
73. See Silberg, pp. 410-1.
74. *JfQ1*, p. 50: no. 80-f.48/52 (he distinguished between natural guardianship and "guardianship relying on the *qāḍī*").
75. Interview with Shaykh Ḥasan Amīn al-Ḥabash. Cf. Schereschewsky, p. 377.
76. See, *e.g.*, *NzḤ19*, p. 123: no. 3/15; *NzI4*, p. 80: no. 8/34-f.83/50, p. 329: no. 5/29-f.100/67; *NzḤ24*, p. 144: no. 2/42-f.75/68; *JfQ1*, p. 115: no. 195-f.1/54; *ṬbḤ1*, p. 74: no. 1/16; *AcQ4*, p. 6: no. 6/59-f.47/59; *AcD6*, p. 48-f.122/65.
77. *ṬbḤ4*, p. 300: no. 6-f.13/68; and *JfQ2*, p. 582: no. 606-f.64/63, respectively.
78. See, *e.g.*, *AcIr*3, p. 168: no. 7-f.47/58; *AcQ5*, p. 79-f.208/63.
79. See, *e.g.*, *NzḤ*19, p. 76: no. 3/76; *JfQ1*, p. 168: no. 277-f.14/55. Cf. Schereschewsky, p. 377.
80. *AcIr3*, p. 67: no. 64/56-f.87/56.
81. High Court of Justice 187/54, quoted by Goitein and Ben-Shemesh, pp. 243-4. Advocate S. Darwish told the author that the *qāḍī* "took the hint" of the Supreme Court that he was not to deprive the woman of her status as natural guardian by the application of religious law. He exerted his good offices to reconcile the mother and the aunt so as to avoid rendering a judgment requiring the child to be handed over to the mother.
82. See, *e.g.*, *NzḤ19*, p. 45: no. 1/43; *NzḤ20*, p. 40: no. 3/20; *AcIr3*, p. 183: no. 20-f.64/58; *AcQ4*, p. 100: f.175/60; *AcD*8, p. 31: f.68/68; *JfQ1*, p. 221: no. 345-f.6/56.

83. See, *e.g.*, *JfQ1*, p. 124: no. 210-f.18/54; *AcIr3*, p. 33: no. 31/55-f.17/55; *NzḤ24*, p. 220: no. 5/32-f.76/69.
84. See, *e.g.*, *JfQ1*, p. 163: no. 270-f.4/54; *NzḤ24*, p. 200: no. 1/8-f.25/69; *AcIr3*, p. 168: no. 7-f.47/58.
85. See High Court of Justice 187/54. Quoted by Goitein and Ben-Shemesh, pp. 243-4.
86. *AcQ5*, p. 24: f.31/63, p. 36: f.71/63 (the girl in question was a daughter of Shaykh Mūsā al-Ṭabarī). The appointment was annulled by Shaykh Amīn Qāsim Mudlij as contrary to Sec. 3 of the Capacity and Guardianship Law. See *AcQ5*, p. 57: f.147/63.
87. See, *e.g.*, *AcIr3*, p. 68: no. 65/56-f.75/56; *AcQ4*, p. 10: no. 10/59-f.75/59.
88. *AcD7*, p. 34: f.184/66. See also *NzḤ24*, p. 86: no. 2/56-f.120/67 (Shaykh Ḥusnī al-Zu'bī).
89. *JfQ5*, p. 16: no. 30-f.123/69. See also *JfQ4*, p. 124: no. 143-f.113/68.

Index

T

U

V

W

Y